OBJECT-ORIENTED DATABASES

D0530698

Prentice Hall International Series in Computer Science

C. A. R. Hoare, Series Editor

BACKHOUSE, R. C., *Program Construction and Verification*
BACKHOUSE, R. C., *Syntax of Programming Languages: Theory and practice*
DeBAKKER, J. W., *Mathematical Theory of Program Correctness*
BARR, M. and WELLS, C., *Category Theory for Computing Science*
BEN-ARI, M., *Principles of Concurrent and Distributed Programming*
BIRD, R. and WADLER, P., *Introduction to Functional Programming*
BJÖRNER, D. and JONES, C. B., *Formal Specification and Software Development*
BORNAT, R., *Programming from First Principles*
BUSTARD, D., ELDER, J. and WELSH, J., *Concurrent Program Structures*
CLARK, K. L., and McCABE, F. G., *micro-Prolog: Programming in logic*
CROOKES, D., *Introduction to Programming in Prolog*
DROMEY, R. G., *How to Solve it by Computer*
DUNCAN, F., *Microprocessor Programming and Software Development*
ELDER, J., *Construction of Data Processing Software*
ELLIOTT, R. J. and HOARE, C. A. R., (eds.), *Scientific Applications of Multiprocessors*
GOLDSCHLAGER, L. and LISTER, A., *Computer Science: A modern introduction (2nd edn)*
GORDON, M. J. C., *Programming Language Theory and its Implementation*
HAYES, I. (ed.), *Specification Case Studies*
HEHNER, E. C. R., *The Logic of Programming*
HENDERSON, P., *Functional Programming: Application and Implementation*
HOARE, C. A. R., *Communicating Sequential Processes*
HOARE, C. A. R., and JONES, C. B. (ed.), *Essays in Computing Science*
HOARE, C. A. R., and SHEPHERDSON, J. C. (eds.), *Mathematical Logic and Programming Languages*
HUGHES, J. G., *Database Technology: A software engineering approach*
HUGHES, J. G., *Object Oriented Databases*
INMOS LTD, *occam 2 Reference Manual*
JACKSON, M. A., *System Development*
JOHNSTON, H., *Learning to Program*
JONES, C. B., *Systematic Software Development using VDM (2nd edn)*
JONES, C. B. and SHAW, R. C. F. (eds.), *Case Studies in Systematic Software Development*
JONES, G., *Programming in occam*
JONES, G. and GOLDSMITH, M., *Programming in occam 2*
JOSEPH, M., PRASAD, V. R. and NATARAJAN, N., *A Multiprocessor Operating System*
KALDEWAIJ, A., *Programming: The Derivation of Algorithms*
KING, P. J. B., *Computer and Communication Systems Performance Modelling*
LEW, A., *Computer Science: A mathematical introduction*
MARTIN, J. J., *Data Types and Data Structures*
MEYER, B., *Introduction to the Theory of Programming Languages*
MEYER, B., *Object-orientated Software Construction*
MILNER, R., *Communication and Concurrency*
MORGAN, C., *Programming from Specifications*
PEYTON JONES, S. L., *The Implementation of Functional Programming Languages*
POMBERGER, G., *Software Engineering and Modula-2*
POTTER, B., SINCLAIR, J., TILL, D., *An Introduction to Formal Specification and 2*
REYNOLDS, J. C., *The Craft of Programming*
RYDEHEARD, D. E. AND BURSTALL, R. M., *Computational Category Theory*
SLOMAN, M. and KRAMER, J., *Distributed Systems and Computer Networks*
SPIVEY, J. M., *The Z Notation: A reference manual*
TENNENT, R. D., *Principles of Programming Languages*
WATT, D. A., *Programming Languages Concepts and Paradigms*
WATT, D. A., WICHMANN, B. A. and FINDLAY, W., *ADA: Language and methodology*
WELSH, J. and ELDER, J., *Introduction to Modula-2*
WELSH, J. and ELDER, J., *Introduction to Pascal (3rd edn)*
WELSH, J., ELDER, J., and BUSTARD, D., *Sequential Program Structures*
WELSH, J. and HAY, A., *A Model Implementation of Standard Pascal*
WELSH, J. and McKEAG, M., *Structured System Programming*
WIKSTRÖM, Å., *Functional Programming using Standard ML*

OBJECT-ORIENTED DATABASES

J. G. Hughes
The University of Ulster

Prentice Hall
New York London Toronto Sydney Tokyo Singapore

First published 1991 by
Prentice Hall International (UK) Ltd,
66 Wood Lane End, Hemel Hempstead
Hertfordshire HP2 4RG
A division of
Simon & Schuster International Group

Printed in Great Britain at the University Press, Cambridge

Library of Congress Cataloging-in-Publication Data

Hughes, John G., 1953–
    Object-oriented databases/J. G. Hughes.
    p. cm. – (Prentice Hall international series in computer science).
    Includes bibliographical references and index.
    ISBN 0-13-629882-6 (cloth);   — ISBN 0-13-629874-5 (pbk.)
    1. Object-oriented data bases. I. Title. II. Title: Object-oriented
data bases. III. Series.
QA76.9.D3H846 1991
005.75—dc20   91-42371
                                                         CIP

British Library Cataloguing in Publication Data

Hughes, John G.
    Object-oriented databases. — (Prentice Hall international series in
computer science).
    1. Databases
    I. Title
    005.74

    ISBN 0-13-629882-6
    ISBN 0-13-629874-5 pbk

---

2 3 4 5 95 94 93 92

Contents

4 Classes and inheritance

5 Object-oriented query processing

8   Object-oriented database implementation

9   Object-oriented knowledge bases

Preface

In the commercial world, relational database systems have now become the *de facto* standard for data processing applications. Their success has largely been due to their flexibility and ease of use, and to the fact that a number of very powerful and efficient relational database management systems are now available commercially. In the past few years these systems have succeeded in providing the level of performance required for large-scale transaction processing environments. However, it is widely recognized that there exists a large class of applications for which the data modelling capabilities of relational systems are too limited. These applications can be characterized as complex, large-scale, data intensive programs, such as those found in the areas of computer-aided design, and computer integrated manufacturing. Object-oriented database systems are being developed to meet the complex data modelling requirements of such applications. Such systems have moved away from the relational model and concentrated on developing the notions of type, data abstraction, inheritance and persistence within a database framework. However, these systems give rise to significant implementation problems, particularly with regard to persistence and concurrency control, which are currently receiving considerable attention in the research community. To investigate some of these problems, numerous object-oriented database programming languages and systems have been designed and implemented over the past few years.

Object-oriented programming languages have, of course, been around for many years. Simula, designed by Dahl and Nygaard at the University of Oslo, first appeared in 1966 and is usually considered as being the first such language. It is essentially an object-oriented extension to Algol 60. During the 1970s several Pascal-based, strongly-typed, modular programming languages appeared (e.g. Pascal Plus, Concurrent Pascal, Ada), which were strongly influenced by Simula but failed to retain some of its fundamental object-oriented features, notably inheritance. Smalltalk was also developed during the 1970s by Kay, Goldberg and Ingalls at Xerox. Although its design was influenced by Simula, its philosophy was rather different, with its emphasis on a free typeless style and dynamic binding.

Programming language objects and database objects are similar in that they encapsulate properties, but there are several important differences. First, database objects must *persist* beyond the lifetime of the program creating them. Second, many database applications require the capability to create and access multiple *versions* of an object. (Examples of this are to be found in historical databases, databases for software management, and computer-aided design.) Third, highly active databases, such as those used for air traffic control and power distribution management, require the ability to associate *conditions* and *actions* with objects where the actions are triggered when the conditions are satisfied. Finally, database integrity control demands the capability to associate *constraints* with objects. Programming languages do not typically support persistent objects or multiple object versions. Nor do they always provide the facilities to associate constraints and triggers with objects.

However, there is a strong trend in the research community toward extending object-oriented languages in the direction of databases, and, at the same time, toward extending database systems with object-oriented facilities. On the one hand, object-oriented database systems must provide a comprehensive set of semantic data modelling concepts to permit modelling of entities and relationships for complex real-world applications, while on the other, application programmers must be able to access and manipulate objects as though they are in an infinite virtual memory.

The major aim of this book is to provide a clean fusion of the advances in both database and programming language research within an object-oriented framework. Chapter 1 gives a comprehensive description of semantic data modelling techniques, starting with the model-independent extended entity-relationship approach, and continuing with a detailed description of the relational data model, the extended relational model, RM/T and the functional data model. Chapter 2 is a treatise on the fundamental principles underlying object-oriented programming, dealing with the important topics of software quality, correctness and reusability and the techniques used in object-oriented programming to support these goals. Chapter 3 introduces the reader to the subject of object-oriented data modelling in which the database takes the form of a collection of complex, highly interconnected objects. This chapter includes several case studies which serve to highlight the differences between the conventional relational approach and the object-oriented approach. Class structure and inheritance, which are central to the object-oriented approach, are discussed in depth in Chapter 4. Examples of class representation and inheritance are drawn from a wide range of object-oriented programming languages and systems.

Chapter 5 deals with object-oriented query processing. This subject is still somewhat immature in relation to database systems and has aroused some controversy over the past few years. We describe some promising approaches to object-oriented query languages, based on extensions to SQL and to the functional data model. Chapter 6 is devoted to persistence, a fundamental property of database systems. Various models of persistence are described, ranging from the use of relations with objects, to database programming languages in which persistence is an orthogonal property of all data. The question of which model is best suited to object-oriented database systems is discussed in depth. The significant implementation issues associated with persistence are deferred until Chapter 8.

The problems associated with concurrency, recovery and distribution in object-oriented databases are described in Chapter 7. This chapter begins with a detailed description of concurrency issues in conventional databases, with the emphasis on serializability theory and two-phase locking. Various models of concurrency, as used in the programming language and database communities, are then described and their relevance to object-oriented databases is discussed. However, conventional database concurrency mechanisms are, in general, too restrictive for the object-oriented environment. Thus, we investigate some of the special problems associated with concurrency in object-oriented databases and the proposed solutions to these problems. The role of the object-oriented paradigm in distributed databases is still the subject of intensive research. We draw attention to some of the advantages of the object-oriented approach in a distributed scenario.

Implementation issues are dealt with in Chapter 8. Efficient implementation is, of course, one of the most challenging problems facing the object-oriented database research community and is likely to remain so for many years. The chapter begins with a description of the techniques used for object storage and memory management in object-oriented systems. Other important implementation issues relevant to databases, such as clustering and version control, are also discussed in this chapter.

Finally in Chapter 9 we turn our attention to object-oriented knowledge bases. This area is still the subject of considerable research and the role of the object-oriented model is not yet fully understood. We concentrate on *knowledge representation* where the advantages of the object-oriented model are well-recognized. In addition, we draw the reader's attention to some aspects of current research and to some of the issues still to be resolved.

This book should be of interest to final year undergraduates, postgraduates, researchers and computer professionals, who are interested in expanding their knowledge of object-oriented programming languages, and systems, and their relevance to database design and implementation.

Acknowledgements

Many useful discussions with colleagues and students helped in the preparation of this book. In particular, I should like to acknowledge collaborative work with David Bell and An Zhi on object-oriented applications in AI, and with Mike Papazoglou of the Australian National University on clustering and on distributed databases. I am also grateful to Helen Martin and Mike Cash of Prentice Hall who encouraged me to write the book and provided invaluable feedback from (anonymous) reviewers.

Above all, I should like to thank my wife Maura for her constant support and encouragement, and my two boys Stephen and Michael who endured my lengthy sessions on their favourite toy (the Apple Macintosh) during the preparation of the book.

1

Semantic data modelling

1.1 INTRODUCTION

The past decade has seen a rapid growth in database systems, not only with respect to the sheer number of such systems, but also with regard to the amount of information being stored and the complexity of applications being developed. This growing demand for systems of ever-increasing complexity and precision has stimulated the need for higher level concepts, tools and techniques for database design and development. Thus the database design methodologies which have been developed in recent years provide the designer with the means for modelling an enterprise at a high level of abstraction, before proceeding with the detailed logical and physical database design. These methodologies have been heavily influenced by advances in programming languages which have developed sophisticated abstraction mechanisms that permit, for example, the specification of data types and objects independently of their implementation.

In this chapter we present the fundamental principles of *semantic* data modelling for database applications. Data models are central to database technology. They provide a basis for conceptualizing data intensive applications and a formal basis for developing languages and systems for implementing such applications. Data modelling is essentially a two-stage process, involving:

1. A *conceptual design* phase, involving the design of a conceptual schema which is an abstraction of the real-world situation under consideration.

2. The design of a logical data structure, representing this schema, which may be mapped onto an actual implementation.

The first step is concerned with analysing the information requirements of the application, preparing a requirements specification, and from this constructing a high-level data model. A data model may be defined as a pattern according to which data are logically organized. It consists of named logical units of data and expresses the relationships among the data as determined by some interpretation of the real world. The data model must capture both the static and dynamic aspects of the underlying application. The static properties of the system are concerned with abstractions of the objects and concepts involved, their properties (or attributes) and their interrelationships. These properties are defined in a schema using some form of data description language. Dynamic aspects of the system are concerned with operations on objects and properties as required by transactions and queries. That is, the dynamic properties model the behaviour of the system and take the form of specifications for operations on the database. In addition, the data model must be able to deal with the dynamic aspects of the system, that is the evolution of the system as the requirements of the application change over time.

Another important function of a data model is to specify *integrity rules* that must be adhered to by the database objects (i.e. the state of an object must not violate an integrity rule) and by operations on objects. Integrity rules or *constraints* often relate static and dynamic properties (e.g. preventing an update that would produce an invalid state for an object). Semantic integrity constraints are highly dependent on the data model. The conventional data models (i.e. the hierarchical, network and relational models) incorporate little semantic integrity and constraints must be explicitly specified by the user. In the more semantically rich data models many such constraints may be inherent to the model itself. Integrity will be an important consideration in our evaluation of data models throughout this text.

In this chapter we discuss a methodology for database design, concentrating on conceptual or *semantic* data modelling. Many semantic data models have been proposed in the literature [see Hull and King, 1987; Tsichritzis and Lochovsky, 1982; Brodie *et al.*, 1984] but few have attracted much interest outside the database research community. This may be due to the fact that many of the proposed models are overly complex and difficult to map onto actual implementations. However, most of the important concepts in semantic data modelling can be adequately represented within the *Extended Entity-Relationship (EER) Model*. This model has, unlike others, attracted a great deal of interest in the commercial applications environment, and it plays a fundamental role in many tools for Computer Aided Software Engineering (CASE). This model was originally proposed by Chen [Chen, 1976] and at that stage was adequate for most traditional data processing applications. However during the past decade database designers have been faced with growing complexity in applications which have given rise to a need for additional semantic modelling concepts. Thus, Chen's proposals have been modified and semantically enriched by many others. Important additions to the original model include the concepts of *subclass* and *superclass*, and the closely related mechanism known as *attribute inheritance*.

Due to its expressiveness and ease of use, the EER model has attracted considerable attention during the last decade in both industry and the research community, and still remains the premier model for conceptual schema design. One of the main reasons for this popularity is that it provides a *top-down* approach to database design, employing the concept of *data abstraction*. In these respects it is compatible with the modern principles of software engineering. We shall use the EER model in our first-level design strategy and study the translation between EER models of data and the implementable models which form the basis of modern database management systems. In later chapters we shall see that the EER model provides a useful first step towards the design of object-oriented databases.

In the second part of this chapter we present the fundamental principles of the relational data model. Due to its ease of use and the availability of efficient implementations, the relational model became the *de facto* standard for commercial database management systems during the 1980s, and thus provides an important yardstick by which the more advanced models (such as the object-oriented model) must be measured. In reviewing the relational model we concern ourselves primarily with issues such as data modelling, data manipulation and integrity. These features will be of primary concern when we compare this model with the object-oriented model.

Finally in this chapter we briefly study two other semantic data models: the model RM/T [Codd, 1979], which extends the relational model to capture more semantics, and the functional data model. Like functional programming, the functional data model has many inherent advantages over other models with regard to capturing semantics and ensuring correctness, but it has yet to prove that it is capable of coping efficiently with large-scale applications.

1.2   THE EXTENDED ENTITY-RELATIONSHIP MODEL

In the extended entity-relationship (EER) model information is represented by means of three primitive concepts:

1. *Entities*, which represent the objects being modelled.

2. *Attributes*, which represent the properties of those objects.

3. *Relationships*, which represent the associations among entities.

Each of these concepts are described in detail in the following sections.

1.2.1   Entities and attributes

A dictionary definition of an entity is: 'Being, existence, as opposed to non-existence; the existence as distinct from the qualities or relations of anything' [*Shorter Oxford English Dictionary*]. For database applications an entity is something about which descriptive information is to be stored, which is capable of independent existence and can be uniquely identified. An entity may be an *object* such as a house, a student or a car; or an *event* or activity such as a football match, a holiday or the servicing of a car.

An entity is meaningfully described by its attributes. For example, a house might be described by the attributes address, style, and colour; a car might be described by the attributes registration number, make, model and year of registration; a football match might be described by attributes such as home team, away team, date, home team score, away team score. If an attribute has itself descriptive information then it should be classified as an entity. For example, if we wish to record additional information on the model of a car (other than the name of the model) then we should introduce the entity type MODEL which will have a relationship with the entity type CAR.

The name of an entity together with its attributes define an *entity type* of which there may be many *instances*. The distinction between entity types and instances is directly analogous to that between data types and their instances in programming languages. An instance of an entity type is an occurrence of that type for which actual values of the attributes have been specified. For example, the attribute values (18 Main Street, detached, blue) define an instance of the entity type HOUSE - a detached house, painted blue on 18 Main Street. The attribute values (Everton, Liverpool, 18/11/87, 2, 1) define an instance of the entity type FOOTBALL_MATCH - a match between Everton and Liverpool on the 18 November 1987 in which Everton was the home team and won the match by two goals to one.

An attribute or set of attributes whose values uniquely identify each instance of an entity type is called a *candidate key* for that entity type. For example, the attribute ADDRESS is a key for the entity type HOUSE; REGISTRATION# is a key for the entity type CAR. Since we defined an entity as a thing which is capable of unique existence, a key must always exist. However, an entity type may have more than one candidate key. For example, a student may be identified by a unique identification number (student number), or by the combined values of his or her name and address. It is useful to choose a *primary key* from among the candidates. The primary key will play an important role when we come to look at the mapping of entity-relationship models onto implementations. When possible we should try to avoid composite primary keys for entities, i.e. keys involving several attributes.

1.2.2   Relationships

A relationship is a named association between two or more entity types. For example, the relationship PLAYS_FOR between the entity types PLAYER and TEAM; the relationship CITIZEN_OF between the entity types PERSON and COUNTRY.

The *functionality* of a relationship may be one-to-one (1:1), one-to-many (1:N) or many-to-many (N:M). As an example, consider a possible company database which might contain the following relationships:

1:1   The relationship HEAD_OF between the entity types MANAGER and DEPARTMENT is 1:1. This means that a department has *at most one* head and that a manager is head of *at most one* department.

1:N   The relationship SUPERVISES between the entity types MAN-AGER and EMPLOYEE is 1:N. This assumes that a manager may supervise *any number* of different employees but a given employee is supervised by *at most one* manager.

N:M   The relationship ASSIGNED_TO between the entity types EMPLOYEE and PROJECT is N:M. Thus an employee may be assigned to *many* different projects and each project may have *many* employees assigned to it.

Some relationships can have properties which may be represented by attributes of the relationship. For example the relationship ASSIGNED_TO between the EMPLOYEE and PROJECT entity types could have attributes such as DATE (date of assignment) and ROLE (the role played by an employee on a project). These attributes cannot be associated solely with the entity type EMPLOYEE or with the entity type PROJECT. Rather they are properties of each employee-project pair connected via the relationship ASSIGNED_TO. Thus if we state that employee John Smith was assigned on 15 October 1989 in the role of 'publicity director', we must identify the project to which these values relate in order for the statement to have full meaning. An employee will in general have a different set of values for these attributes for each project to which he/she is assigned. Thus such properties are best considered as attributes of the relationship.

Membership class
If the semantics of a relationship are such that every instance of an entity type must participate in the relationship, then the membership class of the entity type is said to be *mandatory* in that relationship. Otherwise, the membership class is *optional*.

For example, suppose that in our company database we have an entity type REPORT which has an N:1 relationship PUBLISHES with the entity type PROJECT. That is, each project may publish many reports but a given report relates to exactly one project. The membership class of REPORT in the relationship PUBLISHES is mandatory, since every report must be related to a project. However the membership class of PROJECT in the relationship is optional, since a project might not publish any reports.

The decision as to whether the membership class of an entity type in some relationship is mandatory or optional may sometimes be at the discretion of the data modeller. For example, consider once again the 1:N relationship SUPERVISES between the entity types MANAGER and EMPLOYEE. If we wish to enforce the rule that every employee *must* have a manager, then the membership class of EMPLOYEE in the relationship SUPERVISES is said to be mandatory. However, if we wish to allow a situation in which an employee may exist without being supervised by a manager, then the membership class of EMPLOYEE in the relationship SUPERVISES is said to be optional.

As we shall see later in this chapter, the membership classes of the entity types in a relationship may influence the way in which the relationship is implemented. If an entity type is a mandatory member of some relationship then the implementation should enforce the integrity constraint that no instance of that entity type may exist in the database which does not participate in the relationship.

1.2.3   Schematic representation of EER models

Schematic entity-relationship models use diagrams to depict the natural structure of the data. In these diagrams rectangles represent entity types and diamonds represent relationships. Relationships are linked to their constituent entity types by arcs, and the degree of the relationship is indicated on the arc.

The complete EER model also includes a list of attributes for each entity type and relationship. These are sometimes included on the diagram, but in this text, in the interests of clarity, the attributes will be listed separately.

Example
An EER model for a small company database comprising the entity types DEPARTMENT, PROJECT, EMPLOYEE and REPORT might be represented schematically as shown in Figure 1.1. Each department has many employees but only one manager. An employee belongs to only one department. An employee may work on many different projects which can be managed by different departments. Each report is associated with a

specific project and a project may generate many such reports.

The entity types for this situation (with primary key attributes under-lined) are as follows:

1. Entity type DEPARTMENT with attributes <u>DNAME</u> (a unique depart-ment name), LOCATION, ...

2. Entity type PROJECT with attributes <u>P#</u> (a project number which is unique within the company), TITLE, BUDGET, START_DATE, END_DATE, ...

3. Entity type EMPLOYEE with attributes <u>EMP#</u> (a unique employee number), ENAME, ADDRESS, SEX, ...

4. Entity type REPORT with attributes <u>R#</u> (a unique report number), TITLE, DATE, ...

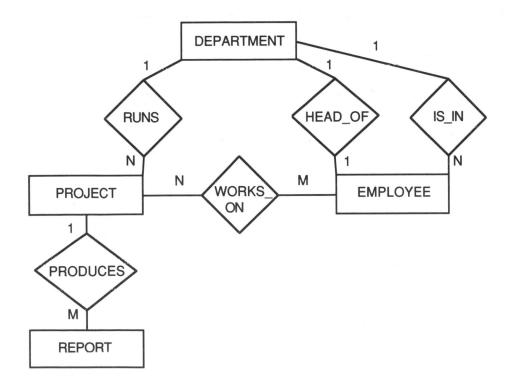

Figure 1.1 Entity-relationship diagram for the company database

The relationships among the entity types are as follows:

1. The 1:1 relationship HEAD_OF between EMPLOYEE and DEPART-
   MENT. The membership class of this relationship is optional for
   EMPLOYEE (i.e. an employee may or may not be head of a department), but mandatory for DEPARTMENT (if we wish to insist that
   every department must have a head).

2. The N:1 relationship IS_IN between EMPLOYEE and DEPART-
   MENT. The membership class of this relationship is mandatory for
   EMPLOYEE. That is, an employee must belong to a department.

3. The 1:N relationship RUNS between entity types DEPARTMENT and
   PROJECT. The membership class of this relationship is mandatory for
   PROJECT, since every project is run by a department.

4. The M:N relationship WORKS_ON between EMPLOYEE and PRO-
   JECT. As described earlier in this chapter, this relationship may have
   attributes such as DATE (the date of assignment) and ROLE, which are
   associated with an employee *and* a project together as a pair and not
   with either individually.

5. The 1:N relationship PRODUCES between PROJECT and REPORT.
   The membership class of this relationship is mandatory for REPORT if
   we require that every report must have an associated project.

1.2.4   More complex relationships

Real-world situations often contain rather more complex relationships
among entity types than the simple binary 1:1, 1:N or N:M relationships
considered so far. For example we may have relationships among entities
of the same type or relationships involving more than two entity types. The
most important of these are described in the following sections.

Involuted relationships
Involuted relationships are relationships among different instances of the
same entity type. Such relationships may also be 1:1, 1:N or N:M as illustrated by the following examples:

Example 1: A 1:1 involuted relationship
An instance of the entity type PERSON may be related to another member
through the relationship MARRY. This relationship, shown in Figure 1.2,
is a 1:1 involuted relationship if we make the simplifying assumption that a
person may be married to at most one other, i.e. past marriages are ignored
and polygamy is forbidden!

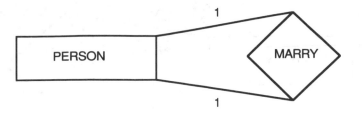

Figure 1.2   A 1:1 involuted relationship

The membership class of PERSON in this relationship is clearly optional. That is, a person may or may not be married.

Example 2:   A 1:N involuted relationship
An instance of the entity type EMPLOYEE may supervise other instances. If we assume that a given employee may have at most one supervisor then we have a 1:N involuted relationship SUPERVISES, as shown in Figure 1.3.

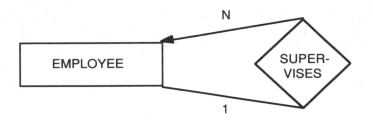

Figure 1.3   A 1:N involuted relationship

(The arrow in this diagram is necessary to indicate the direction of the relationship, namely that one employee supervises many others and not that many employees supervise one other.) The membership class of the entity type EMPLOYEE in this relationship is optional, since not all employees have a supervisor. However, the membership class might be *almost* mandatory if most employees have a supervisor. We shall return to this point later in the chapter.

Example 3:   An N:M involuted relationship
An instance of the entity type PART might be composed of other parts, while a given part may be a component of many other parts. This situation could be represented by an N:M involuted relationship COMPRISES as shown in Figure 1.4.

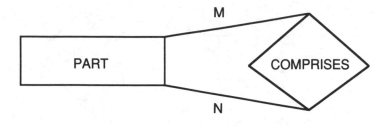

Figure 1.4   An N:M involuted relationship

Ternary relationships

Relationships may involve more than two entity types. Those involving three are not uncommon. As an example, consider the database illustrated in Figure 1.5, which is to hold information on companies, the products that they manufacture, and the countries to which they export these products.

The set of countries to which a product is exported varies from product to product and also from company to company. The relationship SELLS is *ternary*, i.e. it involves three entity types.The functionality of the ternary relationship SELLS is shown in Figure 1.5 to be 'many-to-many-to-many' (N:M:P). This reflects the following facts about the relationship:

For a given (company, product) pair there are in general many countries to which that product is sold. For a given (country, product) pair there may be several companies exporting that product to that country. For a given (company, country) pair there may be many products exported by that company to that country.

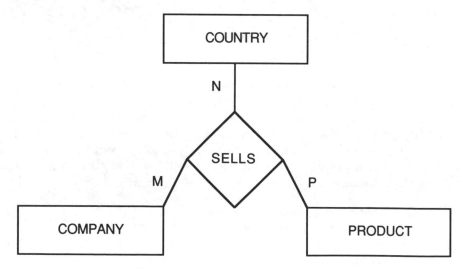

Figure 1.5   A ternary relationship

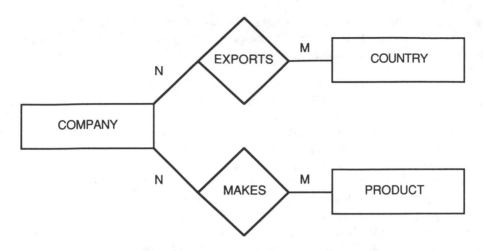

Figure 1.6 Two binary N:M relationships

The functionality of a ternary relationship could also be 'one-to-many-to-many', 'one-to-one-to-many' or even 'one-to-one-to-one', and the semantics of the relationship must be carefully examined to determine its functionality. We shall return to this problem later in the chapter when we consider the representation of ternary relationships in the relational model.

Ternary relationships must be defined carefully and should be introduced only when the relationship cannot be accurately represented by several binary relationships among the participating entity types. Otherwise, as we shall see later, unnecessary redundancy is likely to arise in the resulting database. For example, if a company manufactures many products and exports *all* of these products to a number of different countries, then the two independent binary relationships EXPORTS and MAKES, as shown in Figure 1.6, should be defined instead of a ternary relationship. In this case, it is important to note that the set of countries to which a company exports is independent of the product, and this fact must be reflected by the data model. We shall return to this point later in the chapter when we discuss a concept known as *multivalued dependency*.

Subtypes
A particular weakness of the original entity-relationship model as proposed by Chen was the absence of the concept of a *subtype* and *generalizations* of such subtypes. An entity type E_1 is a subtype of an entity type E_2 if every instance of E_1 is also an instance of E_2. An entity type E is a generalization of the entity types E_1, E_2 ... E_n, if each occurrence of E is also an occurrence of one and only one of the entities E_1, E_2 ... E_n. Smith and Smith [1977] introduced the term generalization in their semantic hierarchy model

and thereby provided a formal basis for subtypes within an abstract data model. These ideas have been extended by others specifically with regard to the entity-relationship model [Scheuermann *et al.*, 1980; Navathe and Cheng, 1983; Sakai, 1983].

As an example of subtypes, consider that in the small company database described above it may be more appropriate to represent heads of departments as *managers*, a special category of employee. Also, there may be other categories of the EMPLOYEE entity type that we wish to distinguish, such as SECRETARY, TECHNICIAN and ENGINEER. Each of these entity sets shares some properties by virtue of the fact that they may all be considered as different categories of an entity type EMPLOYEE. In fact, these entity types are *subtypes* of the entity type EMPLOYEE which is said to be their *supertype*. Note that an instance of a subtype cannot exist in the database without also being a member of the supertype. That is, an instance of the subtype represents the same real-world entity as some instance of the supertype. It is the responsibility of the implementation to ensure that this semantic rule is enforced. However, note that it is not essential that every member of a supertype be a member of one of its subtypes. Also, the subtypes need not be mutually exclusive.

Subtypes may themselves have subtypes, leading to a type hierarchy. For example, in a company concerned with the aerospace industry the subtype ENGINEER may be categorized into the three distinct entity types: AUTO_ENGINEER, AERO_ENGINEER, ELECTRONIC_ENGINEER. This leads to the type hierarchy shown in Figure 1.7. The relationship between a subtype and its parent type is represented by a special kind of 1:1 relationship called an *IS_A* relationship.

Subtypes share all of the attributes of their supertype and some, but not necessarily all, of its relationships. Entities which are members of a subtype are said to *inherit* the attributes of their supertype. Also, a subtype may have additional attributes and relationships which are specific to the subtype. Thus for example, in the company database we may wish to enforce the rule that only instances of the entity type MANAGER, a subtype of EMPLOYEE, may participate in the relationship HEAD_OF. In this case, as shown in Figure 1.8, the relationship would be defined between the entity types MANAGER and DEPARTMENT. A manager shares all the attributes of an employee but may have additional attributes that are relevant only to managers.

It is advantageous to recognize subtypes when they arise since their inclusion adds clarity and precision to the schema and can improve the efficiency of any subsequent implementation. Subtypes often arise in situations where there are many different user views of the enterprise being modelled, and it is important that the data modeller recognize generalizations and type hierarchies when constructing the global data model.

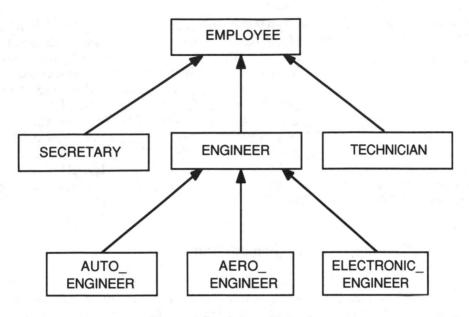

Figure 1.7 A type hierarchy

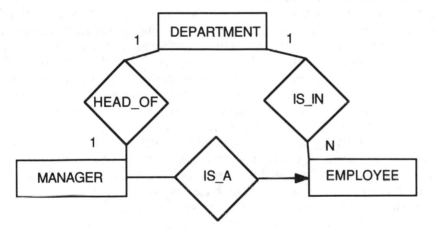

Figure 1.8 MANAGER as a subtype of EMPLOYEE

Generalization and specialization

From an alternative viewpoint, the entity type EMPLOYEE may be considered as a *generalization* of the entity types SECRETARY, ENGINEER and TECHNICIAN if every instance of EMPLOYEE in the database is also an

instance of one of these subtypes. In this case the entity types SECRE-
TARY, ENGINEER and TECHNICIAN form *specializations* of the entity
type EMPLOYEE, where each specialization is distinguished by the value
of an attribute or attributes. In this case the distinguishing attribute could be
JOB_TITLE. A variety of specializations could be defined on the same
entity set, each being distinguished by a different characteristic. For example, another specialization of the entity set EMPLOYEE could be the subtypes FIXED_TERM, LONG_TERM in which employees are distinguished by the value of the attribute TYPE_OF_CONTRACT. Yet another
specialization could be the subtypes WEEKLY_PAID, HOURLY_PAID
which distinguish among all employees on the basis of the value of the
attribute MODE_OF_PAYMENT.

1.2.5   Mapping to an implementation

A great advantage of EER models is that they can be understood by non-
specialists. The number of entities in a database is generally considerably
smaller than the total number of data items. Thus by using the concept of
an entity as an abstraction for those real-world objects about which we
wish to collect information, we greatly simplify the requirements analysis
and conceptual design phases. A schematic EER model may be modified
and extended by a user until it accurately represents the structure of the data
being modelled. In this regard EER models are independent of any particular database management system. These systems generally impose restrictions on the way in which the data may be represented, whereas the EER
model, being at a higher level, can more accurately reflect the natural
structure of the data. Also, unlike many implementations, EER models are
flexible and extensible, and so adapt easily to new developments.

The translation of an EER model into an implementation is reasonably
straightforward. Every database management system provides some mechanism for representing entities and the connections between them
(relationships), but of course compromises have to be made depending on
the facilities available. Network database management systems, for example, often impose restrictions on the types of relationship that can be
directly represented. With such systems it may be necessary to decompose
N:M relationships and involuted relationships into more primitive structures to facilitate implementation.

The relational model on the other hand can, despite its relative simplicity, capture much of the information of EER models and represent that
information by a collection of two-dimensional tables. These tables, or
relations, may be thought of as an abstraction of a restricted form of the
well known data-processing concept of a file.

1.3   THE RELATIONAL DATA MODEL

The relational data model was conceived by Codd in a series of papers published in the early 1970s [Codd, 1970, 1972a, 1972b, 1974]. The model has a sound theoretical foundation, based on the mathematical theory of relations and the first-order logic, but presents the user with a simple view of the data in the form of two-dimensional tables. The strong theoretical foundation of the model permits the application of systematic methods, based on high-level abstractions, to the design and manipulation of relational databases. This greatly reduces the complexities faced by the data modeller and by the end-user.

We shall begin this section by examining the formal definition of a relation, and we shall study the concepts of attribute and key as applied to relations. We shall then present a methodology for translating EER models into relational form.

Definitions

A mathematical definition of a relation may be stated as follows:

Given a collection of sets D_1, D_2, ..., D_n (not necessarily distinct), R is a *relation* on those n sets if it is a set of ordered n-tuples $(d_1, d_2, ..., d_n)$ such that d_1 belongs to D_1 , d_2 to D_2 , ..., d_n to D_n . The sets D_i are called the *domains* of R. The value of n is called the *degree* of R.

It is convenient to represent a relation as a table. The columns of the tabular relation represent *attributes*. Each attribute A has a distinct name, and is always referenced by that name, never by its position. Attribute names have no underlying ordering, and so if the columns of a tabular relation are permuted, the attribute values in each row must be permuted accordingly.

Each attribute A has an associated domain which consists of all the allowable values of A. The relational notion of a domain is closely related to the concept of a *data type* in programming languages and we shall discuss the significance of types and domains in greater depth in later chapters. Attribute values in a relation must be single, non-decomposable data items. That is, an attribute value may not represent a group of data items which are distinguishable by the underlying database management system.

Each row (often called a *tuple*) of a tabular relation is distinct. That is, no two tuples may agree on all their attribute values. Also, the ordering of tuples is immaterial. These properties follow from the fact that a relation, as defined above, is a *set* of tuples.The *cardinality* of a relation is the number of tuples which it contains at any instant in time.

As an example, consider the relation CAR, as defined by the following scheme (a *relation scheme* is simply the name of the relation followed by a list of its attribute names in parentheses).

REG#	MAKE	MODEL	YEAR
ZID654	Ford	Fiesta	1987
BXI930	VW	Golf	1986
COI453	Nissan	Sunny	1987
ZXI675	Ford	Escort	1985
RST786	Fiat	Uno	1983
TXI521	Ford	Orion	1985
HCY675	VW	Jetta	1986
EBZ2308	Toyota	Carina	1989

Figure 1.9 An instance of the relation CAR in tabular format

CAR (REG#, MAKE, MODEL, YEAR)

In tabular format an instance of this relation might appear as shown in Figure 1.9.

The degree of this relation is 4, since it has 4 attributes, and the cardinality of this instance is 7, since there are 7 tuples.

As the reader may have already appreciated, a tuple in a relation corresponds closely to the familiar data processing concept of a record, while attributes correspond with fields. As with attributes, each field has a name and denotes the smallest item of data which has meaning in the real world. Also, each field has a specific data type. A record, like a tuple, has a specific format since its fields have specific data types.

Keys

A key K of a relation R is a subset of the attributes of R which have the following time-independent properties:

1. *Unique identification*: The value of K uniquely identifies each tuple in R.

2. *Non-redundancy*: No attribute in K can be discarded without destroying property 1.

Since each tuple in a relation is distinct, a key always exists. That is, a key consisting of *all* the attributes of R will always have property 1. It then remains to find a subset with property 2. A relation may have more than one candidate key. That is, it may have more than one set of attributes which satisfy properties 1 and 2 above. In this case we must choose one as the *primary key*. An attribute which participates in the primary key is called a *prime attribute*. The value of a prime attribute in any tuple may not be null (undefined). In specifying relation schemes we shall underline the prime attributes.

1.3.1   Transformation of EER models

The following is a set of guidelines for converting an EER model into a relational schema. They are not hard and fast rules and the database designer must use them in conjunction with common sense and an intimate knowledge of the application. However, used wisely, they should lead to a good first approximation to the optimal relational schema.

Transformation of entity types

Each entity type is represented by a relation scheme in which the attributes of the entity type become attributes of the relation. For example, the entity type EMPLOYEE defined in our description of the company database in Section 1.2 may be represented by a relation scheme of the form:

EMPLOYEE (EMP#, ENAME, ADDRESS, SEX, ...)

The primary key of the entity type will serve as the primary key of the relation provided it satisfies the properties of unique identification and non-redundancy defined above.

However, an entity relation such as that defined above may contain additional attributes arising from its participation in relationships. The representation of relationships in the relational model is described in the following sections.

Transformation of binary relationships

The techniques for transforming a relationship depend on the functionality of the relationship and on the membership classes of the participating entity types. The following guidelines are appropriate:

Mandatory membership classes
If entity type E_2 is a *mandatory* member of an N:1 relationship with entity type E_1, then the relation scheme for E_2 contains the prime attributes of E_1. For example, if we insist that every project must be associated with a department then the entity type PROJECT is a mandatory member of the relationship RUNS. The relation scheme for PROJECT should therefore contain the prime attributes of DEPARTMENT, i.e.:

PROJECT (P#, DNAME, TITLE, START_DATE, END_DATE, ...)

A key posted into another relation in this way is often called a *foreign key*. In this example the foreign key DNAME represents the relationship RUNS between DEPARTMENT and PROJECT.

Optional membership classes
If entity type E_2 is an *optional* member of an N:1 relationship with entity type E_1 then the relationship is usually represented by a separate relation scheme containing the prime attributes of E_1 and E_2, together with any attributes of the relationship.

For example, consider the relationship, shown in Figure 1.10, between the entity types BORROWER and BOOK in a library database.

Figure 1.10   A 1:N relationship with optional membership

At any given time a book may or may not be on loan (assume that only current loans are recorded in the database). We might represent this model by the following relational schema:

BORROWER (<u>B#</u>, NAME, ADDRESS, ...)

BOOK (<u>ISBN</u>, B#, TITLE, ...)

where we have included in the BOOK relation the foreign key B#, to hold the identification number of the borrower who currently has a particular book on loan. However, the value of the B# attribute will be *null* in many of the tuples in the BOOK relation, i.e. for all those books which are not currently on loan. The term *null value* in this context means that a value for the attribute is unavailable due to the fact that an instance of the entity type BOOK does not participate in the relationship at present.

The semantics of null values in relations are discussed by [Codd, 1979] and the topic has aroused considerable discussion in the literature in recent years. In particular the presence of null values can add significant complications to the manipulation of a relational database. It should be pointed out that null values do not only arise due to the optionality of relationships as in the above example. For example, their presence may be due to the fact that an attribute value is simply *unknown* at the present time, or it may be that the value of a particular attribute is *undefined* for some instance of an entity type.

In the above example we can avoid the problem of null values by introducing a separate relation to represent the relationship ON_LOAN:

BORROWER (<u>B#</u>, NAME, ADDRESS, ...)

BOOK (<u>CATALOG#</u>, TITLE, ...)

ON_LOAN (<u>CATALOG#</u>, B#)

Thus only those books which are currently on loan appear in the ON_LOAN relation. A separate relation for an optional relationship is particularly advisable if the relationship has attributes. For example, we could associate attributes such as DATE-OF-LOAN and DATE-DUE with the ON_LOAN relationship and these are readily incorporated into the ON_LOAN relation. Posting these attributes in the BOOK relation would compound the problem of null values.

Note, however, that there may be cases where the membership class of an entity type in a relationship is 'almost mandatory' i.e. a large percentage of tuples participate in the relationship. In such cases it may be better to tolerate a small number of null values rather than introduce a separate relation.

Many-to-many binary relationships
An N:M binary relationship is always represented by a separate relation scheme which consists of the prime attributes of each of the participating entity types together with any attributes of the relationship. This transformation applies irrespective of the membership classes of the participating entity types. For example the relationship WORKS_ON between the entity types EMPLOYEE and PROJECT could be represented by the following scheme:

WORKS_ON (<u>EMP#</u>, <u>P#</u>, DATE, ROLE, ...)

Relational schema for the company database
Applying the above guidelines to our entity-relationship model for the company database, we obtain the following relational schema:

DEPARTMENT (<u>DNAME</u>, MANAGER_EMP#, LOCATION, ...)

PROJECT (<u>P#</u>, TITLE, DNAME, START_DATE, END_DATE, BUDGET, ...)

EMPLOYEE (<u>EMP#</u>, DNAME, ENAME, EADDRESS, SEX, ...)

MANAGER (<u>EMP#</u>, OFFICE#, ...)

WORKS_ON (<u>EMP#</u>, <u>P#</u>, DATE, ROLE, ...)

REPORT (<u>R#</u>, P#, TITLE, DATE, ...)

In this schema the foreign key MANAGER_EMP# in the DEPARTMENT relation represents the relationship HEAD_OF with the entity set MANAGERS, indicating that the membership class of this relationship is mandatory for DEPARTMENT. The foreign key DNAME in the PROJECT relation represents the relationship RUNS, the entity type PROJECT being a mandatory member of each of this relationship. The foreign key DNAME in the EMPLOYEE relation represents the relationship IS_IN between DEPARTMENT and EMPLOYEE, of which EMPLOYEE is a mandatory member. The relation WORKS_ON arises from the M:N relationship between EMPLOYEE and PROJECT as described above.

Transformation of involuted relationships
The transformation of involuted relationships follows, to a large extent, the guidelines given above for binary relationships. The techniques involved are best illustrated by a number of examples.

Example 1: A 1:1 involuted relationship
A common example of a 1:1 involuted relationship is the relationship of marriage between instances of the entity type PERSON (shown in earlier Figure 1.2). This is clearly an optional relationship since there will generally be many persons who do not participate in the relationship. Therefore we represent the relationship by a separate relation scheme as follows:

PERSON (<u>ID#</u>, NAME, ADDRESS, ...)

MARRY (<u>HUSBAND ID#</u>, WIFE_ID#, DATE_OF_MARRIAGE)

Note that we must resolve the attribute name clash in the relation MARRY by distinguishing between the ID# of the husband and of the wife. Assuming that each person has only one spouse, either HUSBAND_ID# or WIFE_ID# may serve as the primary key of the relation MARRY. If we wish to store details of remarriages then the functionality of the relationship becomes N:M and all three attributes form the key. (Since a couple could remarry, DATE_OF_MARRIAGE is required as a prime attribute.)

Example 2: A 1:N involuted relationship
An example of an involuted 1:N relationship is that between employees and supervisors, where supervisors are also employees (shown previously in Figure 1.3). If every (or almost every) employee has a supervisor, then we have a mandatory relationship and this may be represented by posting the key of the supervisor into the relation scheme for EMPLOYEE in the following manner:

EMPLOYEE (<u>ID#</u>, SUPERVISOR_ID#, ENAME, ...)

If only some employees are supervised then we should have a separate relation to represent the relationship as in the following schema:

EMPLOYEE (<u>ID#</u>, ENAME, ...)

SUPERVISES (<u>ID#</u>, SUPERVISOR_ID#, ...)

Example 3:   An N:M involuted relationship
An example of an N:M involuted relationship is given by the situation where we have parts which form the components of other parts (shown previously in Figure 1.4). This translates to the following relational schema:

PART (<u>P#</u>, PNAME, DESCRIPTION, ...)

COMPRISES (<u>MAJOR_P#</u>, <u>MINOR_P#</u>, QUANTITY)

The relational schema in this case contains a separate relation for the relationship COMPRISES which, according to our guidelines, should contain the key attributes of the participating entity types. For an involuted relationship however these key attributes come from the same entity type and we must distinguish between them. Thus MAJOR_P# and MINOR_P# both denote part numbers (P#) from the PART relation. The semantics of this relation are that the part represented by MAJOR_P# contains a fixed number (represented by the attribute QUANTITY) of the parts whose identification number in the PART relation is MINOR_P#.

Transformation of ternary relationships
Every ternary relationship is transformed into a separate relation scheme containing the key attributes of the three participating entity types together with any attributes of the relationship. For example the ternary relationship SELLS illustrated in Figure 1.5 would be represented by the following relations:

COMPANY (<u>COMP_NAME</u>, ...)

PRODUCT (<u>PROD_NAME</u>, ...)

COUNTRY (<u>COUNTRY_NAME</u>, ...)

SELLS (<u>COMP_NAME</u>, <u>PROD_NAME</u>, <u>COUNTRY_NAME</u>)

A possible additional attribute of the relation SELLS could be the QUANTITY of the product sold each year by the company to the country. The key attributes of the relation representing the ternary relationship are determined by the functionality of the relationship. If SELLS is M:N:P then all three foreign keys make up the key for SELLS. However, if every company exports each of its products to only one country (but that country varies with product and company) then clearly only COMP_NAME and PROD_NAME are required to form the key for SELLS.

To illustrate this point further, consider a situation in which trainees work on a variety of projects under the supervision of instructors. No instructor can supervise any given trainee on more than one project and no trainee can work on any given project under the supervision of more than one instructor. As shown in Figure 1.11 this situation may be represented by a ternary relationship SUPERVISES involving the entity types TRAINEE, INSTRUCTOR and PROJECT.

The relationship SUPERVISES is 1:1:N and, applying our guidelines, a relational schema for this database is given by:

TRAINEE (<u>EMP#</u>, ...)

INSTRUCTOR (<u>EMP#</u>, ...)

PROJECT (<u>PROJ#</u>, ...)

SUPERVISES (<u>INSTRUCTOR_EMP#</u>, <u>TRAINEE_EMP#</u>, PROJ#)

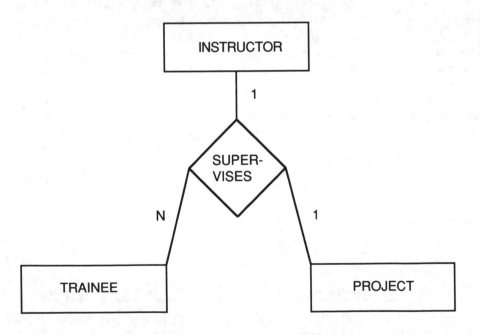

Figure 1.11 A 1:1:N ternary relationship

Note that the SUPERVISES relation has another candidate key, i.e. we could have:

SUPERVISES (<u>TRAINEE EMP#</u>, <u>PROJ#</u>, INSTRUCTOR_EMP#)

As an example of a 1:1:1 ternary relationship, consider the following relationship between teachers, textbooks and subjects. A teacher uses one textbook for a given subject. Different teachers use different textbooks for the same subject. No teacher will use the same textbook for different subjects, but different teachers can use the same textbook for different subjects (e.g. *Macbeth* is used by one teacher for English Literature and by another for Drama). Figure 1.12 illustrates the ternary relationship USES between the entity types TEACHER, TEXTBOOK and SUBJECT.

The relationship USES is 1:1:1 and a relational schema for this database is:

TEACHER (<u>STAFF#</u>, ...)

TEXTBOOK (<u>BOOK NAME</u>, ...)

SUBJECT (<u>SUBJECT NAME</u>, ...)

USES (<u>STAFF#</u>, <u>BOOK NAME</u>, SUBJECT_NAME)

The relation USES actually has three candidate keys. Any combination of two attributes chosen from the three forms a key for the relation.

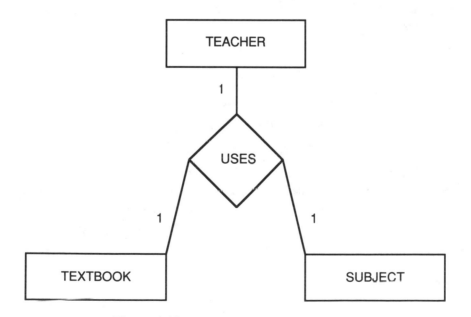

Figure 1.12   A 1:1:1 ternary relationship

Transformation of subtypes

One possible relational representation of a subtype simply contains the key attributes of the supertype, together with any additional attributes specific to the subtype. For example, suppose that we introduce the subtype MANAGER of the entity type EMPLOYEE into our company database. Then the relational schema will require a separate relation for MANAGER of the form:

    MANAGER (EMP#, OFFICE#)

In this relation the key attribute EMP# is a foreign key from the EMPLOYEE relation, which represents the IS_A relationship between the subtype and its supertype. Through this foreign key we have access to the additional attributes of a manager which he shares with other employees.

In general, if we use this scheme, the transformation of a type hierarchy into a relational schema results in a separate relation for the root entity type and for each subtype. The key of each relation is the key of the root entity relation, which also contains attributes which are common to all of the subtypes. The relation for each subtype contains, together with the key, attributes which are specific to that subtype.

Thus consider again the type hierarchy illustrated in Figure 1.7, which has the root entity type EMPLOYEE with subtypes SECRETARY, ENGINEER and TECHNICIAN. The subtype ENGINEER has its own subtypes of AUTO-ENGINEER, AERO-ENGINEER and ELECTRONIC-ENGINEER. This hierarchy could be represented by a relational schema of the following form:

    EMPLOYEE (EMP#, attributes common to all persons)

    ENGINEER (EMP#, attributes specific to engineers)

    SECRETARY (EMP#, attributes specific to secretaries)

    TECHNICIAN (EMP#, attributes specific to technicians)

    AERO_ENGINEER (EMP#, attributes specific to aero-engineers)

    AUTO_ENGINEER (EMP#, attributes specific to auto-engineers)

    ELECTRONIC_ENGINEER (EMP#, attributes specific to electronic
                             engineers)

where the attribute EMP# is a key attribute whose value uniquely identifies one instance of the entity type EMPLOYEE. The EMPLOYEE relation will contain a tuple for every engineer, secretary and technician. The ENGINEER relation will have a tuple for every auto-engineer, aero-engineer and electronic engineer. It is the responsibility of the implementation to ensure that consistency is maintained among all of these relations.

1.4   NORMALIZATION OF RELATION SCHEMES

A relational schema designed according to the guidelines of the previous section may still contain ambiguities or inconsistencies which must be resolved before implementation. This process of refinement is known as *normalization*.

Normalization theory is built around the concept of *normal forms*. Relation schemes designed according to the guidelines of Section 1.3 should, at the very least, be in *first normal form* (1NF). A first normal form relation is a relation in which every attribute value is an atomic, non-decomposable data item. This property was inherent in our definition of a relation. In Codd's seminal paper on the relational model [Codd, 1970] he defined two further normal forms, *second normal form* (2NF) and *third normal form* (3NF). Later, third normal form was shown to have certain inadequacies and a stronger form was introduced called *Boyce–Codd normal form* (BCNF) [Codd, 1974]. Subsequently Fagin introduced *fourth normal form* (4NF) [Fagin, 1977] and also *fifth normal form* (5NF) [Fagin, 1979].

Before we consider these normal forms in some detail, it must be stressed that normalization theory is nothing more than a formalization of good database design principles. The derivation of appropriate entities, attributes and relationships from the initial requirements analysis will have a crucial influence on the level of normalization present in the resultant relational schema. Any ambiguities or inconsistencies present in this schema will most likely have arisen due to an inadequate or incorrect entity-relationship model. Entity normalization will be preserved under the transformations described in Section 1.3.

Further discussion of normalization requires a definition of the term *functional dependence*.

1.4.1   Functional dependence

Given a relation R, attribute B of R is functionally dependent on attribute A of R (written as A —> B) if and only if whenever two tuples of R agree on their A-value they also agree on their B-value. That is, at any instant in time each value of A has exactly one value of B associated with it. (Attributes A and B may be composite.)

As an example, consider the following (badly designed) relation scheme:

REPORT (S#, C#, TITLE, LNAME, ROOM#, MARKS)

A tuple <s, c, t, l, r, m> in this relation indicates that student s obtained marks *m* on course number *c* which has title *t* and is given by lecturer *l* who has room number *r*. Assume that each course has only one lecturer and each lecturer has one room. Some of the functional dependencies existing in this relation are as follows:

1. [S#, C#] —> MARKS

This implies that for a given pair of (S#, C#) values occurring in the relation REPORT there is exactly one value of MARKS.

2. C# —> TITLE

3. C# —> LNAME

4. C# —> ROOM#

For a given value of C# there is exactly one value of TITLE, LNAME and ROOM#.

5. LNAME —> ROOM#

Each lecturer has exactly one associated value of ROOM#.

The attribute MARKS is said to be *fully* functionally dependent on the key since it is dependent on the key attributes S# and C# as a composite pair, but not on either individually. In general, an attribute B of relation R is fully functionally dependent on a set of attributes A of R if it is functionally dependent on A and not functionally dependent on any proper subset of A.

The attributes TITLE, LNAME and ROOM# are said to be *partially* dependent on the key since they are dependent only on C# and not on S#. The attribute ROOM# is said to be *transitively* dependent on C# since it is dependent on LNAME which in turn is dependent on C#. Such partial and transitive dependencies in relation schemes can give rise to serious problems when manipulating the database, and so they must be removed before implementation.

1.4.2 Second normal form

A relation is said to be in second normal form (2NF) if it is in 1NF and every non-prime attribute is fully functionally dependent on the primary key.

The relation REPORT defined above is not in 2NF and this can give rise to the following anomalies:

1. If we wish to insert details of a new course into the database we cannot do so until at least one student has registered for the course (we cannot

have a null value in the prime attribute S#). Similarly, if we wish to insert details of a new lecturer and his room number we cannot do so until he is assigned to a course and at least one student has registered for that course.

2. If we wish to change the title of course 361 from Database Technology to Database Systems then we must search for every tuple containing this value of C# and update all of them. There will be as many tuples as there are students enrolled for course 361.

3. If every student enrolled for course 361 drops out of that course and we delete the corresponding tuples, then all details of the course will disappear from the database.

To convert to 2NF and overcome these anomalies we split the relation into two, bringing together into a separate relation scheme those attributes which are partially dependent on the key.

REPORT (S#, C#, MARKS)

COURSE (C#, TITLE, LNAME, ROOM#)

These relations are in 2NF since in each of them the non-prime attributes are fully dependent on the key. However the relation COURSE requires further normalization due to the existence of the transitive dependency:

C# —> LNAME —> ROOM#

1.4.3   Third normal form

A relation R is said to be in third normal form (3NF) if it is in 2NF and every non-prime attribute of R is non-transitively dependent on the primary key.

Actually, our definitions of 2NF and 3NF are restricted in that they deal only with dependencies between non-prime attributes and the *primary* key. A more general definition of a 3NF relation R is that it is a relation in which every non-prime attribute is fully functionally dependent on *every* key of R, and non-transitively dependent on *every* key of R. More precisely,

*   *a relation R is in 3NF if whenever X —> A holds in R and A is not in X then either X contains a key for R, or A is prime.*

The relation COURSE defined above is not in 3NF since we have the dependency LNAME —> ROOM# and LNAME is not a key and ROOM# is non-prime. This transitive dependency can also give rise to anomalies:

1. We cannot insert details of a new lecturer and his room number until he is assigned to a course.

2. To change the room number for a lecturer we must change it in every tuple corresponding to a course given by that lecturer.

3. If a lecturer ceases to give any course then all details of that lecturer and his room# are deleted from the database.

To convert to 3NF we split the relation COURSE into two relations, separating out the transitive dependency. This gives a final relational schema defined by the following:

REPORT (<u>S#</u>, <u>C#</u>, MARKS)

COURSE (<u>C#</u>, TITLE, LNAME)

LECTURER (<u>LNAME</u>, ROOM#)

These relations are now fully normalized. Note however, that had we started with a good design (i.e. an EER model in which students, courses and lecturers were represented by entity types) and applied our transformation guidelines, we would have obtained the above schema directly.

The reduction of the original REPORT relation into the three relations above constitutes what is known as a *non-loss decomposition*. In general, a relation R(A, B, C) in which we have the functional dependency,

$$A \longrightarrow B$$

can always be non-loss decomposed into its 'projections' $R_1(A, B)$ and $R_2(A, C)$. This result is known as Heath's theorem [Heath, 1971]. No information is lost in such a decomposition since the original relation can always be reconstructed by 'joining' the projections. Thus, any information that can be derived from the original structure can also be derived from the new structure. As we have seen from the anomalies described above, the converse is not necessarily true. Thus a non-loss decomposition may be regarded as a more precise representation of the real world.

1.4.4   Boyce–Codd normal form

Third normal form does not deal satisfactorily with relations which have multiple candidate keys, where those keys are composite and overlap (i.e. have at least one attribute in common).

In order to define a further normal form, called Boyce–Codd normal form (BCNF), it is convenient to introduce the concept of a *determinant*. A determinant is an attribute, or group of attributes, on which some other attribute is fully functionally dependent. Then we have that,

* *A relation R is in BCNF if and only if every determinant is a candidate key.*

This is more restrictive than 3NF. Thus any relation that is in BCNF is also in 3NF.

As an example, consider a college in which each subject is taught by several teachers but each teacher teaches only one subject. Each student takes several subjects and has only one teacher for a given subject. This might be represented by the following relation scheme:

ENROLS (S#, TEACHER_NAME, SUBJECT_NAME)

However, this relation is not even in 2NF since we have the partial dependency,

TEACHER_NAME —> SUBJECT_NAME

Alternatively, we could have

ENROLS (S#, SUBJECT_NAME, TEACHER_NAME)

This relation is in 3NF but not in BCNF since we have the dependency,

TEACHER_NAME —> SUBJECT_NAME

and TEACHER_NAME is not a candidate key. Thus we cannot insert the fact that a teacher teaches a certain subject until at least one student enrols for that subject. Also, the fact that a teacher teaches a certain subject is recorded, with great redundancy, for every student to whom he teaches that subject. The solution, once again, is a non-loss decomposition given by:

CLASS (S#, TEACHER_NAME)

TEACHES (TEACHER_NAME, SUBJECT_NAME)

These relations are fully normalized. The fact that a teacher teaches a certain subject is recorded only once in the TEACHES relation and the problems described above are avoided.

In entity-relationship modelling, the relation ENROLS would arise from an incorrect representation of the interrelationships between the entity types STUDENT, TEACHER and SUBJECT, as a single ternary relationship. The problems with this relation would have been avoided if we had realized at the data analysis stage that we actually have two independent binary relationships in this situation - an N:M relationship between STUDENT and TEACHER, and a 1:N relationship between SUBJECT and TEACHER. A transformation of these two binary relationships would have led to the relations CLASS and TEACHES.

COMPANY	PRODUCT	COUNTRY
IBM	PC	France
IBM	PC	Italy
IBM	PC	UK
IBM	Mainframe	France
IBM	Mainframe	Italy
IBM	Mainframe	UK
DEC	PC	France
DEC	PC	Ireland
DEC	Mini	France
DEC	Mini	Spain
ICL	Mainframe	Italy
ICL	Mainframe	France
...	...	...

Figure 1.13   An instance of the relation SELLS

1.4.5   Multi-valued dependency and fourth normal form

Fourth normal form is best described by an example. Thus, consider the following relation representing the relationship between companies, products and countries:

SELLS (COMPANY, PRODUCT, COUNTRY)

A tuple $<x, y, z>$ in this relation indicates that company x sells product y in country z. An instance of this relation might have the form shown in Figure 1.13.

It is straightforward to check that this relation is in BCNF. However, if we know that each manufacturer sells *all* its products in *every* country to which it exports, then it is clear that this relation contains a great deal of redundancy.

For example, to add a new product for IBM we must add a tuple for every country to which IBM exports. In a properly normalized relational schema this information should only have to be added once. Similarly, if DEC starts exporting all its products to China, then a separate tuple must be inserted for each product.

It is clear that the redundancy is eliminated if we replace SELLS by a non-loss decomposition consisting of two relations, MAKES and EXPORTS, whose schemes are as follows:

MAKES

EXPORTS

COMPANY	PRODUCT
IBM	PC
IBM	Mainframe
DEC	PC
DEC	Mini
ICL	Mainframe

COMPANY	COUNTRY
IBM	France
IBM	Italy
IBM	UK
DEC	France
DEC	Spain
DEC	Ireland
ICL	Italy
ICL	France

Figure 1.14   Instances of the relations MAKES and EXPORTS

MAKES (<u>COMPANY</u>, <u>PRODUCT</u>)

EXPORTS (<u>COMPANY</u>, <u>COUNTRY</u>)

The information that is held in the instance of SELLS shown in Figure 1.13 can then be represented by the instances of the MAKES and EXPORTS relations shown in Figure 1.14.

The normalization rules that we have studied so far do not help us to eliminate the redundancy in the relation SELLS. This is because the redundancy is not caused by partial or transitive functional dependencies. Rather, the problem arises in the relation SELLS because we have two *multi-valued dependencies*:

COMPANY —>—> PRODUCT

COMPANY —>—> COUNTRY

Given a relation R (A, B, C), the multi-valued dependency,

A —>—> B

holds in R if and only if the *set* of B-values matching a given (A-value, C-value) pair in R depends only on the A-value and is independent of the C-value (A, B, and C may of course be composite.) Thus in the above example the set of countries to which a company exports a product is determined by the company name and is independent of the product name. Similarly the set of products exported to a country by a company is independent of the country name.

It is possible of course that in the real-world situation the multi-valued dependencies described above do not hold. For example, the set of countries to which a company exports a product may vary from product to product. In this case the relation SELLS would be in fully normalized form.

We are now in a position to define fourth normal form:

- *A relation R is said to be in fourth normal form (4NF) if and only if, whenever there exists a multi-valued dependency in R, A —>—> B, then all attributes of R are functionally dependent on A.*

Equivalently, R is in 4NF if it is in BCNF and all multi-valued dependencies in R are in fact functional dependencies. In the relation SELLS, neither of the multi-valued dependencies are functional dependencies. That is, neither PRODUCT nor COUNTRY is functionally dependent on COMPANY.

It is important to realize that violations of fourth normal form arise from errors made at the data analysis stage. In the above example, the relation SELLS results from a ternary relationship involving the three entity types COMPANY, PRODUCT and COUNTRY. A proper data analysis however, should have revealed (at the entity-relationship modelling stage) that the relationships between the entity types COMPANY and PRODUCT, and COMPANY and COUNTRY were independent.

1.4.6   Limitations of normalization

As we have seen, normalization to a large extent removes the anomalies present in some 1NF and 2NF relations which may arise due to incorrect entity-relationship modelling. For most practical applications reduction to 3NF is adequate, but sometimes further refinement to BCNF or 4NF is warranted. There is in fact a fifth normal form (5NF), which is designed to cope with a type of dependency called 'join dependency' which is not covered by the other normal forms. However such dependencies are rare and 5NF is of little practical significance. For a comprehensive description of 5NF see Fagin [1979] or Date [1990], or the more informal description given by Kent [1983].

It should be borne in mind, however, that full normalization may not always be desirable and the database designer may take advantage of his intimate knowledge of the real world and choose not to normalize in some particular instances. For example, consider the following relation:

CUSTOMER (<u>NAME</u>, STREET, CITY, POSTCODE)

Strictly speaking, the attribute POSTCODE uniquely identifies STREET and CITY so that we have the transitive dependencies:

POSTCODE —> STREET

POSTCODE —> CITY

Thus CUSTOMER is not in 3NF. However, in practice the attributes STREET, CITY and POSTCODE are always used together as a unit and decomposing the relation would not be advisable in this case. This rather contrived example is given to illustrate the point that, as in many other aspects of database design, the data modeller must use common sense when normalizing and should not consider the rules given above as absolute.

It is also important to bear in mind that from a practical point of view normalization, while often facilitating update, tends to have an adverse effect on retrieval. Related data which may have been retrievable from one relation in an unnormalized schema may have to be retrieved from several relations in the normalized form. The database designer may therefore be tempted to take account of performance requirements when deciding whether to normalize all relations fully. A 'pragmatic' approach such as this is valid provided the integrity of the database is not compromised for the sake of efficiency.

1.5   RELATIONAL DATABASE DESIGN METHODOLOGY

We are now in a position to define a methodology for relational database design (adapted from Teorey *et al*. [1986]) which leads us from the initial requirements analysis to a set of normalized relations which are an accurate representation of the real-world situation. The steps involved in this methodology, as illustrated in Figure 1.15, are described below.

Step 1.   Requirements analysis
The objectives of the requirements analysis stage are to identify the data requirements of the enterprise and to describe informally the information to be recorded about the data objects and their interrelationships. For a large enterprise with many different classes of users, *multiple views* of data and relationships occur. These views must be amalgamated into a single global view, eliminating redundancy and inconsistency from the model in the process. For example, the modeller must be able to recognize among the differing views, *synonyms* (words of different forms having the same meaning), and *homonyms* (words of the same form having different meanings). In addition, it is important to identify data objects which may belong to the same type hierarchy.

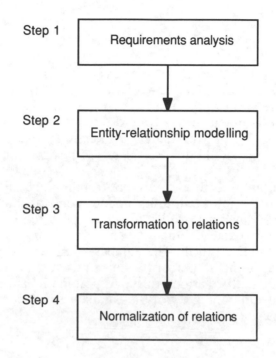

Figure 1.15   A methodology for relational database design

The requirements analysis stage should also involve an analysis of the types of transactions (operations) to be performed on the database since these may have a significant influence on the information content of the database. Requirements analysis is a crucial step in the design process since we must ensure that we incorporate all the necessary information for the particular application.

Step 2.   EER modelling of requirements
At this stage we construct an EER model to describe the data objects and their interrelationships. We identify key attributes, decide on the functionality of relationships and whether the membership classes of the participating entity sets are optional or mandatory. We then construct a schematic EER model which gives a global view of the entire database.

Step 3.   Transformation of EER model to a relational schema
We apply the guidelines from Section 1.3 to map the EER model onto a set of relations. Particular attention must be paid at this stage to the membership classes of entity types in relationships, to involuted relationships, to subtypes and generalizations, and to ternary relationships.

Step 4. Normalization of the relational schema

For each relation produced at Step 3, derive a list of functional dependencies and, if present, multi-valued dependencies. If necessary, reduce each relation to the highest stage of normalization required using the techniques described in Section 1.4.

This methodology provides a disciplined approach to relational database design which is particularly advantageous for large databases. Using entity types as abstractions for real-world objects and focusing on the relationships among entity types, reduces the number of data elements to be considered and simplifies the analysis stage. The reduction of an EER model to a set of normalized relations is to a large extent a mechanical process, though a designer may wish to use intimate knowledge of the application to refine the resultant schema in order to improve processing efficiency.

1.6   DATABASE INTEGRITY

The preservation of the integrity of a database system is concerned with the maintenance of the correctness and consistency of the data. In a multi-user database environment this is a major task, since integrity violations may arise from many different sources, such as typing errors by data entry clerks, logical errors in application programs, or errors in system software which result in data corruption. Many commercial database management systems have an integrity subsystem which is responsible for monitoring transactions which update the database and detecting integrity violations. In the event of an integrity violation, the system then takes appropriate action, which should involve rejecting the operation, reporting the violation, and if necessary returning the database to a consistent state. However, these integrity subsystems are in general rather primitive and the problems of maintaining the correctness of the database are left largely in the hands of the database implementor.

Integrity rules may be divided into three broad categories:

1. *Domain integrity rules*, which are concerned with maintaining the correctness of attribute values within relations. The rule, given in Section 1.3, by which the values of the primary key attributes in any tuple should not be null, also falls into this category (this is sometimes called *entity integrity*).

2. *Intra-relation integrity rules*, which relate to the correctness of relationships among attributes of the same relation (e.g. functional dependencies), and to the preservation of key uniqueness.

3. *Referential integrity rules*, which are concerned with maintaining the correctness and consistency of relationships between relations.

In this chapter we discuss each of these in more detail. In subsequent chapters we describe those features of modern software development systems which are designed to assist software engineers in the construction of large, correct and easily maintainable systems, and which may be applied very effectively to the problem of maintaining database integrity.

1.6.1   Domain integrity

As described in Section 1.3, a relation of degree n is defined to be a subset of the Cartesian product of n domains $D_1, D_2, ...D_n$, not necessarily distinct. That is, the values that appear in the relation in column i must belong to D_i. The columns are given names, called attributes, and it is these attribute names which are referenced in queries. Thus, every attribute of every relation, R, has an underlying domain, D_i, and any value submitted as a candidate value for R.A must belong to D_i. Entity integrity is equivalent to enforcing the rule that the domain for any primary key attribute must not include null.

A domain integrity rule, therefore, is simply a definition of the *type* of the domain, and domain integrity is closely related to the familiar concept of type checking in programming languages. The definition of the type of a domain must be as precise as possible in order to avoid violations of domain integrity. Thus for example, if we have an attribute AGE, it is not sufficient to describe its type as INTEGER since this does not prevent unrealistic values for AGE (e.g. negative values) being entered into the database. At the very least we should be able to specify that the domain type for attribute AGE is POSITIVE_INTEGER, and ideally it should be possible to specify upper and lower bounds for values of AGE. Unfortunately, commercial database management systems typically provide only simple types for domains. For example, the ORACLE database management system provides the domain types: NUMBER (integers and real numbers), CHAR (variable length character strings), DATE, TIME, and MONEY. INGRES and DB2 provide similar restricted domain types. In this respect these systems are comparable with programming languages such as FORTRAN, COBOL and PL/1 which provide limited facilities for type definition and rather weak type checking. On the other hand, as we shall see in later chapters, many object-oriented programming languages and systems provide *abstract data types* and *strong type checking*. The advantages of each of these for database applications are a major concern of this book.

1.6.2   Intra-relational integrity

Intra-relational integrity rules are concerned with maintaining the correctness of relationships among the attributes of a relation. One of the most important of these is *key uniqueness*. As we saw earlier in this chapter, the set property of a relation guarantees that no two tuples in a relation have the same values in all their components. A generalization of that property leads to a class of integrity rule that enforces the uniqueness of distinguished key components of tuples. Unfortunately, many relational database management systems do not enforce key uniqueness.

The implementation of key uniqueness requires that the system guarantees that no new tuple can be accepted for insertion into a relation if it has the same values in all its prime attributes as some existing tuple in the relation. In addition, we must also guarantee that no existing tuple in a relation is *updated* in such a way as to change its prime attribute values to be the same as those of some other tuple in the same relation. In fact, changing the values of prime attributes is an operation that should not be undertaken lightly, since as described in the next section, it may have significant consequences elsewhere in the database.

1.6.3   Referential integrity

Whereas domain integrity is concerned with maintaining the correctness of attribute values, referential integrity is concerned with the correctness of relationships between relations, and may be defined as follows:

Let R_1 be a relation with an attribute, or group of attributes, A which forms the primary key of another relation R_2. Then, at any given time, R_1.A must either be equal to the primary key value of some tuple in R_2, or it must be null (provided it is not prime). The attribute R_1.A is said to be a *foreign key*.

As we have already seen, foreign keys play an extremely important role in relational databases in that they serve to represent many different classes of relationship between entity types. As an example, consider once again that part of the simple company database from Section 1.2 which is concerned with the entity types EMPLOYEE and PROJECT and the many-to-many relationship between them, WORKS_ON. This part of the database is represented by the following three relation schemes:

EMPLOYEE (EMP#, ENAME, FLOOR)

PROJECT (P#, PNAME, LEADER)

WORKS_ON (EMP#, P#, ROLE)

The relation WORKS_ON contains two foreign keys, EMP# which is the key of EMPLOYEE and P# which is the key of PROJECT. When updating these relations, we must adhere to the following rules in order to preserve referential integrity.

Rule 1
Before inserting or updating a tuple w in WORKS_ON, check that a tuple e exists in EMPLOYEE with e.EMP# = w.EMP#, and that a tuple p exists in PROJECT with p.P# = w.P#.

Rule 2
Before deleting a tuple e from the EMPLOYEE relation, delete all tuples w in WORKS_ON where w.EMP# = e.EMP#.

Rule 3
If changing the EMP# component of any tuple e in EMPLOYEE, make the same change to the EMP# component of any tuple w in WORKS_ON where w.EMP# = e.EMP#.

Rule 4
Before deleting a tuple p from the PROJECT relation, delete all tuples w in WORKS_ON where w.P# = p.P#.

Rule 5
If changing the P# component of any tuple p in PROJECT, make the same change to the P# component of any tuple w in WORKS_ON where w.P# = p.P#.

Clearly in any large relational database environment the maintenance of referential integrity is a complex and tedious task and it is highly desirable that the users be absolved of this responsibility. This means that an update operation on any of the relations should automatically lead to the application of the appropriate referential integrity rules.

The application of these rules may or may not be transparent to users. For example, a user who deletes a PROJECT tuple from the database should be made aware of the fact that this will, by virtue of Rule 4 above, trigger the deletion of all tuples in the WORKS_ON relation which reference the deleted project (this is sometimes called *cascade* delete). However, in general the details of how these rules are implemented may be hidden from an end-user, with an underlying integrity subsystem taking responsibility for the task.

1.7   THE SEMANTIC DATA MODEL RM/T

The relational model offered a significant step forward in data modelling, moving as it did away from the machine-oriented, pointer-based techniques which symbolized the older network and hierarchical models. At the same time it offered a realistic framework for efficient implementation as evidenced by the large number of successful relational database management systems now in the marketplace. However, inadequacies in the relational model quickly become apparent when it is applied to complex, highly structured application domains. Within the simple framework offered by the model it is impossible to represent and maintain control over situations involving large numbers of interrelated, complex entities. The problem lies in the fact that the relational model is incapable of representing much of the semantic information in real-world applications [Haskin and Lorie, 1982].

Recognizing the inadequacies of the relational model, many authors have defined new models, often called semantic data models, which attempt to capture more of the semantics of application domains. Such models include SHM [Smith and Smith, 1977], TAXIS [Mylopoulos *et al.*, 1980] and SDM [Hammer and McLeod, 1981].

In 1979, Ted Codd, the founder of the relational model, published a paper entitled 'Extending the relational model to capture more meaning' [Codd, 1979], in which he defined a new semantic data model called RM/T. In RM/T a database is considered to consist of a set of entities that represent the objects and concepts, and their interrelationships, present in real-world situations. That is, relationships are modelled as entities (unlike the EER model in which relationships are a separate concept). Each entity has a set of associated properties and entities may be manipulated by a set of operations consisting of *create_entity*, *delete_entity* and *update_entity*.

Every entity in the database is defined to be an instance of at least one entity type, and all entities of a given type share the properties of that type. The model incorporates the notion of a subtype/supertype hierarchy in which the instances of a type inherit all the properties of its supertypes in the hierarchy. Also, all entity types are classified as either *associative*, *characteristic*, *kernel* or *designative*. The purpose of this classification is to provide the model with built-in integrity constraints, over and above those enforced in the conventional relational model. These classifications have the following semantics:

•   *Associative*   An associative entity represents a (potentially) many-to-many relationship between two otherwise independent entities. Associative integrity enforces the rule that an associative entity can only exist if all the entities that participate in the association also exist. This form of integrity is enforced by referential integrity rules in relational databases. An example of an associative entity might be the *assignment* of employees to projects.

- *Characteristic* A characteristic entity describes some aspect of another, superior entity. Thus, the characteristic entity is existence-dependent on the superior entity. (The entity relationship model incorporates a similar concept, often called weak entities.) The integrity rule associated with a characteristic entity is that the characteristic entity can only exist if the corresponding superior entity also exists. Once again, explicit referential integrity rules are required to enforce such a condition in the relational model. An example of a characteristic entity might be the *job history* of an employee. The job history can only exist if the employee exists.

- *Kernel* A kernel entity is a fundamental entity that is neither associative nor characteristic. Employee and project are kernel entities.

- *Designative* A designative entity is a (potentially) many-to-one relationship between two otherwise independent entities. For example, a designative entity might represent the relationship between employee and department. An employee belongs to only one department and therefore is said to designate that department. A designative entity can only exist if all the entities it designates also exist.

RM/T supports two kinds of subtype/supertype relationships. In *unconditional generalization*, each instance of the subtype must be a member of the supertype. *Alternative* (or conditional) generalization is used to form subsets of a union of types. For example, if EMPLOYEE is modelled as an alternative generalization of SECRETARY, ENGINEER and TECHNICIAN, then each employee must be either a secretary, engineer or technician. However, the set of employees does not have to contain all secretaries, engineers and technicians.

Although RM/T provides additional semantics at the conceptual level, as is the case with the EER model, RM/T maps easily to the pure relational model at a lower level of abstraction. This of course has many practical advantages considering the extensive availability of efficient relational database management systems. Additional operators have been defined at the entity level that essentially extend the declarative and operational capabilities of the relational model. These entity level operations serve to enforce greater semantic integrity.

An important concept in the RM/T model is that every entity is identified by a unique, system-generated identifier called a *surrogate*. Users can never explicitly access or manipulate surrogates. Each entity type has an associated one-column E-relation which holds the surrogates of all the instances of that type. This obviates the need to define primary keys for entities. The concept of a surrogate also plays an important role in the object-oriented model and we shall return to this concept in later chapters.

1.8 THE FUNCTIONAL DATA MODEL

It has been demonstrated by many authors [e.g. Sibley and Kerschberg, 1977; Buneman and Frankel, 1979; Shipman, 1981] that the relationships among data can simply be represented by means of the mathematical notion of a function. In this section we shall follow closely the notation of Shipman, and the functional programming language DAPLEX. Implementations of this language are reported by Fox *et al.* [1984] and Atkinson and Kulkarni [1984].

The relationship between an entity set and an attribute is a function that maps the entities in that set into the domain of the attribute. Thus, for example, rather than defining an entity STUDENT with an attribute NAME which is a STRING, NAME may be regarded as a function which maps STUDENT into STRINGs. In this way, a relation scheme of the form:

STUDENT (ID_NO, NAME, ADDRESS)

may be regarded as a set of functions:

STUDENT ( ) —> ENTITY

ID_NO (STUDENT) —> INTEGER

NAME (STUDENT) —> STRING

ADDRESS (STUDENT) —> STRING

Thus in this *Functional Data Model* we define an entity by means of the functions that may be applied to it. The representation of the entity is left to the implementor and defined at a lower level of abstraction. As we shall see in Chapter 2, this concept is similar to that of an abstract data type.

The function STUDENT defined above, with zero arguments, evaluates to a set of entities. ENTITY is a system provided type and all entities are subtypes of that type. The other functions defined above return scalar values and define attributes or properties of the entity type STUDENT. The entity types INTEGER, STRING and BOOLEAN are built-in entity types.

Functions defined over entities may also return entities (single-valued functions), or sets of entities (multi-valued functions). Multi-argument functions are also permitted and these provide a convenient means for representing relationships involving several entities. Thus the introduction of artificial entities to model many-to-many relationships or non-binary relationships is unnecessary.

A DAPLEX schema for a simplified version of a college database is given below. This is similar to the example given in Shipman's paper and we have used upper/lower case to conform with the conventions of that paper.

```
DECLARE Student ( )            —>>   ENTITY
DECLARE ID-No (Student)        —>    INTEGER
DECLARE Name (Student)         —>    STRING
DECLARE Address (Student)      —>    STRING
DECLARE Sex (Student)          —>    STRING
DECLARE Level (Student)        —>    INTEGER
DECLARE Course (Student)       —>>   Course

DECLARE Course ( )             —>>   ENTITY
DECLARE Course-No (Course)     —>    INTEGER
DECLARE Title (Course)         —>    STRING
DECLARE Department (Course)    —>    Department
DECLARE Lecturer (Course)      —>    Lecturer

DECLARE Department ( )         —>>   ENTITY
DECLARE Name (Department)      —>    STRING
DECLARE Head (Department)      —>    Lecturer

DECLARE Lecturer ( )           —>>   ENTITY
DECLARE Name (Lecturer)        —>    STRING
DECLARE Room (Lecturer)        —>    INTEGER

DEFINE Lecturer (Student)      —>>   Lecturer(Course(Student))
```

Following the notation of Shipman, we may schematically represent this functional description of the college database as shown in Figure 1.16. The similarity between this diagram and an entity-relationship diagram should be obvious to the reader. The difference is that relationships among entities or between entities and their attributes, are represented by single-valued and multi-valued functions.

A DECLARE statement introduces a new function which, if it has no arguments, is a new entity type. A single-headed arrow (—>) indicates a single-valued function, while a double-headed arrow (—>>) implies a multi-valued function. A DEFINE statement introduces a 'derived function' which is defined in terms of other declared or defined functions.

The statement:

DECLARE Department (Course) —> Department

indicates that Department is a function which, when applied to a Course entity, returns an entity of type Department. That is, a department entity is returned, not a department name or other identifier.

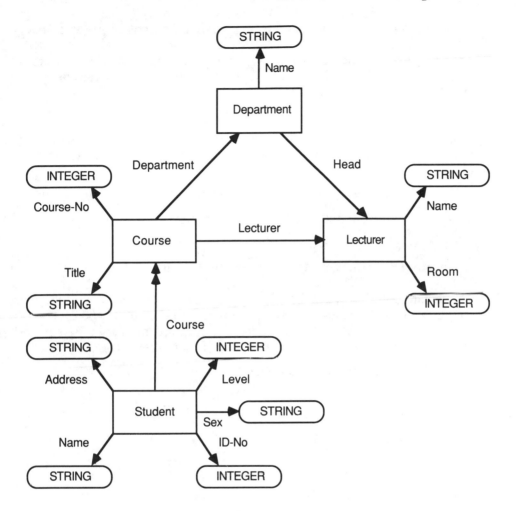

Figure 1.16 A functional model for the college database

The statement:

DECLARE Course (Student) —>> Course

is an example of a multi-valued function. That is, the Course function when applied to a Student entity returns a *set* of entities of type Course (i.e. the courses taken by the student).

An example of a multi-argument function might be:

DECLARE Marks (Student, Course) —> INTEGER

which returns the marks obtained by a specified Student entity on a specified Course entity.

For database applications it is important that functions do not map in
only one direction. That is, as well as being able to find the lecturer of a
course by means of the function,

> Lecturer (Course) —> Lecturer

we should also be able to find the course taught by a lecturer. This is provided by an explicit function inversion mechanism in DAPLEX, as illustrated by:

> DEFINE Course (Lecturer) —> INVERSE OF Lecturer (Course)

Note that the inverse function is a *derived* function.

1.8.1   Representation of subtypes in the functional model

An important concept in the functional data model is that of a *subtype*. For
example, instead of declaring students and lecturers to be of type ENTITY as
in the schema of Figure 1.16, we could introduce an entity type Person and
declare Student and Lecturer to be subtypes of that type as follows:

> DECLARE Person ( ) —>> ENTITY
>
> DECLARE Name (Person) —> STRING
>
> DECLARE Student ( ) —>> Person
>
> DECLARE Lecturer ( ) —>> Person

These declarations imply that the set of Student entities, and the set of Lecturer entities, are subsets of the set of Person entities. The two sets
(Students and Lecturers) may overlap (e.g. if a Lecturer can also be a Student), or they may be disjoint. Any Student entity and any Lecturer entity
has the Name function defined over it, and the individual Name functions
defined for these entities in the schema of the previous section are no
longer necessary. Subtypes inherit all the properties of their supertypes.

Thus the functional data model arranges types into a *type hierarchy*.
For example, we could extend the hierarchy defined above by introducing
an entity type Professor which is a subtype of the type Lecturer (i.e. all Professors are Lecturers and share the properties of Lecturers, but may have
additional properties of their own). This type hierarchy is illustrated in Figure 1.17.

Introducing Professor into the functional schema requires an additional
function declaration of the form:

> DECLARE Professor () —>> Lecturer

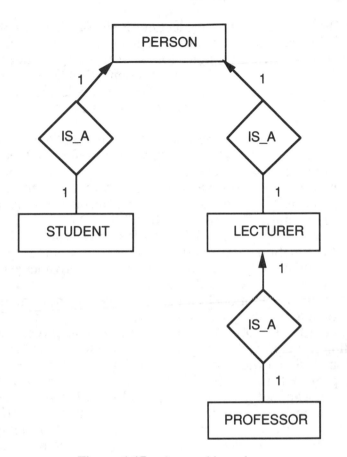

Figure 1.17   A type hierarchy

The same kind of hierarchy could be represented in the relational model with a schema of the following form:

      PERSON (<u>ID#</u>, NAME, ADDRESS, SEX)

      STUDENT (<u>ID#</u>, LEVEL)

      LECTURER (<u>ID#</u>, ROOM#, APPOINTMENT_DATE)

      PROFESSOR (<u>ID#</u>, CHAIR_TITLE)

In this schema the PERSON relation holds an identifying number (ID#) for all persons in the database, together with their names, addresses and sex. The LECTURER relation holds a subset of these ID#s, for all those persons who are lecturers, together with attributes which apply specifically to lecturers, namely room number and date of appointment. The relation

PROFESSOR holds a subset of the lecturer ID#s together with the attribute CHAIR_TITLE, an attribute which pertains only to professors. Thus the complete set of attributes held for a professor includes ID# and CHAIR_TITLE (in the PROFESSOR relation), ROOM# and APPOINT-MENT_DATE (in the LECTURER relation), and NAME, ADDRESS and SEX (in the PERSON relation). This arises by virtue of the fact that a professor is a lecturer who is a person.

It should be obvious to the reader that, in a database such as that defined by the above schema, the maintenance of referential integrity, is of crucial importance. That is, the database management system must not allow a situation to arise in which a 'subtype relation' contains a tuple which has no corresponding tuple in the appropriate 'supertype relation'. Similarly, for example, if we delete a PROFESSOR tuple, the system must ensure that the corresponding LECTURER and PERSON tuples are also deleted. In the functional data model such referential integrity constraints are *implicit* in the model itself. This is an important advantage of the functional approach over the relational data model.

The functional data model is a simple, user-friendly model with an easily understood visual representation and a sophisticated level of in-built semantic integrity. The ability to reference functions directly makes data manipulation in the model very elegant. These attractions have led to the model being used in a wide range of research projects. For example, in the Multibase project {Smith, 1981} it has been used to provide a unifying interface to distributed heterogeneous databases. However, the inherent power of the model gives rise to significant implementation difficulties for large-scale applications which have yet to be adequately resolved. For this reason, the model has not yet provided the basis for a commercial database management system.

1.9   SUMMARY

In this chapter we have studied semantic data modelling, concentrating on four of the classical models in database technology, namely:

* The Extended Entity-Relationship Model

* The Relational Data Model

* The Relational Model RM/T

* The Functional Data Model

The extended entity-relationship model concentrates on conceptual modelling and provides a convenient diagrammatic technique for representing data models. The relational model has an inherent simplicity which lends itself to ease of understanding and straightforward implementation. The relational model RM/T extends the conventional relational model to capture more of the semantics of real-world applications. It retains the simple, tabular representational format of the relational model but provides enhanced facilities for representing entities and relationships. In many respects RM/T can be viewed as an amalgamation of the relational model and the entity-relationship model. The functional data model is also characterized by an inherent simplicity but incorporates a high level of semantic integrity. This can have significant advantages for representing complex relationships among entities.

We shall see in later chapters that semantic data modelling plays an important role in object-oriented database design.

1.10 BIBLIOGRAPHIC NOTES

Two general references to semantic data models are the books by Tsichritzis and Lochovsky [1982] and Teorey and Fry [1982]. The first of these discusses and compares a wide range of data models. A more modern survey and analysis of semantic data models appears in Hull and King [1987].

Entity-relationship modelling has received a great deal of attention in the research literature and an international conference devoted entirely to this model is held at regular intervals. A formal description of the model is given by Ng [1981]. The review paper by Teorey *et al.* [1986] is an excellent study of the extended entity-relationship model and the transformation of EER models to relational schemes.

Detailed descriptions of the relational model can be found in many texts, notably those of Ullman [1982] and Yang [1986]. Date's second volume on database systems [Date, 1983] gives a more extensive description of the relational model RM/T than that given in this chapter. A description of this model can also be found in the paper by Codd [1979].

The functional data model is discussed with great clarity in Shipman [1981], and more recently in Buneman and Frankel [1979].

2

Principles of object-oriented systems

2.1 SOFTWARE ENGINEERING AND DATABASES

The term 'software engineering' implies the application of scientific knowledge and discipline to the construction of computer software systems. In practice, this involves the production of a specification, a problem solution, and a program design prior to the inception of actual coding. Ideally therefore, software development should be like mathematics or any other branch of science or engineering, where one adopts a methodical approach to solving a problem and, most importantly, one is required to show that the solution is correct, i.e. that it solves the given problem.

One of the most important techniques for dealing with complexity in software systems is the *principle of abstraction*. Abstraction is used to construct solutions to problems without having to take account of the intricate details of the various component subproblems. The system design phase of any software project involves abstraction as a means for developing representations of the complex data objects and concepts inherent in the application. Abstraction allows the system designer to apply the principles of *stepwise refinement* by which at each stage of the system design unnecessary details associated with representation or implementation may be hidden from the surrounding environment. This ability to decompose a large problem into a number of smaller ones, and to specify unambiguously the interactions among the components, is a vital tool in the construction of large software systems.

Database systems are typically large software systems, which are distinguished by the fact that they involve the processing of data with three important characteristics:

1. There is a large amount of data which, in general, must be held in external storage and which must be organized such that individual data

objects can be retrieved and updated efficiently.

2. The data objects have complex interrelationships.

3. The data must be shared among many different users, and the system must maintain the integrity of the data in the face of the many difficulties imposed by such sharing.

Very few of the popular programming languages provide adequate constructs for the efficient processing of large volumes of interrelated data. The simple sequential and random file structures found in most languages offer only minimal facilities in this area. However many modern languages do offer very powerful algorithmic constructs for the representation of complex data objects. The ability to define such abstract objects, together with appropriate operations, is invaluable for database applications.

Conventional database management systems, on the other hand, in general provide highly efficient facilities for organizing and accessing data on external storage devices, but rather primitive constructs for logical data structuring. For example, most commercial database management systems offer only very simple data types such as integer, character, string, etc., and the database designer and applications programmer is limited to these types even when communicating with the database from within a sophisticated programming language. However there is a strong trend in the research community toward extending programming languages in the direction of databases and, at the same time, toward extending database systems with enhanced semantic data modelling concepts. These research efforts have led to the development of *object-oriented databases*.

Object-oriented databases differ from their more conventional counterparts in that they incorporate much greater sophistication with regard to type definition and data abstraction. Of course, these concepts have been extensively researched in the programming language domain and the database community has drawn heavily on the experience gained from that research. At the same time, a number of research efforts within the programming language community have been attempting to develop more sophisticated models of persistence and concurrency, two concepts which are fundamental to database applications.

Although programming language objects and database objects are similar in that they encapsulate properties, there are several important differences. First, database objects must *persist* beyond the lifetime of the program creating them. Second, many database applications require the capability to create and access multiple versions of an object (examples of this are to be found in historical databases, databases for software management, and for computer-aided design). Third, highly active databases such as those used for air traffic control and power distribution management, require the ability to associate conditions and actions with objects where the actions are triggered when the conditions are satisfied. Also, database integrity control demands the capability to associate constraints with objects. Finally, databases require predicate-based query capabilities on objects. Programming languages do not typically support persistent objects or multiple object versions. Nor do they often provide the facilities to associate constraints and triggers with objects.

In this chapter we first of all outline the basic principles of software engineering as applied to database system design and development. We then describe the concepts underlying object-oriented systems, concentrating on the fundamental concepts of data abstraction, inheritance and polymorphism.

2.2   THE DATABASE LIFE CYCLE

Any large software project may be divided up into several *project phases* (see for example the book by Pomberger [1984]). The five phases of the database life cycle are [Hughes, 1988]:

- *requirements analysis* ;
- *data modelling and applications software design* ;
- *implementation* ;
- *testing* ;
- *maintenance.*

Each of these are examined in detail below. However, it must be stressed that database development is an *iterative* process. Often the data modelling phase will highlight ambiguities or inconsistencies in the requirements analysis, while the implementation and test phases may indicate that errors were made in constructing the data model. A common scenario is for the user to place additional demands on the system following the implementation and testing phases. If the original design and implementation is poorly structured this iterative process can easily lead to a system which is of poor quality and which is difficult to maintain.

2.2.1   Requirements analysis

The objective of the requirements analysis phase is to describe precisely the information content of the proposed database system and to determine the transaction demands that will be placed on the system. This analysis should lead to the production of a *requirements specification*, which is a detailed and precise description of the database system, its functions and its user interfaces. This requirements specification must be accepted by both users and database designer as complete and consistent and must therefore be clearly understood by everyone involved. For this reason, natural languages tend to be widely used for drafting requirements specifications. However, the imprecision and ambiguity of such languages tend to make it very difficult to test specifications for completeness and consistency. The discipline of software engineering has attempted to provide some methodical aids for constructing specifications, ranging from elementary aids such as flowcharts and decision tables to more elaborate techniques such as *SSADM* (Structured Systems Analysis and Design Methodology) as described by Downs *et al.* [1988], or SADT [Shoman and Ross, 1977].

The use of tools for Computer Aided Software Engineering (CASE) has increased substantially over the past few years, particularly in the area of information systems design. These tools are typically stand-alone, PC-based products, containing a data dictionary (or encyclopedia), graphical interfaces, documentation tools, tools for analysis and consistency checking, and (limited) application generators. These products automate parts of the system development life cycle and attempt to overcome the productivity and quality crisis in software development.

CASE is a mechanism for automating the techniques inherent in structured systems development methodologies. The methodologies provide a framework for rigorously defining the process to be automated and the tools provide the support for automation. Structured methodologies have been around since the 1970s but prior to the advent of CASE they had made little impact on organizations concerned with systems development. This was largely due to the fact that when a manual approach was adopted the detailed diagrammatic techniques of most of these methodologies were exceedingly tedious to use. CASE tools however are bringing new life to structured methodologies by transforming systems development into a fully automated process [Crozier *et al.*, 1989].

To a large extent however, requirements specification remains, like data modelling and programming, a creative task for which a precise and comprehensive methodology has not yet been developed. We shall continue our discussion therefore with a somewhat informal description of the requirements analysis phase.

The first step in the requirements analysis phase is to identify the data objects present in the real-world situation to be modelled, the properties of those objects, and the associations among them. Functionally different applications (user views) must be identified, not only so that such views may be incorporated in the overall system design, but also to identify access rights for the purposes of security and privacy. Thus the database designer must discuss the requirements in depth with every possible class of user and study the manner in which data is currently processed. In the existing environment, data may be processed manually or possibly in a computerized system using files and application programs. In the former case the data processing needs may not be well defined, and decisions must be made as to what can and should be automated. Where a file-based computerized system exists, the various application programs may be rather loosely related. Some may be grossly inefficient, while others may be redundant or of historical interest only.

The objectives of the database designer at the requirements analysis stage are:

1. To obtain a clear and concise description of the infrastructure of the enterprise to be modelled.

2. To derive information about the nature and volume of data to be stored and processed. In particular, the properties of the data objects must be ascertained together with their domains, ordering requirements, sort criteria, units of measurement, etc. The frequency with which the data objects are accessed or updated and the expected growth in the volume of the data are also important factors which may influence the implementation phase, as are the requirements for data protection.

3. To compile information on the nature and volume of the transactions (functions) occurring in the enterprise and the relationships between those transactions. Important factors which must be determined include the exact purpose of the transaction, the frequency with which it is performed, the data requirements of the transaction, and the data and information which it produces. It is also important to ascertain the nature of any interactions which may take place between the various transactions. In particular, information is required on the data flow between transactions and the sequence in which they must be performed.

2.2.2   Data modelling and design of applications software

The quality of a database system is significantly influenced by the quality of the data model, and thus data modelling occupies an important position in the database life cycle. For that reason, a large portion of this book is devoted to the subject. The purpose of data modelling is to develop a global design for the database with the ultimate objective of achieving an efficient implementation which satisfies the requirements. As with any design process, data modelling requires a certain amount of ingenuity and creativity, but meaningful and effective guidelines can still be laid down.

In Chapter 1 we presented a detailed methodology for database design which uses an extended version of the *entity-relationship model* [Chen, 1976] as a first step in the design process. This model has been very successful as a tool for communication between the designer and the end-users during the requirements analysis and design phases because of its ease of understanding and clarity of representation. One of the main reasons for its effectiveness is that it is a *top-down* approach which makes use of the *principle of abstraction*. These factors are central to the object-oriented paradigm and will be discussed in greater detail later in the chapter.

In the design of applications software the principal issues relating to quality are:

*   *Reliability* - the software should behave strictly according to the original specifications and should function correctly under both normal and abnormal conditions;

*   *Extensibility* - the applications software should be capable of adapting easily to changes in the specifications or in the data model;

*   *Reusability* - the software should be developed using a modular approach which permits modules to be reused by other applications.

2.2.3   Implementation

By implementation we mean the transformation of our data model and applications software design into a fully functioning database system which operates on a particular machine, usually under the control of a database management system. The design of the system should ideally be independent of any particular DBMS, but not all such systems are equally well suited to the task of transforming the design into an efficient and easily-maintainable implementation.

In order to provide for the phases of the database life cycle which follow implementation (testing and maintenance), a good implementation should be able to reflect good design decisions. In particular, the level of abstraction employed in the design should also be realized in the implementation. The DBMS used for implementation should provide high-level structures for the representation of complex data objects and their interrelationships. It should also provide a range of software tools (languages and utilities) which enable users to interact with the database at a level suited to their requirements, but in a manner which preserves the consistency and correctness of the database.

In object-oriented programming systems, important issues which influence efficient implementation are:

- *Configuration management* - by which software developers may keep track of inter-module dependencies and obtain information about the current state of modules;

- *Garbage collection* - by which objects which are no longer used by the system are automatically deallocated by the underlying run-time system and the resulting memory space made available for reuse.

For database applications we must add to these the issues of persistence and the efficient associative retrieval of objects via indexing and other fast access techniques. Persistence is discussed briefly below and in detail in Chapter 6. A detailed discussion of performance issues relating to object-oriented databases is deferred to Chapter 8.

2.2.4   Testing

The quality of a database system is measured first by its correctness and reliability, and second by the degree to which it satisfies the demands of the initial requirements analysis. The purpose of the testing phase therefore is twofold:

1. To discover any errors that may have arisen during the modelling and implementation phases.

2. To ascertain, in conjunction with the user community, whether the system satisfies the information demands of users and the requirements of application programs.

By error we mean any deviation from the behaviour stipulated by the requirements analysis. Such errors may be caused by a faulty or inadequate requirements analysis, incorrect data modelling, or programming errors made during the implementation phase. Testing therefore is an activity which relates to the entire project and rather than be treated as an isolated phase, it should be distributed over all phases of the database life cycle, including the maintenance phase. For a complex database with a large number of different user groups, it may be necessary to develop *prototype* database systems in a number of iterations. At each stage of the iteration these prototypes can be discussed with the users to ensure that the needs of all applications are satisfied.

At the current level of sophistication in software engineering there is no universal recipe for testing software systems. The scope and number of tests will vary considerably from system to system. The effort put into this phase will depend on the complexity of the enterprise and the level of expertise available for the data modelling and implementation phases.

Note that it is also important to test the *robustness* of the system against incorrect user interaction and against errors in application programs. Protecting the database against such errors is an important aspect of database technology.

2.2.5   Maintenance

As described above it is almost impossible to devise an exhaustive test phase for a large database system, and in practice many errors and inadequacies in the system first come to light during actual use. These must be monitored and eliminated within the framework of the maintenance phase of the database life cycle. An exact requirements analysis is also very difficult in many cases and so new user demands are often added during the operation of a database system which require system modifications.

The maintenance phase involves three tasks:

1. The correction of errors which arise during operation.

2. The implementation of system modifications which arise due to new user requests or changes in the original user requirements.

3. The implementation of performance enhancements and improvements to user interfaces.

The responsibility for maintaining a multi-user database system must reside centrally with the database administrator through whom all user requests and complaints are channelled. Database usage and performance must be constantly monitored with the assistance of DBMS utilities (such as a data dictionary) which provide statistics on important factors such as access times, storage utilization and transaction throughput. Corrections, modifications and enhancements to the system, whether at the logical or physical levels, must be carried out with the minimum of disruption to the user community. Thus it is desirable to have a high degree of *data independence* by which applications are insulated from the physical organization of the database.

Maintenance can be a very expensive part of any database project and it is therefore prudent to pay particular attention to the *maintainability* of the system. Designing and implementing a database system which is easily maintained means ensuring a good *modular* structure with good supporting documentation. The techniques presented in this book for database design and development are designed to improve the maintainability of database systems.

2.3   OBJECT-ORIENTED SYSTEMS

The advent of the software crisis in the late 1960s led to a rethink on the design of programming languages. Simplicity of structure, modularity and reusability became central to language design and the discipline of software engineering was born. Better languages and the development of structured programming techniques led people to consider programs not as sequential lines of code, but as collections of interacting modules. This more disciplined approach to software development led in turn to the emergence of structured systems design methodologies which have now gained widespread acceptance, particularly in the area of applications programming. These methodologies ultimately view the structure of software systems as collections of interacting, autonomous components (or modules) each of which realizes a single conceptual function of the system. Thus, languages such as Ada and Modula/2 support various kinds of modules ranging from conventional functions and procedures to packages, concurrent processes and generic modules which can be parameterized by types.

Object-oriented languages offer modularity but much more besides. A language is said to be object-oriented if it supports objects as a language feature, where each object instance belongs to a *class* and classes support *inheritance* (each of these concepts will be explained presently). An object represents a single entity and describes both the structure and behaviour of that entity. Thus an object has a set of operations, representing the allowable operations for the entity that it describes, and a local state which is shared by these operations and which 'remembers' the effects of invoked operations. That is, the effect of invoking an operation on an object may depend on the state of the object prevailing at the time of invocation, as well as on the arguments of the operation. Thus, other previously executed operations may influence the effect of an operation. This means that an object can 'learn' from its experience, recording in its state the cumulative effect of its invocation history. This is extremely important for database and artificial intelligence applications.

An object can be manipulated like a data structure but it defines its own manipulation protocol by means of the operations declared in its external interface. The state of an object is manipulated by sending the object a message using a symbolic name (or selector) by which the receiving object selects the appropriate operation to be invoked. Thus, the receiving object responds to messages by invoking its own operations (often called 'methods'). The important point is that the receiver of the message determines how the manipulation is to be performed. That is, the selector describes what the sender of the message wants to happen but not how it should happen. This is consistent with the principles of data abstraction, modularity and 'information hiding'.

Programming language support for objects is advantageous for software development because these object abstractions can directly model real-world entities such as customers, cars, accounts, orders, etc. which clearly have a state and a behaviour. It is also desirable to be able to classify objects which have the same structural and behavioural pattern. Thus a class in an object-oriented programming language defines a structure and a set of operations which are common to a group of objects. A new object is generated by creating a new instance of the appropriate class. Objects which are instances of the same class have a common set of operations, specified in the class interface, and therefore a common object behaviour. However, such instances will in general have different states.

A class can inherit properties and operations from other classes (its superclasses) and its own properties and operations can be inherited by subclasses. An object which is an instance of a class C has available to it the operations defined in C (its base class) and in the superclasses of C. If a class may inherit from more than one superclass, we say that the language permits *multiple inheritance* [Cardelli, 1984]. Inheritance permits programmers to create classes which are *specializations* of others. Alternatively, superclasses may be *generalizations* of their subclasses. As we shall see in subsequent chapters, specialization (or particularization) and generalization are extremely useful concepts in database and artificial intelligence applications.

Although the term 'object-oriented' has become popular only during the last decade, object-oriented programming languages have been around for many years. Simula, designed by Dahl and Nygaard at the University of Oslo [Dahl and Nygaard, 1966], first appeared in the late 1960s and is usually considered as being the first such language. It is essentially an object-oriented extension to Algol 60, and features classes with single inheritance, and co-routines which simulate parallel processes. During the 1970s several Pascal-based modular programming languages appeared (e.g. Pascal Plus [Welsh and Bustard, 1981], Concurrent Pascal [Brinch-Hansen, 1976], Ada [Ichbiah *et al.*, 1979], Modula/2 [Wirth, 1982]), which were strongly influenced by Simula but which concentrated on modularity and in the process discarded the concept of inheritance and in some cases the essential features of the class. Smalltalk was developed during the 1970s by Kay, Goldberg and Ingalls at Xerox [Goldberg and Robson, 1983] and was the first substantial interactive, graphics-based implementation of an object-oriented development environment. Although the design of Smalltalk was clearly influenced by Simula, its style was rather different, with its emphasis on a free, typeless mode of programming with dynamic binding. Other developments which have made important contributions to the subject include the work on message passing in the concurrent programming language Actors [Agha, 1981], and on multiple inheritance in FLAVORS, a language for artificial intelligence [Moon, 1986].

It might be expected that after almost 25 years of development there might be some agreement on the fundamental principles of object-oriented programming languages and systems. On the contrary, the programming language community is still experimenting, while the database and AI communities are faced with considerable difficulties with regard to efficient implementation of a wide range of powerful object-oriented concepts.

The remainder of this chapter provides an introduction to the basic principles of programming with objects. We concentrate on those issues, such as data abstraction, inheritance, polymorphism and dynamic binding, which are of importance for applications in the areas of database technology and artificial intelligence.

2.3.1   Schema evolution and reusability

Database systems, perhaps even more so than other software systems, tend to evolve around a number of fundamental object types which form the kernel of the system. As the system evolves, new views of the data are added by restricting or extending existing object descriptions, and new applications on these views are generated using existing code modules as a basis. Conventional database management systems tend to offer very limited facilities for the expansion or modification of existing data structures. For example, commercial relational systems typically allow the dynamic creation and deletion of relations and the addition of new columns to a relation. Changes to domain types will usually involve the rewriting of the relations involved and changes to the applications that use them. This is largely due to the fact that the data structures comprising the database schema and the application programs are very loosely coupled. In addition, the long-standing failure of conventional database systems to provide well-defined interfaces to strongly-typed, modular programming languages makes code refinement and reuse more difficult than necessary.

Both of these features, namely schema evolution through the extension and refinement of existing data structures and the effective reuse of applications code, are major concerns of the object-oriented data model. The nature of the object-oriented model permits the semantics of schema evolution to be rigidly defined and validated [Banerjee *et al.*, 1987], while the inheritance capability of the model allows for the creation of generic components that can be reused in many parts of the system. These issues are discussed in more detail in Chapter 3.

2.3.2   Concurrency

When several application programs or terminal users are interacting with a shared database simultaneously, their operations on the database must be carefully controlled. Specifically, the effect of a database procedure (often called a *transaction*) must be that which would be obtained if no other transaction were executing concurrently. The effect of executing several transactions concurrently, therefore, must be the same as if they had been executed serially in some order. By 'effect' here, we mean the final state of the database together with any results produced by the transactions. Concurrently executing transactions whose effect is equivalent to that of some serial execution are said to be *serializable*, and most conventional database management systems impose severe restrictions on transactions in order to guarantee serializability.

To prevent any transaction from reading or updating data that are being updated by another transaction we could provide a *locking* mechanism which guarantees exclusive access to an item of data while a lock is in force. However, locking requires considerable system overheads to maintain and may cause bottlenecks, particularly if the items are large (e.g. entire relations). Thus, in recent years, alternatives to locking, such as timestamping and optimistic concurrency control, have been investigated.

Object-oriented databases have the capability to offer more concurrency than conventional systems [Weihl, 1985]. This stems from the fact that in an object-oriented system the operations on the database are not simple reads and writes but rather have more inherent semantics. The system can possibly take advantage of such semantics in scheduling transactions, but in environments involving large-scale cooperative applications the task is non-trivial. Another important issue is that serializability is in general too stringent a correctness criterion for many object-oriented systems where transactions may be long-lived and highly cooperative.

Object-based concurrency control in database management systems is still the subject of much current research that has led to the development of new models of concurrency control for cooperative transactions. The basic principles and the state-of-the-art are described in detail in Chapter 7.

2.3.3   Correctness

Program correctness has been a strong motivation for much of the work in software engineering and programming language design. Ideally, correctness should be determined by a formal mathematical proof that a program conforms to its specification. However the current widespread practice of using natural language for specifications and machine-oriented languages for implementation is not conducive to presenting mathematical proofs of programs, and this obligation is normally discharged by testing, i.e. by showing that the solution solves *some* instances of the problem.

The construction of formal proofs of correctness of programs is beyond the scope of this text and is adequately covered by other authors (e.g. Brady [1977]; McGettrick [1982]). However, we shall in this book be intimately concerned with those aspects of programming language design and programming style which influence the ease of program verification. It has long been recognized that both the characteristics of a given programming language and the practices used to write programs in the language have a significant influence on program correctness. Support in a language for concepts such as data abstraction and strong type-checking greatly ease program testing and verification. Also highly desirable is the ability to break a large program down into modules which may be separately compiled, and tested in isolation.

For a database system, correctness implies not only that it conforms to its specification, but also that the values and relationships maintained in the system obey the consistency constraints inherent in the data model, and *at all times* are an appropriate representation of the state of the enterprise. The preservation of the consistency and integrity of the data in a large multi-user database environment is a major problem. A relatively minor update to the database may require multiple changes to be propagated throughout the storage structures which represent the database at the physical level. An update which is only partially carried out may result in the database being inconsistent with the underlying data model, and incorrect with respect to its representation of the enterprise.

Correctness in programming languages is often specified in terms of *preconditions*, *postconditions* and *invariants*. In database systems correctness is maintained through the use of declaratively specified knowledge about the data and its application in the form of *integrity constraints* or *triggers*. An integrity constraint is a predicate which must be true at all times. A trigger is defined by a predicate and a body of code - whenever the predicate becomes true the code is executed (the trigger is *fired*). This knowledge is monitored by the database system at all times. Any transaction which violates an integrity constraint will be rejected, while triggers may be fired at any time when the effect of a transaction causes the appropriate predicate to become true. The body of the trigger may perform operations necessary to maintain the correctness and consistency of the database.

Maintaining correctness is a primary objective of object-oriented database systems and the model provides many advantages in this regard. Database integrity is discussed in detail in Chapter 3.

2.3.4   Persistence

The idea of extending programming languages to embrace database management concepts may be extended to allow *all* data objects (not just files or relations) to have *persistence*. That is, any data object may exist for an arbitrarily long time, beyond the lifetime of the program in which it is created. Now that virtual memory is commonplace, the distinction between primary and secondary memory should be less important. Thus the database applications programmer should be able to specify persistence as an orthogonal property of data, independent of type. One of the primary motivations for persistent programming languages is to relieve the database applications programmer of the considerable effort normally required to transfer data between the database storage system and his program. In programming database applications with conventional programming languages, a large fraction of the code is devoted to performing translations between the form of data in the program (arrays, records, sets, etc.) to the form required for external storage (operating system files, or an embedded database system interface).

The lack of adequate support for persistence has been recognized as a serious shortcoming of program language design, and languages are now appearing that address this issue. PS-algol [Atkinson *et al.*, 1983] was one of the first languages which was designed to support orthogonal persistence. That is, support for persistence does not involve the addition of new data structures to the language, but rather persistence is provided as a property applicable to all existing data structures.

Persistence, in relation to object-oriented database programming languages and systems, is a complex issue and is discussed in detail in Chapter 6.

2.4   DATA ABSTRACTION

The message sending convention described briefly above, for invoking operations on an object, supports an important principle in structured programming, namely data abstraction. The principle is that program units should not make assumptions about the implementation and internal representation of the *data types* that they use. In this way, it is possible to change the underlying implementation of data types without having to change the program units which use them. Thus the purpose of abstraction in programming is to separate behaviour from implementation. This makes large software projects more intellectually manageable since it allows for separate and independent development of different parts of the system.

Perhaps the simplest programming abstraction mechanism is the procedure. A procedure is designed to perform some task and other parts of the program may call the procedure by name in order to carry out this task. The user of a procedure needs only to know what the procedure does and not how this task is performed. Any implementation that performs the required task will suffice provided it performs correctly and with reasonable efficiency. In the early seventies however, it was realized that for large software systems a more powerful abstraction mechanism than the procedure was required [Parnas, 1972; Liskov, 1972]. From these ideas, the concept of an *abstract data type* arose [Hoare, 1972b; Liskov and Zilles, 1974]. As with procedures, the basic concept of abstract data types is to separate the user's view of the abstraction from details of its implementation in such a way that implementations of the same abstraction can be substituted freely. This is achieved by encapsulating the representation of the data object being abstracted with a set of operations that manipulate it, and restricting users to those operations. Code which uses the abstract data type will not be affected by changes in its implementation. Thus we have the following definition:

*   *An abstract data type (ADT) defines a class of objects, which have the same abstract data structure, by the operations applicable to them and the formal properties of those operations.*

Thus an abstract data type defines a class of objects that can be manipulated directly only by a specified set of operations. Such abstractions have always been used in computing. For example, programs using integers manipulate them via a built-in set of well-defined operations and do not need to be concerned with the underlying implementation strategy for integers, such as whether the representation is 2's complement or not. The contribution of abstract data types was to extend this principle of data abstraction to more complex user-defined object types.

Many modern programming languages offer very general algorithmic facilities for type definition. Module or 'information-hiding' mechanisms are provided so that arbitrary new types can be defined by both the necessary details for representation, which are hidden from the surrounding program, and the allowable operations to be maintained for objects of that type. Furthermore, since these mechanisms may be applied repeatedly, types may be mapped, step by step, from higher, user-oriented levels to lower levels, ending with the built-in language constructs. At each level, the view of the data may be abstracted from those details which are unnecessary for data usage, i.e. details with regard to representation, constraints, access rights, etc. This leads to a decoupling of the data structures which define the database, and the application programs which operate on them.

For database applications, ADTs play three inter-related roles. First they may be used to extend the typing system of the language to provide for more complex attribute types. For example, types such as date, time, colour, name, etc., which are commonly occurring attribute domains in databases but are not always provided as built-in types, may be implemented conveniently via ADTs. This may be extended to arbitrarily complex user-defined types. Second, ADTs may be constructed to represent the high-level database objects themselves. In this case we are using ADTs to represent time-evolving entities as opposed to inert data. In this regard ADTs provide a convenient vehicle for implementing integrity constraints and triggered procedures which govern the behaviour of an object at run-time. Finally, ADTs may represent relationships among entities via aggregation and generalization abstractions. Aggregation is an abstraction in which a relationship between objects is represented by a higher-level aggregate object (or type). Generalization is an abstraction in which a set of objects with similar properties is represented by a generic object. This provides a natural mechanism for the representation of the IS_A class of relationships described in Chapter 1. We shall describe aggregation and generalization (and other object-oriented abstractions) in Chapter 3.

2.4.1 Formal specification of abstract data types

As an example of an abstract data type representing a domain type, consider the familiar and commonly occurring case of the *set*. In a database system for instance we might wish to include a set of hobbies in the attributes of an entity type PERSON. That is, each person has a list of hobbies and this list varies substantially from person to person: Mr Smith may have no hobbies (the empty set), Mr Jones may have the set of hobbies (football, chess, badminton), and Ms Evans may like (hockey, badminton, swimming, dancing). We are not interested in the hobbies themselves (i.e. a hobby has no attributes other than its name), only in the set associated with each person. Relational databases however, would force us to treat hobbies as a repeating group and extract them into a separate relation:

```
PERSON ( ID#, ... )
HOBBIES ( ID#, HOBBY_NAME )
```

Thus the set of hobbies is fragmented and held remotely from the person details despite the fact that it is a simple attribute of a person.

Other examples of sets as domain types in databases might be: the set of facilities offered by a hotel (pool, sauna, restaurant, ...); the set of keywords associated with a document; the set of optional extras available on a new car (air conditioning, sunroof, alloys, ...). The important point to note is that in each case the set members are not entity types - we are not interested in their individual attributes. Thus the proper role for the set is as a domain type.

Many mathematical models have been proposed for specifying ADTs but the most appropriate for our purposes is *algebraic specification* [Guttag and Horning, 1977]. This approach can be characterized as *operator-driven* since it places the emphasis on the operators (or functions) associated with a type. A formal specification of the abstract data type *set*, for any base type X, is given in Figure 2.1. (The base type of a set is the type associated with the individual elements of the set.) We assume that X has an associated equality function, equal (X, Y) which returns true if X=Y and false otherwise. The algebraic specification consists of three parts: types, functions and axioms. The types and functions specify the syntax of the ADT while the axioms express its semantics.

The TYPES section

The TYPES section lists the types of the specification. The first such type will always be the ADT being specified. The other types are assumed to be defined elsewhere. In this case the ADT is the set of all sets, set(X) with type parameter X. X represents any type but we may require that certain operations are defined for that type. In this case we require that X has an equality operator, so that set(X) is defined only for base types that have an equality operator. The type set(X) is said to be a *generic* ADT in that it captures the common properties of sets for any type X. Actual set types are obtained by providing an explicit type for X when an instance of the ADT is declared. For example,

set(Integer)

represents the ADT *set of integer*. We shall return to the concept of genericity later in the chapter.

The FUNCTIONS section

The FUNCTIONS section lists the operations applicable to instances of the type. The syntactic notation used for specifying a function *f*, with *n* arguments of types $T_1, T_2, ..., T_n$, and returning a value of type S is

$$f: T_1, T_2, ... \ T_n \longrightarrow S$$

At least one of the types $T_1, ..., T_n$ or S must be the ADT being specified.

The functions in the specification of an ADT fall into the following three categories:

ADT *set*

TYPES
　　set(X with equal: X - X -> Boolean), Boolean, Integer

FUNCTIONS
　　new_set:　　-> *set(X)*
　　empty:　　　*set(X) -> Boolean*
　　insert:　　　*X, set(X) -> set(X)*
　　delete:　　　*X, set(X) -> set(X)*
　　member:　　*X, set(X) -> Boolean*
　　union:　　　*set(X), set(X) -> set(X)*
　　intersect:　*set(X), set(X) -> set(X)*
　　subset:　　*set(X), set(X) -> set(X)*
　　card:　　　*set(X) -> Integer*

AXIOMS
　　for all *x, y : X, s, t : set(X)*:

　　1. *insert(x, insert(y, s))* =　　if *equal(x, y)*
　　　　　　　　　　　　　　　　　then *insert(x, s)*
　　　　　　　　　　　　　　　　　else *insert(y, insert(x, s))*
　　2. *delete(x, new_set)* =　　　*new_set*
　　3. *delete(x, insert(y, s))* =　if *equal(x, y)*
　　　　　　　　　　　　　　　　　then *delete(x, s)*
　　　　　　　　　　　　　　　　　else *insert(y, delete(x, s))*
　　4. *member(x, new_set)* =　　*false*
　　5. *member(x, insert(y, s))* =　*equal(x, y) or member(x, s)*
　　6. *union(s, new_set)* =　　　*s*
　　7. *union(s, insert(x, t))* =　*insert(x, union(s, t))*
　　8. *intersect(s, new_set)* =　*new_set*
　　9. *intersect(s, insert(x,t))* =　if *member(x, s)*
　　　　　　　　　　　　　　　　　then *insert(x, intersect(s, t))*
　　　　　　　　　　　　　　　　　else *intersect(s, t)*
　　10. *subset(new_set, s)* =　　*true*
　　11. *subset(insert(x, s), t)* =　if *member(x, t)*
　　　　　　　　　　　　　　　　　then *subset(s, t)*
　　　　　　　　　　　　　　　　　else *false*
　　12. *card(new_set)* =　　　　*0*
　　13. *card(insert(x, s))* =　　*1 + card(delete(x, s))*

Figure 2.1　A formal specification of the abstract data type *set*

(i) *Constructor functions*: These are functions for which the ADT appears only on the right-hand side of the arrow. Such functions yield new elements of the ADT. The only constructor in the above example is the function *new_set*.

(ii) *Accessor functions*: These are functions for which the ADT appears only on the left-hand side of the arrow in the specification. Such functions yield properties of existing elements of the type. In the above example accessor functions are *member* (which returns a Boolean result indicating whether the first argument belongs to the second argument, which is of type set), *empty* (which returns a Boolean result indicating whether the set argument is empty), and *card* (which returns the cardinality of the set argument).

(iii) *Transformer functions*: These are functions for which the ADT appears on both the left- and right-hand sides of the arrow. These functions yield new elements of the ADT from existing elements and (possibly) other arguments. All of the functions in the set specification are transformer functions with the exception of *new_set*, *member*, *empty* and *card*.

The AXIOMS section
The AXIOMS section expresses the semantic properties of the ADT. For example, the first axiom in the set specification states the semantics of the *insert* function:

```
for all x, y : X; s : set
  insert(x, insert(y, s))  =   if x=y
                               then insert(x, s)
                               else insert(y, insert(x,s))
```

This axiom permits us to permute the order of insertions arbitrarily and to introduce or eliminate duplicate elements without changing the meaning of expressions. These correspond with the mathematical properties of a set.

2.4.2   Data abstraction and strong typing

A language is said to be *statically* typed if it is possible to determine the types of all expressions at compile time. A *strongly* typed language on the other hand offers the ability to determine the type compatibility of all expressions representing values from the static program representation at compile time [Wegner, 1989]. Static typing clearly implies strong typing but strongly typed programming languages do not have to determine the types of expressions at compile time provided they offer operand/operator compatibility. This implies the provision of some form of *dynamic binding* by which some variables or expressions are bound to their types at run-time.

The provision of a wide variety of data types, accompanied by strong type checking, are the central concepts of any programming language that aims to achieve a high degree of software integrity and maintainability. For database applications in particular, the programmer should be able to specify well-defined properties of data objects, and the rules of the language should guarantee that these properties are maintained throughout the program. Properties which are common to several objects should be separated out into a single type declaration, and referred to by name. If such a property is changed during system maintenance, only one declaration is affected rather than the individual object declarations. The advantage of this is that there is only one mechanism, namely the type checker, which is responsible for guaranteeing the legitimate usage of objects and their properties.

Statically typed languages are able to resolve many errors at compile time and, as discussed earlier, the resolution of errors at the earliest possible stage in the life cycle is highly desirable. In particular, static typing of object data structures permits a higher level specification of the data model since the types of objects and their attributes must be explicitly specified in the model. Also, static typing absolves the system of the necessity to carry out run-time type checks, thereby reducing execution time, and removes the need to store type information with data, which economizes on storage. However, the association of static typing with data abstraction is not entirely an unqualified benefit and many popular object-oriented languages (such as Smalltalk) have deliberately avoided static typing in order to enhance the flexibility of the language. Also, it has been demonstrated [Morrison *et al.*, 1987] that static binding can be particularly restrictive in database environments and that some measure of dynamic binding is often desirable. This is due to the fact that with static type checking the bindings are established at the beginning and are immutable, and any subsequent change in the database schema or application programs requires recompilation of the schema and/or the programs.

Clearly, as in many walks of life, there is a trade-off between structure and discipline on the one hand, and flexibility and speed of development on the other. Data abstraction associated with static typing can be rather burdensome for example in a situation which demands rapid prototyping. However, the lessons of software engineering, learned at great cost over the past two decades, are that *strongly* typed object-oriented languages are highly desirable for both systems and applications development. This point will be stressed at many stages throughout this text. The relationship between inheritance and dynamic binding is reconsidered in later in this chapter.

2.4.3   Implementing abstract data types with classes

In order to implement an abstract data type, we must first choose a representation for the object and implement the functions in terms of that representation. Obviously we must choose a representation which will permit these functions to be implemented in a reasonably efficient manner, but to users of the ADT this representation should be invisible. Thus the set abstraction specified above might have a representation which employs an array or a linked-list, but such a choice is left to the implementor of the abstraction and should have no bearing on the use of the ADT.

Although it is possible to implement ADTs in a language that provides no special support for them, it is more convenient if an abstract type can be implemented as a single program module. In object-oriented languages an ADT is implemented via such a module, which is usually called a *class*. For example, in C++ a class definition takes the following form:

```
class name
{
      private components

public:
      public components

};
```

The private components are the attributes and functions necessary for the implementation of the class, and these cannot be accessed by other program units which use the class. The public components of the class represent the user interface in that they are the components of the class that a user may reference. These components can be functions returning the values of attributes, constructor (and destructor) functions, accessor functions and transformer functions. Instances of classes (i.e. object instances) are typically generated at run-time via operations such as *new* or *create*.

We shall defer a detailed look at classes and their representation until Chapter 4. In the remainder of this chapter we shall specify a class by giving its name, its parameters (if any), and its user interface. This interface will consist of a series of properties, which represent the visible part of the state of the object, and a series of functions by which the user can control the behaviour of the object. Thus a template for our class specifications is as follows:

```
class <class name> [(<parameter list>)]

    properties
        {visible properties of the class}

    operations
        {operations on objects of this class which are
            visible to the user}

end <class name>.
```

For example, consider the object type *book* as might exist in a library database. Information to be held on a book include its title, date of publication, publisher and author. Typical operations on a book might be:

- Take a book out on loan;

- Reserve a book for taking out on loan when available;

- A Boolean function which returns true if the book is currently on loan and false otherwise.

The class book may be defined by the following structure:

```
class book

    properties
        title : string;
        date_of_publication : date;
        published_by : publisher;
        written_by : author;

    operations
        create () -> book;
        loan (book, borrower, date_due);
        reserve (book, borrower, date_reserved);
        on_loan (book) -> Boolean;
        ...

end book.
```

An important point to note here (and one to which we shall return in subsequent chapters) is that data abstraction as provided by the class mechanism allows one to define properties of entities in terms of other entities. Thus we see from the above example that the properties published_by and written_by are defined in terms of the classes publisher and author respectively. An outline description of these classes is given below.

```
class author

    properties
        surname : string;
        initials : string;
        nationality : country;
        year_of_birth : integer;
        year_of_death : integer;

    operations
        create () -> author;
        ...

end author.


class publisher

    properties
        name : string;
        location : city;

    operations
        create () -> publisher;
        ...

end publisher.
```

As described in Chapter 1, semantic data models offer this form of abstraction, but in the relational model a property which has structure must be separated from its owner and linked artificially through foreign keys. In this way, a single entity must be modelled as multiple tuples in multiple relations. In object-oriented data modelling with classes, the database designer is able to construct high-level models, rich in semantic integrity, without having to decompose objects into forms suitable for machine representation. We shall discuss object-oriented data modelling in greater detail in Chapter 3.

2.5   INHERITANCE

It can be seen that classes provide a good facility for modular decomposition, and their advantages for semantic data modelling will be further explored in Chapter 3. However, as seen so far they do not fully achieve the goals of reusability and extensibility. In particular, additional facilities are required to enable the class mechanism to support those frequent situations where we wish to define a new class as a specialization of an existing class. That is, we often wish to define a class of objects which has all (or almost all) of the characteristics of an existing class but has some additional properties or additional aspects to its behaviour. Examples of this were illustrated in Chapter 1 where the concepts of IS_A hierarchies and generalization/specialization were introduced.

In object-oriented systems, the concept of inheritance permits objects to be organized in taxonomies in which specialized objects inherit the properties and operations of more generalized objects. Similar classes of objects which share properties and functions can be modelled by specifying a *superclass*, which defines the common part, and then deriving specialized classes (*subclasses*) from this superclass. This feature clearly provides powerful support for reusability and extensibility since the definition of new objects can be based on existing classes.

As an example, consider the (partially complete) inheritance hierarchy shown in Figure 2.2.

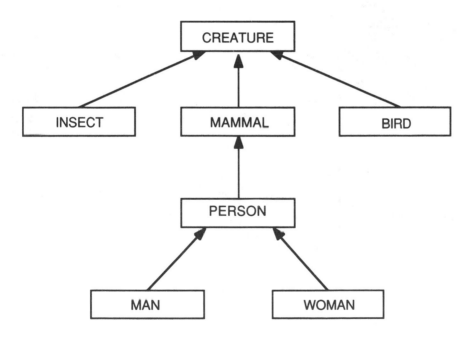

Figure 2.2 An inheritance hierarchy

The object classes mammal, bird and insect are defined as subclasses of creature, the object class person as a subclass of mammal, and man and woman as subclasses of person. Class definitions for this hierarchy might take the following form:

```
class creature

    properties
        type : string;
        weight : real;
        habitat : ( ... some habitat type ... );
        ...

    operations
        create () -> creature;
        predators (creature)  -> set (creature);
        life_expectancy (creature)  -> integer;
        ...

end creature.


class mammal

    inherit creature;

    properties
        gestation_period :  real;

    operations
        ...

end mammal.


class person

    inherit mammal;

    properties
        surname, firstname : string;
        date_of_birth : date;
        origin : country;

end person.
```

```
class man

    inherit person;

    properties
        wife : woman;
        ...

    operations
        ...

end man.


class woman

    inherit person;

    properties
        husband : man ;
        maiden_name : string;
        ...

end woman.
```

2.5.1   Inheritance for extensibility

In software engineering inheritance is a powerful mechanism for dealing with the natural evolution of a system and with incremental modification [Meyer, 1988]. That is, the inheritance mechanism may be used not only for specialization as described above, but for extending software modules to provide additional services (operations). For example, if we have a class (or module) A with subclass B, then B provides the services of A as well as its own. Thus B may be considered as an extension of A since the properties and operations applicable to instances of A are a subset of those applicable to instances of B.

This ability of inheritance to specify system evolution in a flexible manner is invaluable for the construction of large software systems. For database applications inheritance has the added advantage of providing the facility to model natural relationships among entities which have some commonality in their structure and behaviour.

2.5.2   Inheritance and polymorphism

In object-oriented programming, polymorphism refers to the ability of a single program entity to refer at run-time to instances of a variety of types or classes. A simple form of polymorphism is *overloading*, which permits the use of the same name for more than one entity in a program, ambiguities being resolved by the system by examination of the context of each occurrence of the name. Overloading is essentially a syntactic facility which permits programmers to use the same name for different implementations of similar operations. For example, one may wish to use the name *add* for operations to add two integers, two real numbers, or even two character strings. An *add* operation on variables *v1* and *v2* is invoked by the call:

```
add (v1, v2)
```

and the system decides which function to apply by examining the types of *v1* and *v2*. Ambiguities may be resolved either at compile time, in the case of statically typed languages, or at run-time. Such operator overloading is commonly provided in conventional programming languages such as Ada and Algol 68.

   A more powerful form of polymorphism is offered by *parametric polymorphism* which allows us to abstract over types. In the above example parametric polymorphism would permit us to define the function *add* with the type *T* of its arguments being specified as a *parameter* of the function, e.g.

```
add (T: type; v1, v2 : T)
```

That is, the actual type *T* is passed to the function only when it is called. This form of polymorphism was pioneered by the language ML [Milner, 1984], and also appears in the languages Poly [Matthews, 1985] and Napier [Morrison *et al.*, 1987]. Its advantages for software reuse are obvious and it can significantly reduce the amount of code in a large system.

   Generic modules (or packages), as provided by languages such as Ada, offer a similar but slightly more restrictive form of polymorphism. With genericity, one could for example, define a *list* abstraction in which the type of the elements to be held in the list is a formal parameter of the abstraction, e.g.

```
class list [ T : type ]

    properties
        maximum_length : integer;
```

operations
     create -> list [T];
     insert (x : T ; l : list [T]) -> list [T];
     delete (x : T ; l : list [T]) -> list [T];
     member (x : T ; l : list [T]) -> Boolean;
     empty (l : list [T]) -> Boolean;

end list.

Actual instances of the list abstraction are obtained by providing an actual type for the formal parameter. Thus a list of integers, a list of reals and a list of characters may be generated by the instance declarations

     Int_list : list [integer];
     Real_list : list [real];
     Char_list : list [char];

Genericity provides module implementors with a method by which they can write the same code to describe all instances of the *same implementation* of a data structure (e.g. list, stack, queue, etc.) applied to different types of objects.

Unrestricted polymorphism would clearly conflict with the notion of strong type checking, and in an object-oriented environment polymorphism is often constrained by inheritance. Obviously, an instance of a specialized type B can be viewed also as an instance of any of its ancestor types A. However, the reverse is not true since B may contain additional properties and operations which are undefined for its ancestors. Thus at run-time variables of type A in a program can be assigned to variables of type B but not vice versa. That is, returning to the example of inheritance described in the preceding section, if we have the type declarations

     p is of type person ;
     m is of type male ;

then the assignment

     p := m ;

is allowable, even in a strongly typed language. It implies that the object of type person referenced by the variable *p* is to become the object of type *male*, referenced by the variable *m*, which is of course also a person. However, the assignment

     m := p ;

is illegal, since in this statement we are attempting to assign an object of
type male to an object of type person which may not have the characteristics
required of a male object. Note that polymorphism does not allow for
objects changing their types during the lifetime of a program, but rather it
allows a variable to refer to objects of various types.

2.5.3   Inheritance and dynamic binding

Operations which are defined for a class and its subclasses need not necessarily be implemented identically in each class. Many object-oriented languages provide the capability to *redefine* an operation which has been
inherited from an ancestor. The operation retains its original name but the
implementation is tailored to the specialized class. For example, the operation which calculates the life expectancy of a creature in the inheritance
hierarchy defined above, might be redefined for the *person* class. This
would permit the software engineer to take account of factors which influence the life expectancy of persons but perhaps not those of other crea-
tures.

When this feature is considered in conjunction with polymorphism it
raises the question of how the system is to decide which form of an operation is to be applied to a polymorphic object when the precise form of the
object may not be known at compile time. For example, suppose the variable *c* in a program refers to an object of type *creature*. Then the function
call,

```
x := c.life_expectancy;
```

will clearly invoke the operation defined in the class *creature*. Similarly, if
the variable *p* refers to an object of type *person*, then the call

```
x := p.life_expectancy;
```

will invoke the redefined operation in the class *person*. However we may
have a situation in which the polymorphic variable *c*, statically declared as a
creature, refers dynamically to a *person* object. That is, we could have the
following ,

```
c := p;
...
x := c.life_expectancy;
```

The technique used is known as dynamic binding, a process by which the version of the operation to be applied is determined by the dynamic form of the object at run-time. With dynamic binding the redefined version of the *life_expectancy* operation in the class *person* will be applied in this case.

The ability of software to adapt automatically to the form of the objects which it encounters is of crucial importance in object-oriented systems.

2.6 SUMMARY

In this chapter we discuss the principal features of object-oriented programming systems and their relation to database technology. In the early sections we outline the requirements for the design and development of reliable, robust and extensible database systems using sound software engineering techniques. We define data abstraction and describe its role in the system development process. The relationship between data abstraction and object-orientation is discussed in depth. The main characteristics of the object-oriented paradigm are identified and analysed and shown to be particularly relevant to database technology through their provision of sophisticated data abstraction facilities and mechanisms for the control of data integrity and consistency.

In subsequent chapters we return frequently to many of the issues discussed here and in particular to the following important concepts:

- data abstraction,

- inheritance,

- persistence,

- concurrency.

Each of these plays a crucial role in object-oriented database design and development.

2.7 BIBLIOGRAPHIC NOTES

Abstract data types have received a great deal of attention in the literature over the past two decades. Two early seminal papers are those of Liskov and Zilles [1974] and Guttag and Horning [1977]. More modern treatments can be found in the review paper of Cardelli and Wegner [1985] and the book of Liskov and Guttag [1986].

An excellent treatment of object-oriented software construction is provided by Bertrand Meyer's book [Meyer, 1988]. Much of the subject matter in the book is based on the language Eiffel which was designed by Meyer, but the treatment is comprehensive and the book can be regarded as the definitive work in this area. In particular, the concepts of inheritance, polymorphism and genericity are given an in-depth treatment.

3

Object-oriented data modelling

3.1   BASIC CONCEPTS

The fundamental concepts underlying the object-oriented data model are straightforward. Human beings can perceive the real world as a variety of inter-related objects, and we can view these objects at different levels of detail. When we look at a tree for example, we need not concern ourselves with the intricate arrangement of leaves, branches, trunk and roots, but simply view the tree as an indivisible object with certain properties. In some circumstances we may wish to consider the leaves in more detail, but we can still view a leaf as an object with properties such as colour, texture and shape. We may wish to go down to the molecular structure of a leaf, but even a molecule can be viewed as an object with well-defined properties and behaviour.

Breaking down an application area into objects and relationships is a common technique in systems analysis and the extended entity-relationship model, described in Chapter 1, is one of many such *top-down* approaches. However, traditional database models, including the relational model, tend to break objects down into artificial structures which are more easily implemented on the rather restrictive computer architectures available today. Object-oriented databases on the other hand preserve the same high-level representation of the application throughout the analysis and implementation phases. This approach permits users to see a database as a collection of interrelated complex objects which may be viewed at whatever level of detail is necessary for their application. In this way, the object-oriented model provides a more natural representation of the real world.

In an object-oriented database every object is an instance of a *class*. The objects belonging to a class are collectively described by a class definition. That is, instead of describing individual objects, the object-oriented approach concentrates on the patterns of both state and behaviour that are common to an entire class of objects, e.g. the class of persons, of vehicles, of books, of aircraft, etc. The state of an object is implemented through properties or attributes, but unlike relational databases such properties are not restricted to non-decomposable data types and may in fact be complex objects themselves. Thus for example, a tree object may have a property 'leaf type' which as described above is itself a complex object and will have a corresponding class definition. The behaviour of an object is implemented as a set of procedures (sometimes called methods) that are encapsulated with the properties. This class structure, encompassing both properties and behaviour, is the natural unit of abstraction in object-oriented systems. An arbitrary number of *instances* of a given class may co-exist, having different identities but conforming to the same structural and operational pattern. Such objects are said to be objects of the same class.

In defining a class it is important, according to the principles of step-wise refinement, not to consider prematurely any particular representation of the data. That is, we should like to have a complete, precise and unambiguous description of the class without being encumbered by, for example, details of its underlying representation. The choice of visible details is made by considering both the intended application of the class and also its users. The primary objective is to permit users to ignore details of the system which are irrelevant to the application and concentrate on those which are important. In the design of large software systems, *data abstraction* has long been recognized as a means to develop high-level representations of the concepts that relate closely to the application being programmed and to hide the inessential details of such representations at the various stages of system development.

Object-oriented systems development is primarily a data abstraction technique, though it embellishes this technique with the notion of *inheritance*. In this chapter we discuss the relationship between data abstraction and object-oriented database design. Inheritance is briefly described, but a detailed discussion of this important concept and all its implications is deferred until Chapter 4.

3.2   OBJECT-ORIENTED SYSTEMS ANALYSIS

Traditional systems development methodologies view an information system from two separate perspectives, the *data* perspective and the *process* perspective. The data perspective is concerned with entity-relationship modelling, relational analysis, and ultimately database schema generation and the physical implementation of the database. The process perspective is

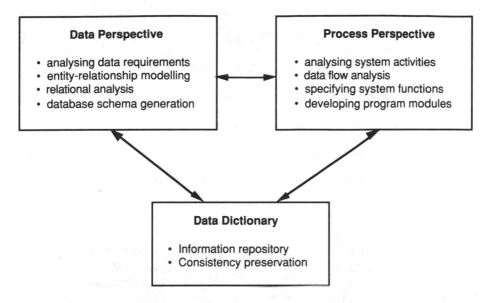

Figure 3.1   Conventional structured analysis

concerned with the functional requirements of the system and involves business activities, data flow diagrams, system functions and, at the low end, compilable units of program code (modules). In traditional tools for computer-aided software engineering (CASE tools) a *data dictionary* serves to integrate these two perspectives and maintain consistency (Figure 3.1).

In this traditional approach, often termed *data flow analysis*, processes are introduced to represent transformations of input data to output data and, by the principle of stepwise refinement, processes are successively decomposed into simpler sub-processes. Thus we have a principle of aggregation in which functions are grouped together if they are constituents of the same higher level function. These constituent functions may operate on different data stores. Data flow analysis thus places rather weak emphasis on the principle of data abstraction by which the functions operating on a particular data object should be encapsulated with that object. As a result the data flow technique can lead to great complexity for large systems.

In an object-oriented perspective (Figure 3.2), the principle of aggregation is centred on the underlying data abstractions. That is, every function must be associated with a particular object, and thus functions are grouped together if they operate on the same data abstraction. In this way, objects encapsulate both state and behaviour. Functions which are constituents of a higher level process may reside in different objects and a sequence of messages (or function calls) between objects is necessary to perform a higher level process.

Object-Oriented   Perspective

- Identifying entities/objects and their attributes

- Identifying the functions to be applied to each object

- Establishing the interface each object presents to other objects

- Implementing the objects

Figure 3.2   Object-oriented analysis

Because of the difference in aggregation principles, proceeding from a traditional structured analysis approach to an object-oriented design can be awkward. This can be avoided by adopting an object-oriented viewpoint during the analysis phase. A number of object-oriented requirements specification methods have been proposed in the literature [Booch, 1986; Seidewitz and Stark, 1987; Bailin, 1989; Ward, 1989] and it is interesting to note that the entity-relationship model occupies a central role in many of these techniques.

3.2.1   Identifying objects

One of the first questions to be answered when adopting an object-oriented approach to database design is 'how do we find the objects?'. In fact the real task is to find sets or *classes* of objects with a common structure and behaviour. There is of course no definitive approach to this problem which provides an infallible solution in every case (skill and experience play important roles), but it is possible to offer some general guidelines.

The first step in object-oriented design is to extract the meaningful objects and concepts from the real-world enterprise being modelled. That is, one of the key ideas of object-oriented design is to consider database construction as operational modelling and use the object classes of the real world as a basis for the classes in the database system. However, how do we decide what is an object and what is a property of an object? For example, if offices are located in cities, should *city* be a property of the object class *office* or should it be an object class in its own right? The general guideline lies in the theory of data abstraction: something should only be represented by a class if it represents a set of similar objects or concepts with meaningful properties and operations which are required to be maintained by the system. Thus if city has its own properties which must be recorded by the system (such as name, area, population, etc.), and its own operations, and exists in its own right, independently of its relationship with office, then city should be an object class in the database. If city exists solely as a property of office then it should be an attribute of the object class office.

A look back to Chapter 1 will show that this is very closely related to the approach that one adopts in extended entity-relationship modelling. However it is important to realize that in the object-oriented approach to database design the data modeller is not constrained by implementation or normalization considerations which are often introduced into EER modelling. For example, the attributes of object classes need not be non-decomposable or single-valued. Thus the EER approach is a valid and indeed extremely valuable approach for object-oriented database design, provided one maintains a high level of data abstraction and does not introduce the decompositions which are typically demanded by the network and relational models. Unnecessary modifications to the EER model include the elimination of repeating groups, the decomposition of many-to-many and non-binary relationships, and the introduction of token identifiers for entities. Actually, none of these factors *should* play a role in the EER model, which is supposed to be implementation independent. However, many textbooks present the model in a rather low-level form, in which the constraints of the traditional data models are incorporated into the EER model itself.

Having selected the objects relevant to the enterprise being modelled, they may be organized into several different categories:

- Families of objects that have much in common. Inheritance will be used to model such objects in order to obviate the need to duplicate shared properties and operations. The existence of an inheritance hierarchy is indicated by the presence of properties or operations which only apply to certain instances of an object class. For example, if we are modelling bank accounts then the property *overdraft_limit* applies only to current accounts and not to savings accounts. Similarly the operation *calculate_interest* might apply only to interest-bearing savings accounts.

- Part/whole relationships: we need to identify objects which have an 'IS_PART_OF' relationship with another object. This gives rise to the concept of a *complex object* - an object which has a complex structure consisting of other sub-objects. For example, the object *engine* might be a part of the complex object *vehicle*.

- Groups or *clusters* of closely inter-related classes that together describe a coherent part of the enterprise. Clustering is an aid to both conceptual modelling of large systems and also to physical implementation (objects that tend to be accessed together are placed near each other in physical storage).

- General purpose classes that are used by many applications (often called *base* classes). Implementations of such base classes may already be available via class libraries which often provide ready-to-use abstractions for commonly used data structures such as lists, sets, etc. The availability of an extensive class library, together with the use of inheritance, greatly facilitates the rapid definition of application specific classes.

3.2.2   Identifying the operations

Identifying the operations serves to characterize the behaviour of each class of object by determining the operations that may be performed on objects of that class or by objects of that class on another object. This involves a detailed analysis of the *processing* requirements of the system. As described earlier, in the conventional data flow approach the processing requirements of the system are considered separately from the data structures in the system. In object-oriented analysis these processing requirements are mapped onto sequences of operations, each of which is uniquely identified with a specific class. The analyst must identify those operations which are used only internally to a class (private operations) and those that are public and will appear in the class interface.

In Chapter 2 we described how the functions applicable to a data abstraction may be classified into three categories:

- *Constructor (and destructor) functions*

- *Accessor functions*

- *Transformer functions*

Operations in classes can be considered under the same three headings, and we shall illustrate the different types of function by considering the following example of a class for current accounts in a banking system. The properties maintained for an account are an account number, the owner (of type Customer), and the current balance. Operations applicable to current accounts include deposit, withdrawal and a function to calculate the charges due over a specified period.

```
class Current_Account

inherit Account

properties
        account_number : Integer;
        owner : Customer;
        current_balance : Money;

operations
        create;
        calculate_charges (from_date, to_date : Date) :
                            charge : Money;
        deposit (amount : Money);
        withdraw (amount : Money);

end Current_Account.
```

(i) *Constructor (and destructor) operations*

Constructor operations yield new instances of the class. In object-oriented systems such an operation is often called *create* or *new* and provides users with the capability to generate new objects dynamically and assign actual values to their properties. Destructor operations allow users to discard unwanted object instances. In some systems the deallocation of unwanted objects may be automatic. If we consider as an example a class representing bank accounts, then clearly we need an operation which will generate a new account given values for properties such as account number, customer details, etc. Similarly we may also require an operation to discard an instance of an account which is no longer required.

(ii) *Accessor operations*

Accessor operations yield properties of existing instances of the type. Such operations might provide, for example, an associative access capability, i.e. the ability to locate objects on the basis of their property values. Such operations may also perform calculations for an object or on behalf of another object. Considering again the example of the bank account, a typical accessor operation might be an operation to evaluate the service charges for an account over a specified period.

(iii) *Transformer operations*

Transformer operations yield new instances of the class from existing instances and (possibly) other arguments. Examples of such operations for the bank account might be *deposit* and *withdrawal* operations which alter the property *current_balance* of a specified account.

3.3   OBJECT-ORIENTED ABSTRACTIONS

In this section we discuss five abstraction concepts which have emerged from studies in semantic data modelling and which form the fundamental basis of the object-oriented data model. These are the concepts of:

- classification/instantiation

- identification

- aggregation

- generalization/specialization

- association

The paired concepts of classification and instantiation are inverses of each other, as are generalization and specialization.

3.3.1   Classification and instantiation

As already described in the introduction, the process of classification is central to the object-oriented approach and is concerned with the grouping of objects with similar properties and behaviour into object classes. The objects belonging to a class are collectively described by a class definition. That is, instead of describing individual objects, the object-oriented approach concentrates on the patterns of both state and behaviour that are common to an entire class of objects. As we shall see below, we may additionally classify objects into subclasses based on additional semantics. The state of an object is represented by its properties and its behaviour by a set of procedures that are encapsulated with the properties. This class structure, encompassing both properties and behaviour, is the natural unit of abstraction in object-oriented systems and may be used to model both entity objects and relationship objects. This differs from the EER model in which entities are classified according to their structure, with no regard for their behaviour, and a separate concept, namely the relationship type, is used to model interactions among entities.

Instantiation is the inverse of classification and concerns the generation of distinct objects of a class. The distinction between a class and its instances is similar to the distinction between a type definition and variable declarations in conventional programming languages. However, most object-oriented systems dynamically create instances by sending a 'new' or 'create' message to the class.

The following example of a *Hotel* entity type illustrates the general notion of class definitions and instantiations. Note that the class definition is an abstract specification and does not include any mention of the instance variables (i.e. the actual hotels). Any number of databases might use the Hotel class definition with the instances being described as part of an actual implementation.

```
class Hotel

        properties
                name : String;
                address : String;
                owner : Company;
                manager : Person;
                facilities: Set (OptionType);
                ...

        operations
                Create (...);
                ReserveRoom (room# : Integer; guest : Person;
                        arrive_date, depart_date : DateType)
                ...

    end Hotel.
```

In this example we define a class Hotel which has five properties: name, address, owner, manager and facilities. Note that these properties may themselves be defined in terms of other classes. Thus the owner of a hotel is an instance of a class Company, the manager is an instance of the class Person, and the facilities that it offers are defined as an instance of the class *set* with actual type parameter OptionType. OptionType might take the form:

OptionType = (Swimming_Pool, Sauna, Tennis, Golf, ...)

The classes Company and Person might have the structures illustrated below. (Only the main properties are shown. Such classes will have their own operations in a real application.) An instance of the class Hotel might take the form illustrated in Figure 3.3.

Note that the properties Owner and Manager represent entire objects, not key values as in the relational model, or pointers as in network or hierarchical databases. Thus it is possible to access the properties of the Owner or Manager from within a Hotel object, without the need for explicit joins. The underlying system may indeed require to perform a join operation or follow a pointer but such implementation details are hidden from the user.

```
class Company

    properties
        name, headquarters, telephone : String;
        ...

    operations
        ...

end Company.

class Person

    properties
        Name, Address : String;
        DOB : Date;
        ...

    operations
        ...

end Person.
```

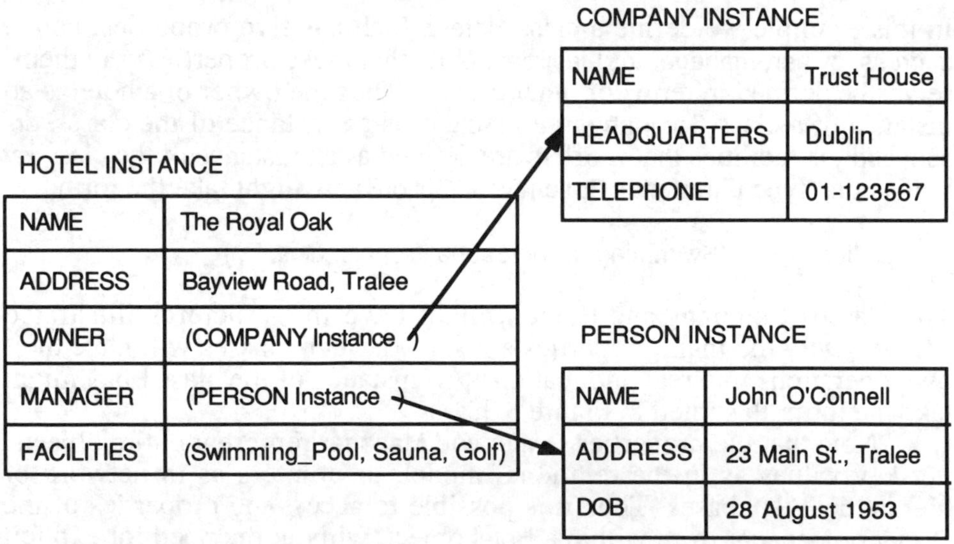

COMPANY INSTANCE

NAME	Trust House
HEADQUARTERS	Dublin
TELEPHONE	01-123567

HOTEL INSTANCE

NAME	The Royal Oak
ADDRESS	Bayview Road, Tralee
OWNER	(COMPANY Instance)
MANAGER	(PERSON Instance)
FACILITIES	(Swimming_Pool, Sauna, Golf)

PERSON INSTANCE

NAME	John O'Connell
ADDRESS	23 Main St., Tralee
DOB	28 August 1953

Figure 3.3   Class instances

3.3.2   Identification

Identification is concerned with the process whereby both abstract concepts (i.e. classes) and concrete objects (i.e. instances) are uniquely identifiable. For example, the name of a class should uniquely identify that class and distinct object instances must be assigned some unique object identity. In the EER model all entity and relationship types must have a unique name, and within each type definition the attribute names must be distinct. At the implementation level, relational databases distinguish between entities of a given type by means of key values, while instances of a relationship are identified by means of a combination of key values of the participating entities. These key values are often used as a basis for the placement of objects in physical storage and their rapid retrieval by means of hash functions, indexes, or some other access method. However, key values represent an aspect of the *state* of an object which may change with time, whereas the identity of an object should be immutable despite changes to the object's state, position or structure. In programming languages, class instances may be identified by variable names and these do provide a measure of immutability within the scope of a single program. However, providing instances of a class with a unique identity is a much more difficult problem when those instances persist beyond the lifetime of the program creating them and when they are shared among many applications. We shall return to this problem in Chapter 6 when we deal with the issue of *persistence*.

3.3.3   Aggregation

Aggregation [Smith and Smith, 1977] is an abstraction in which a relationship among objects is represented by a higher level, aggregate object (or type). Usually, a meaningful name is assigned to this aggregate type and one may use this name without reference to the underlying properties of the type. It may be used for example as a property of some other object type, and thus by applying such aggregation repeatedly, a hierarchy of objects can be created. In the EER model for example, we aggregate attributes of an object to form an entire object. However in the object-oriented model, aggregation is much more powerful in that it permits the combination of objects that are related via some particular relationship into a higher level aggregate object. Such abstraction is not catered for by the EER model, but is particularly useful if the aggregate object has additional properties or is itself to be related to another object.

For example, consider the relationship RESERVES between a person and a flight. The EER diagram for this relationship is shown in Figure 3.4.

Figure 3.4   The relationship RESERVES

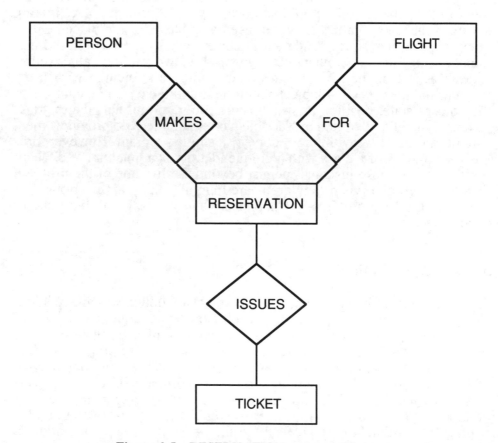

Figure 3.5   RESERVATION as an entity type

As shown in the Figure 3.4, the object types person and flight are themselves aggregations of attributes (or more precisely, they are aggregations of *component objects*). Suppose, however, that we wish to regard reservation as an object type in its own right, which has its own associated properties and operations, and takes part in other relationships. For example, properties of reservation might include the date of the reservation, the class of seat reserved and whether it was confirmed or cancelled. We might also wish to relate the object type reservation to the object type representing the tickets issued. To represent this situation in the EER model we have to create a new 'weak' entity type reservation which depends for its existence on the entity types PERSON and FLIGHT. This weak entity type may then be related to the ticket entity type as shown in Figure 3.5.

However, in the object-oriented model we may create a new higher level aggregate class *reservation* encompassing person, flight and the relationship reserves, and relate this class to the class ticket as shown in Figure 3.6. In considering such a high-level aggregate abstraction we do not need to concern ourselves with the details of persons and flights.

CLASS RESERVATION

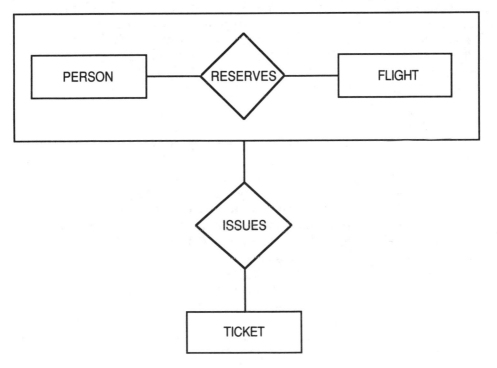

Figure 3.6 RESERVATION as a class

Thus in an object-oriented data model, aggregation abstractions permit us to model relationships among the objects. In the relational model the relationship 'reserves' would be represented by a relation containing the key attributes of the entities 'Person' and 'Flight' together with the additional attributes of the relationship (e.g. 'date' and 'confirmed'). Thus the information about a reservation is scattered across several relations. If we require the source or destination airports of a particular reservation we must perform a join of the reserves relation and the flight relation. In the object-oriented model reservation is represented by a class which contains properties of the class types person and flight, together with those operations pertaining to reservations. The important point is that the user of the Reservation class does not need to be concerned with the representation details (such as key values) of persons and flight. All of the properties of the person and flight associated with a particular reservation are encapsulated by the class and may be accessed without explicit joins.

The explicit support provided by some object-oriented database systems for *inverse relationships* is useful. For example, the class reservation contains a property set (Ticket) which has as its inverse the property issued_for in the Ticket class. Whenever an instance is modified on one side of an inverse relationship, it is automatically modified on the other side. This feature of the system solves the problem of referential integrity which arises in relational databases. That is, one-to-one, one-to-many and many-to-many relationships can all be supported and maintained automatically using the inverse construct.

Composite objects

Aggregation provides a convenient mechanism for modelling the relationship *IS_PART_OF* between objects. The *IS_PART_OF* relationship occurs very frequently in database applications and represents a situation where one class is an *assembly* (or aggregate) of *component* objects. Each instance of an assembly is comprised of a set of component instances, and for this reason it is often referred to as a *composite object*. We may add the notion of existence dependency to the *IS_PART_OF* relationship. A dependent object is one whose existence depends on the existence of another object and is owned by exactly one instance of that object.

The *IS_PART_OF* relationship is quite different from inheritance, although this fact is not always appreciated and the two concepts are sometimes confused. As an example, let us return to the example of a car abstraction illustrated in Chapter 2. Recall that the class *car* inherits the properties and operations of the class *vehicle*. However, a car object is not a part of a vehicle object. Nor is it associated with an instance of a vehicle. However, as illustrated in Figure 3.7 a car may be considered as consisting of three major components - the *body*, the *engine* and the *transmission*.

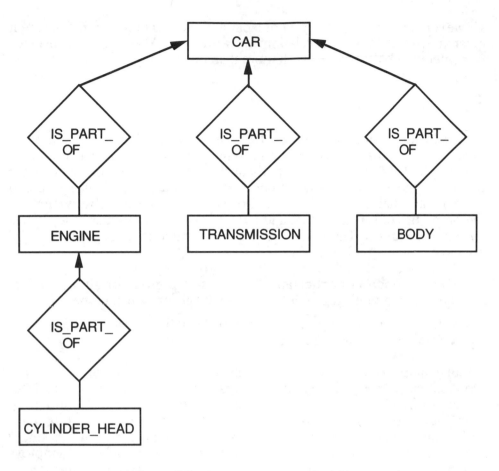

Figure 3.7 A car as a composite object

Each of these components is an object in its own right with its own associated properties and functions. Also, each may have its own constituent components, such as the cylinder head of the engine. Each instance of a *body*, an *engine* and a *transmission* belongs exclusively to one instance of *car*. The classes *body*, *engine* and *transmission* are related to *car* through the *IS_PART_OF* relationship and their existence depends on *car* (assuming that we are dealing with an application in which these objects are of interest only as components of cars and are not regarded as having an independent existence).

Note that the *IS_PART_OF* relationship is different from that which relates a car with, for example, its owner. Owner is a property of car and, like body, engine and transmission, it has its own class structure.

However, an owner is not a part of a car and the owner has an independent existence separate from its relationship with a car. Also, the same instance of owner may be associated with more than one instance of car.

3.3.4   Generalization

Generalization [Smith and Smith, 1977] is an abstraction in which a set of objects with similar properties is represented by a generic object. Within an object-oriented framework, it is perhaps the most important mechanism for modelling the real world, since it permits us to graduate from the specific to the general. That is, generalization allows us to move from observations of the properties of specific objects to a model which represents those objects by generic classes. There are two ways in which generalization may be effected:

(i)   The common properties and functions of a group of similar object types are grouped together to form a new generic object type.

(ii)   Subtypes of a given object type may be defined, using predicates to constrain the values of attributes.

As an example of the first method, consider the employees of a company, who may have many diverse functions ranging from managers to maintenance staff. However, they have many properties in common (e.g. employee number, name, address, etc.) and for some purposes (e.g. payroll) it may be convenient to group these common properties into a single generic object type 'employee'. In fact, the sub-classifications of employees may themselves be generic object types, such that we have a *generalization hierarchy* as illustrated in Figure 3.8.

Each generic object type in the hierarchy can be thought of as defining a class of individual employees. For example, *analysts*, *programmers* and *operators* can be generalized to the object type *computer staff*. In turn, *computer staff* together with *managers* and *maintenance staff* may be generalized to the object type *employee*. An individual programmer will be a member of the classes *programmer*, *computer staff* and *employee* but the relevant attributes of this programmer will vary from class to class. When this programmer is considered as a member of the generic class employee, any attributes of programmers which are not shared by other employees (e.g. the projects they are assigned to) will be irrelevant. Similarly, when a programmer is being considered as a member of the generic class *computer staff*, any attribute which distinguishes programmers from other computer staff (e.g. knowledge of programming languages) will be irrelevant.

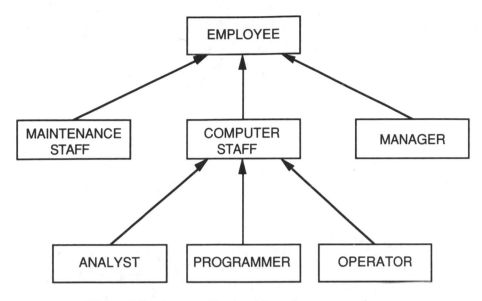

Figure 3.8 A generalization hierarchy over employees

As in the case of aggregation, generic object types are explicitly named and one may use the new object type without reference to its underlying properties. The generic type may be used as a property in other object type specifications which allows the data modeller to specify relationships in which generic objects participate. For example, computer staff (analysts, programmers and operators) may be assigned to projects. This relationship does not concern the other classes of employees and is therefore most precisely defined as a relationship between the generic object type *computer staff* and the object type *project*.

The generalization hierarchy shown in Figure 3.8 has two characteristics which are not necessarily shared by all such hierarchies. First it is a tree in that no object type is a descendant of more than one generic object type. This need not be always the case. For example, as shown in Figure 3.9 a senior analyst may be both a manager and a member of the computer staff. That is, he may have the status of a manager and therefore have properties in common with other managers, but may also have particular skills associated with computer staff.

The second characteristic of generalization hierarchies which should be borne in mind, is that the immediate descendants of any node need not be mutually exclusive object classes. For example, as mentioned above, managers and computer staff need not be mutually exclusive but it may be convenient to treat them as two distinct object classes.

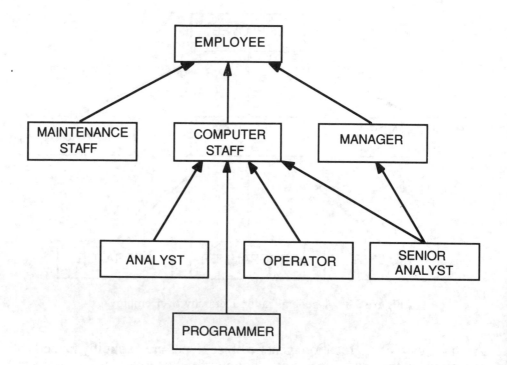

Figure 3.9   A generalization hierarchy which is not a tree

3.4   THE ROLE OF INHERITANCE

As described in Chapter 2, inheritance permits objects to be organized in taxonomies in which specialized objects inherit the properties and functions of more generalized objects. Similar classes of objects which share properties and functions can be modelled by specifying a *superclass*, which defines the common part, and then deriving specialized classes (or subclasses) from this superclass. Inheritance will be discussed in detail in Chapter 4, but in order to convey the general principles concerning its role in data modelling we shall look briefly at a simple example of a database application in which inheritance is useful.

Consider a database which maintains details of various types of vehicle (cars, trucks, buses, etc.) in an organization. We require a class definition for each type of vehicle in the database. However, vehicles may have certain properties and functions in common. For example they are all likely to have a registration number, make, model, colour, mileage, fuel type and year of registration. Thus rather than duplicating these properties for every class of vehicle, we may choose to define a superclass, *vehicle*, and permit the class definitions for cars, trucks, buses, etc. to inherit the properties and functions of this superclass. The specification for the vehicle class might take the following form:

class Vehicle

    properties
        reg_no, make, model : String ;
        colour : ColourType ;
        mileage : Integer ;
        fueltype : (leaded, unleaded, diesel);
        year : Integer ;

    operations
        New_vehicle (...)
        Value (...)
        Drive (...)
        Sell (...)

  end Vehicle.

Now suppose that we wish to define a new class specifically for cars. A car is a special class of vehicle and all the properties and functions defined for vehicles are applicable to cars. However, a car may have additional features such as size (compact, medium, large) and optional extras (a set of options). Also we may wish to re-define a property or operation applicable to vehicles in a manner that makes it more applicable to cars. For example, if all cars use either leaded or unleaded fuel, we may wish to re-define the property fueltype. We can take advantage of the commonality among cars and vehicles by defining car as a descendant of vehicle as follows:

class Car

    inherit Vehicle

    properties
        fueltype : (leaded, unleaded); {re-defined}
        {additional properties of cars}
        size : (compact, medium, large);
        extras : set (OptionType);

  end Car.

Similar classes may be defined for trucks, buses, etc., each of which may have its own additional properties. Note that a descendant class may inherit some or all of the properties and functions of its superclass. In addition, recall from Chapter 2 that it may be possible to re-define an inherited property or function.

It is clear that inheritance represents the IS_A relationship which, as shown in Chapter 1 arises frequently in database and knowledge base applications. Thus, in the above example inheritance is used to represent the relationship 'every car is a vehicle'. However, there are important semantic differences in the way that IS_A relationships are represented by inheritance and the way that such relationships are represented in the relational model.

- If we consider the objects in each of the classes Vehicle and Car, it is important to note that instances of the class Car are not a subset of Vehicle instances. Rather, objects that may be referenced by variables of type Car are a subset of objects that may be referenced by variables of type Vehicle. This is in contrast to the relational representation where all tuples in the Car relation would have a corresponding tuple in the Vehicle relation, connected via a common key value.

- If we say that every car is a vehicle then every property and operation applicable to instances of type Vehicle is inherently applicable to instances of type Car (though re-definition may permit the class Car to provide its own implementation for an operation). The relational model provides no mechanism for incorporating such semantic information.

Thus inheritance provides the data modeller with a semantically sound mechanism for representing IS_A hierarchies which involve any number of specializations.

The concept of *multiple inheritance* permits a new class to be derived from several existing classes, inheriting an appropriate selection of properties and functions from each. Further discussion of inheritance is deferred until Chapter 4.

3.5   INTEGRITY CONTROL IN OBJECT-ORIENTED SYSTEMS

Since many object-oriented programming languages deal only with memory resident (i.e. transient) objects, they generally ignore the problem of corruption of objects due to faulty programs. However, protection of the integrity of data has always been a primary consideration of database technology. As we have seen, the typing mechanisms in object-oriented systems (particularly strongly typed systems) are sufficient to guarantee a high degree of integrity and consistency. However, many situations demand complex, application specific integrity control which is beyond the capabilities of the typing system alone. Thus, many object-oriented languages and systems provide the capability to associate explicit *constraints* with a class definition, as well as *triggers* which specify action to be taken in the event that some condition becomes true.

3.5.1 Constraints

Constraints are typically Boolean expressions that refer to the properties of the class and are checked for validity following execution of operations of the class. Instances of the class must at all times satisfy the constraints associated with that class. Any operation giving rise to a constraint violation is rejected, the object is restored to its original state and an exception may be raised. Examples of constraints are given in the following class definition.

```
class Car

    inherit Vehicle

    properties
            fueltype : (leaded, unleaded);  {re-defined}
            {additional properties of cars}
            size : (compact, medium, large);
            extras : set (OptionType);

    constraints
            if year > 1985 then fueltype = unleaded;

            if make = 'Saab' then extras include sunroof;

    end Car.
```

The constraints specified in the above class assert that:

*   all cars registered after 1985 use unleaded fuel;

*   all Saab cars have a sunroof.

Similar constraints can be specified in some relational database management systems using the SQL ASSERT statement [Date, 1990]. However, the more advanced typing provided by object-oriented systems permits more sophisticated constraints to be constructed. For example, used in conjunction with inheritance, constraints can be used to provide more specialized classes, as the following example illustrates:

class Woman

    inherit Person
    ...

    constraints
      sex = Female

end Woman.

Such constraint-based specializations are often useful in artificial intelligence applications.

3.5.2 Triggers

Often it is convenient to be able to specify the action to be taken if a certain condition becomes true or if a constraint violation takes place. That is, rather than simply rejecting the operation which gave rise to the condition, it should be possible for the user to specify other actions. For example, in the case of a constraint violation it might be desirable, especially in an interactive environment, to inform the user of the violation and permit him to redo the operation.

Triggers monitor the database at run-time and when a trigger condition becomes true, the associated trigger action is initiated. For example, a 'delete trigger' could be used to ensure deletion of all references to an object when it is deleted from the database. Of course, such actions can be incorporated into the transactions operating on the system, but many benefits accrue from the ability to specify declaratively such actions within the database schema. The advantages of triggers for supporting highly active database systems have been recognized for many years and they are supported by a number of conventional database management systems. A DEFINE TRIGGER statement is provided in SQL, though most SQL implementations do not support it.

A trigger specifies a *condition* and an *action* to be taken when that condition becomes true. A simple example of a trigger is given in the following class definition:

```
class Inventory_Item;

    properties
        item : Part;
        qty_in_stock, reorder_level, reqd_level : Integer;

    operations
        add (qty);
        remove (qty);
        issue_order (qty);
        ...

    triggers
        if qty_in_stock < reorder_level
        then issue_order (reqd_level - qty_in_stock);

end Inventory_Item.
```

As can be clearly seen, this trigger automatically issues an order when the quantity of an item in stock falls below its reorder level.

Object-oriented systems which provide triggers include ODE [Agrawal and Gehani, 1989], Vbase [Andrews and Harris, 1987] and OOPS [Schlageter *et al.*, 1988]. In ODE, triggers are specified with class definitions and may take two forms: *once-only* (which is the default) and *perpetual*. A once-only trigger is automatically deactivated once the trigger has 'fired' (i.e. been put into effect) and may then be reactivated explicitly if required. A perpetual trigger, on the other hand, fires every time its associated condition becomes true, without having to be explicitly reactivated. In addition, ODE provides *timed triggers* which can be used to specify time limits within which the actions are to be executed.

3.6   CASE STUDIES

In this section we consider two case studies. The first is a relatively simple example of a medical research group, the viruses it studies and the papers it publishes. The second is a more elaborate application involving a hospital. In each case we follow the database design methodology outlined in this and in previous chapters. We begin by developing an EER model of the enterprise, using the techniques described in Chapter 1. We transform this EER model into a normalized relational schema, and then an object-oriented model which takes the form of a list of class definitions. The final section of the chapter compares the relative merits of the two models with reference to these applications.

3.6.1   Case study 1: A medical research group

Consider the following situation:

A medical research group maintains a database of all published papers relating to certain kinds of virus. The information recorded about a virus includes its scientific name and a free text description. Each paper is published in a particular issue of a journal which is identified by the name of the journal, the volume number and the number of the issue. A paper may have one or more authors and may be concerned with one or more viruses. The abstract of the paper is recorded in the database, together with the name of each author and the name of the institution at which the research was carried out. Each paper contains a list of references to other papers and this information is recorded in the database. Papers published by the research group itself are also stored and for these papers, additional information is stored consisting of details of any associated research contract (e.g. contract no., amount, start date, finish date).

Typical operations performed by users of the database are:

*   Enter a new paper with all its associated information.
*   List the details of all papers concerning a specified virus.
*   List the papers of a specified author.
*   List the papers associated with a specified research contract.

The entity-relationship model

The entities of this application, together with their attributes, are as follows:

1. Entity PAPER with attributes TITLE, JOURNAL, VOL#, ISSUE# and YEAR.

2. Entity INTERNAL_PAPER which is a specialism of PAPER.

3. Entity VIRUS with attributes VIRUS-NAME and DESCRIPTION.

4. Entity AUTHOR with attribute ANAME, NATIONALITY and DATE-OF-BIRTH.

5. Entity INSTITUTE with attributes INAME, ADDRESS and TYPE.

6. Entity CONTRACT with attributes CONTRACT#, AMOUNT, START-DATE and END-DATE.

These entities and the associated relationships are illustrated in Figure 3.10.

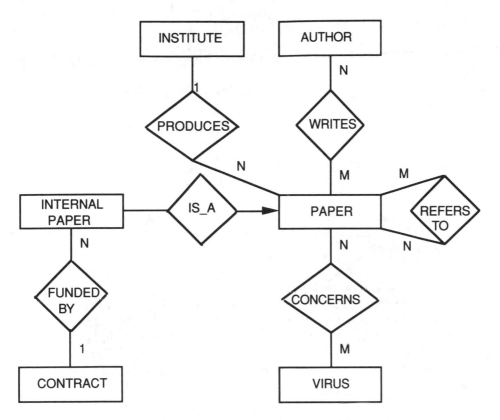

Figure 3.10 EER model for the Research Institute

The relational schema
A fully normalized relational schema for this model, designed according to
the guidelines of Chapter 1, is as follows:

        PAPER (P#, TITLE, INSTITUTE-NAME, JOURNAL, VOL#,
                       ISSUE#, YEAR)
        INTERNAL_PAPER (P#, CONTRACT#)
        AUTHOR (AUTHOR-NAME, NATIONALITY,
                       DATE-OF-BIRTH)
        INSTITUTE (INSTITUTE-NAME, ADDRESS, TYPE)
        CONTRACT (CONTRACT#, AMOUNT, START-DATE,
                       END-DATE)
        WRITES (P#, AUTHOR-NAME)
        REFERENCES (P#, REF-P#)
        VIRUS (VIRUS-NAME, DESCRIPTION)

CONCERNS (P#, VIRUS-NAME)

Note that the details concerning a research paper are stored in many different relations:

- The title, journal details and institute name are stored in the relation PAPER;

- The names of the viruses discussed in a paper are stored in the relation CONCERNS;

- The authors are stored in the relation WRITES;

- The references are stored in relation REFERENCES.

In the object-oriented model, all of the information associated with a paper, including the operations that may be applied to a paper, are encapsulated in one class structure.

The object-oriented schema
The object-oriented database schema is a set of class definitions, one for each entity in the EER model. The class Paper is clearly the central component of the object-oriented design and its specification includes properties which define the relationships CONCERNS, REFERS_TO and WRITES. That is, *all* of the information relating to a paper is represented in a single class definition.

```
class Paper

    properties
        title : String;
        publication : JournalEntry;
        institute : Institute;
        written_by : Set (Author)
                    inverse is Author.papers;
        concerns : Set (Virus)
                    inverse is Virus.covered_by;
        refers_to : Set (Paper);

    operations
        create (...)
        ...

    end Paper.
```

(Note: In the above class, the type JournalEntry is a type or class holding the properties journal, vol#, issue# and year.)

Note the use of *inverse* relationships. This feature is supported by several object-oriented database systems and is a powerful mechanism for preserving integrity. Whenever an instance is modified on one side of an inverse relationship, it is automatically modified on the other side. This feature of the system solves the problem of *referential integrity* which arises in relational databases and was described in Chapter 1. Thus, one-to-one, one-to-many and many-to-many relationships can all be supported and maintained automatically using the inverse construct.

The other class definitions which comprise the object-oriented schema are outlined below.

```
class Internal_Paper

    inherit Paper

    properties
        associated_contract : Contract
                    inverse is Contract.reports;

    operations
        create (...)
        ...

end Internal_Paper.

class Virus

    properties
        name, description  : String;
        covered_by : Set (Paper)
                    inverse is Paper.concerns;

    operations
        create (...)
        ...

end Virus.

class Contract

    properties
        contract#, amount  : Integer;
        start, finish : Date;
        reports : Set (Internal_Paper)
                inverse is
                Internal_paper.associated_contract;
```

```
        operations
                create (...)
                ...

    end Contract.

    class Author

            properties
                    name : String;
                    nationality : NationalityType;
                    date_of_birth : Date;
                    ...

            operations
                    create (...)
                    ...

    end Author.

    class Institute;

            properties
                    name, address : String;
                    type : InstituteType;

            operations
                    create (...)
                    ...

    end Institute.
```

3.6.2   Case study 2: A hospital database

In this section we shall apply the methodology described in this and in previous chapters to a rather more complex situation. The objective is to design both a relational and an object-oriented database for a (somewhat) simplified hospital application. The hospital wishes to maintain a database to assist with the administration of its wards and operating theatres, and to maintain information relating to its patients, surgeons and nurses. In accordance with our database design methodology we begin with a requirements analysis.

Requirements analysis
A requirements analysis yields the following informal description of the information to be recorded:

The patients occupying each ward
Most patients are assigned to a ward on admittance and each ward may contain many patients. However, consultants (senior surgeons) at the hospital may have private patients who are assigned to private rooms, each of which has a unique identification number. The information to be recorded about a patient upon registration at the hospital includes a unique patient number, name, address, sex, phone number, date of birth and blood group.

The nurses assigned to each ward
A nurse may or may not be assigned to a ward and he/she cannot be assigned to more than one ward. A ward may have many nurses assigned to it. Nurses are identified by their staff numbers and their names, addresses, phone numbers and grades are also recorded. Each ward has a unique number and is dedicated to a particular type of patient (e.g. geriatric, pediatric, maternity, etc.).

The operations undergone by patients
A patient may have a number of operations. The information to be recorded about an operation includes the type of operation, the patient, the surgeons involved, date, time and location.

The surgeons who perform operations
Only one surgeon may perform an operation, any other surgeons present being considered as assisting at the operation. Surgeons come under the direction of senior surgeons, called consultants, who may also perform or assist at operations. Information recorded about a surgeon includes name, address and phone number. Each consultant has a specialism.

The theatres in which operations are performed
An operation can be performed in only one theatre but a given theatre may be the location of many operations. Each theatre has an identifying number and some may be specially equipped for certain classes of operation.

The nurses assigned to each theatre
A nurse may or may not be assigned to a theatre and he/she cannot be assigned to more than one theatre. A theatre may have many nurses assigned to it.

The entity-relationship model

The following is a list of entities, attributes and relationships which represent the informal description of the database outlined above:

1. Entity type SURGEON, with attributes NAME, ADDRESS and PHONE-NO.

2. Entity type CONSULTANT which is a subtype of the entity type SURGEON. Every consultant is a specialist in a particular branch of surgery and this is recorded as an additional attribute SPECIALITY.

3. Entity type PATIENT, with attributes PATIENT# (a unique patient number), NAME, ADDRESS, PHONE-NO, DATE-OF-BIRTH, SEX and BLOOD-GROUP.

4. Entity type PRIVATE-PATIENT which is a subtype of the entity type PATIENT. The number of the private room to which such a patient is assigned is recorded as an additional attribute, ROOM#.

5. Entity type NURSE, with attributes STAFF# (a unique staff number), NAME, ADDRESS, PHONE-NO, SEX and GRADE. A nurse may be assigned either to a ward or to a theatre.

6. Entity type WARD, with attributes WARD# (a unique ward number), WARD-TYPE and NO-OF-BEDS.

7. Entity type THEATRE, with attributes THEATRE# (a unique theatre number) and THEATRE-TYPE.

8. Entity type OPERATION, with attributes OPERATION-TYPE, DATE and TIME.

The attribute lists are by no means complete since this information depends to a large extent on the specific application. Also, a number of the attributes listed may be composite, i.e. it may be necessary to break them down into smaller components.

Appropriate relationships, as extracted from the requirements analysis, are as given in the following list:

1. PERFORMS, a 1:N relationship between entity types SURGEON and OPERATION, with the entity type OPERATION being a mandatory member of this relationship, i.e. every operation must be performed by a surgeon.

2. ASSISTS, an N:M relationship between entity types SURGEON and OPERATION indicating those surgeons who assist at each operation. A possible attribute of this relationship is the ROLE played by each surgeon.

3. SUPERVISES, a 1:N relationship between the entity types CONSUL-TANT and SURGEON. The membership class of SURGEON in this relationship is optional since there may be surgeons (e.g. consultants) that are not supervised.

4. TREATS, a 1:N relationship between the entity type CONSULTANT and the subtype PRIVATE-PATIENT. The membership class of PRIVATE-PATIENT in this relationship is mandatory. That is, every private patient is assigned to a consultant for treatment.

5. UNDERGOES, a 1:N relationship between entity types PATIENT and OPERATION. The entity type OPERATION is a mandatory member of this relationship since an operation must always have an associated patient.

6. OCCUPIES, a 1:N relationship between entity types WARD and PATIENT, where the membership class of PATIENT is 'almost' mandatory since most patients are assigned to a ward on entry to the hospital.

7. LOCATED, a 1:N relationship between entity types THEATRE and OPERATION. The entity type OPERATION is a mandatory member of this relationship since clearly every operation must be located in a theatre.

8. WARD-ASSIGN, a 1:N relationship between entity types WARD and NURSE. A possible attribute for this relationship is DATE-ASSIGNED giving the date on which a particular nurse was assigned to a ward. The NURSE entity type is an optional member of this relationship since a nurse may or may not be assigned to a ward at any given time.

9. THEATRE-ASSIGN, a 1:N optional relationship between THEATRE and NURSE, with attribute DATE-ASSIGNED giving the date on which a particular nurse was assigned to a theatre. As is the case with WARD-ASSIGN, the NURSE entity type is an optional member of this relationship since a nurse may or may not be assigned to a theatre at any given time.

In addition to the above relationships, we have an IS_A relationship between the subtype CONSULTANT and the entity type SURGEON, and another between the subtype PRIVATE-PATIENT and the entity type PATIENT.

A schematic EER model for the hospital application is illustrated in Figure 3.11.

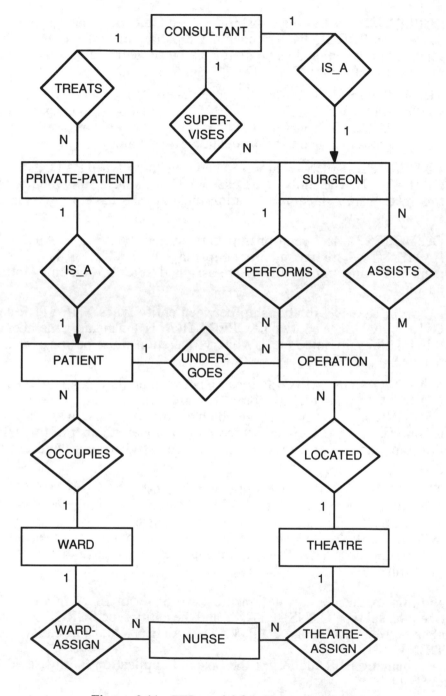

Figure 3.11   EER model for the hospital database

The relational schema

We are now ready to apply the guidelines of Section 1.3 to transform our EER model into a set of relations. Recall that each entity type is represented by a separate relation, but that the representation of a relationship depends on its semantics and its functionality. In applying our guidelines we obtain the following normalized relational schema:

SURGEON (SNAME, ADDRESS, PHONE-NO)

CONSULTANT (SNAME, SPECIALITY)

PATIENT (PATIENT#, WARD#, PNAME, ADDRESS,
         PHONE-NO, DATE-OF-BIRTH, SEX, BLOOD-GROUP)

PRIVATE-PATIENT (PATIENT#, SNAME, ROOM#)

NURSE (STAFF#, NNAME, ADDRESS, PHONE-NO, SEX,
       GRADE)

THEATRE (THEATRE#, THEATRE-TYPE)

OPERATION (OP#, SNAME, THEATRE#, PATIENT#, OP-TYPE,
           DATE, TIME)

SUPERVISES (SURGEON-SNAME, CONSULTANT-SNAME)

ASSISTS (OP#, SNAME, ROLE)

WARD-ASSIGN (STAFF#, WARD#, DATE-ASSIGNED)

THEATRE-ASSIGN (STAFF#, THEATRE#, DATE-ASSIGNED)

In the relational schema the relationship OCCUPIES is represented by the foreign key WARD# in the PATIENT relation since this relationship is 'almost mandatory' for PATIENT. That is, most patients are assigned to wards. The relationship TREATS is represented by the foreign key SNAME (the name of the consultant) in the PRIVATE-PATIENT relation. Also, the foreign keys SNAME, PATIENT# and THEATRE# in the OPERATION relation represent respectively the PERFORMS, UNDER-GOES and LOCATED relationships of which OPERATION is a mandatory member.

The M:N relationship ASSISTS is represented by a separate relation scheme containing the key attributes of SURGEON and OPERATION, together with the attribute ROLE which indicates the role played by a surgeon at an operation. The optional 1:N relationships WARD-ASSIGN and THEATRE-ASSIGN are each represented by a separate relation scheme containing the key attributes of the participating entity sets together with the additional attribute DATE-ASSIGNED. If the majority of nurses were assigned to wards we might choose to represent the WARD-ASSIGN relationship by posting the foreign key WARD# into the NURSES relation (together with the attribute DATE-ASSIGNED).

The optional 1:N relationship SUPERVISES is represented by a separate relation, but could be represented by posting the name of the supervising consultant (C-SNAME) into the SURGEON relation, as follows:

SURGEON (<u>SNAME</u>, SADDRESS, PHONE-NO, C-SNAME)

The attribute C-SNAME in this case will be null for all those surgeons who do not come under the direction of a consultant.

The object-oriented schema

The object-oriented database schema is a set of class definitions, one for each entity in the EER model. Relationships are typically represented by properties (or operations) rather than separate classes, unless the relationship itself has attributes (apart from those of the participating entities). In this case a class may be constructed for the relationship, as was done for the Reservation example in Section 3.4.3. For the hospital database the many-to-many relationship ASSISTS between SURGEON and OPERATION is probably best incorporated in the class for surgeon.

Once again it is important to note that all the information associated with a particular entity is represented in the class definition, rather than being scattered across several relations. For example, in the class Surgeon we have represented not only the simple properties of surgeons (name, address, phone number) but also the supervising consultant and the operations the surgeon has performed and assisted at.

```
class Surgeon

        properties
                name, address, phone_no : String;
                sex : (Male, Female);
                supervised_by : Consultant
                        inverse is Consultant.supervises;
                performs : Set (Operation)
                        inverse is Operation.performed_by;
                assists_at : Set (Operation)
                        inverse is Operation.assisted_by;

        operations
                create (...);
                assign_duties (...);
                role (Surgeon, Operation) —> RoleType;

end Surgeon.
```

```
class Consultant

    inherit Surgeon

    properties
            supervises : Set (Surgeon)
                    inverse is Surgeon.supervised_by
            treats : Set (Private_Patient)
                    inverse is Private_Patient.treated_by;

    operations
            create (...);
            calculate_fees (hours, ...);
            ...

end Consultant.

class Patient

    properties
            number : Integer;
            name, address, phone_no : String;
            sex : (Male, Female);
            date_of_birth : Date;
            blood_group : Blood_Type;
            on_ward : Ward
                    inverse is Ward.patients;
            undergoes : Set (Operation)
                    inverse is Operation.performed_on;

    operations
            create (...);
            admit (...);
            discharge (...);
            ...

end Patient.

class Private_Patient

    inherit Patient

    properties
            room# : Integer;
            insurance : InsuranceType;
            treated_by : Consultant
                        inverse is Consultant.treats;
```

operations
    create (…);
    calculate_charges (...);
    …

end Private_Patient.

class Ward

properties
    ward# : Integer;
    no_of_beds : Integer;
    occupancy : Integer;
    type : (Geriatric, Pediatric, Maternity, ...);
    patients : Set (Patient)
            inverse is Patient.on_ward;
    nurses : Set (Nurse)
            inverse is Nurse.ward_assign;

operations
    create (…);
    …

end Ward.

class Operation

properties
    date : Date;
    type : OperationType;
    performed_on : Patient
        inverse is Patient.operations;
    performed_by : Surgeon
        inverse is Surgeon.performs;
    assisted_by : Set (Surgeon)
        inverse is Surgeon.assists_at;
    located_in : Theatre
        inverse is Theatre.holds;

operations
    create (…);
    schedule (...);
    cancel (…);
    …

end Operation.

```
class Nurse

    properties
        staff#, name, address, phone# : String;
        sex : (Male, Female);
        grade : (Student, SEN, SRN, ...);
        ward_assign : Ward
                    inverse is Ward.nurses;
        theatre_assign : Theatre
                    inverse is Theatre.nurses;

    operations
        create (...);
        ...

end Nurse.

class Theatre

    properties
        theatre# : Integer;
        type : TheatreType;
        nurses : Set (Nurse)
                inverse is Nurse.theatre_assign;
        holds : Set (Operation)
                inverse is Operation.located_in;

    operations
        create (...);
        ...

end Theatre.
```

3.7   COMPARISON OF THE OBJECT-ORIENTED AND RELATIONAL DATA MODELS

The relative merits of the relational and object-oriented approaches to data management may be summarized under the headings: data types; data integrity; schema evolution (i.e. the ability of the data model to evolve with changing requirements); and data manipulation. The first three of these are discussed below. The important subject of data manipulation is discussed in Chapter 5.

3.7.1   Data types

In relational database management systems there is only one generic type for data structuring, namely the relation type. By definition, attributes of normalized relations are non-decomposable and in practice they tend to have relatively simple data types (integer, real, string, date, etc.). Operations on relations are restricted to retrieving and updating tuples identified by attribute values. Efforts have been made to extend the typing capabilities of relational systems (e.g. POSTGRES [Stonebraker *et al.*, 1987]) and also to relax the requirement that attributes must be non-decomposable (see the work on non-1NF relations [Dadem *et al.*, 1986; Deshpande and Van Gucht, 1988; Ozsoyoglu, 1988]). The primary motivation in this work is to extend the semantic capabilities of the relational model while retaining its spartan simplicity.

An object-oriented database stores class definitions and instantiations of these classes. Class definitions are the analogue of schemes in other database systems, but with the important additional feature that classes encapsulate the behaviour of the object by packaging operations with the data structure. There is a class definition associated with each object type and the operations that can be applied to instances of that class may be customized to the object.

The properties of classes need not be simple data types but can be references to other classes of arbitrary complexity. Object-oriented systems typically provide a range of classes implementing frequently used data types. Users can tailor these to the needs of their own applications using the facilities afforded by genericity and inheritance.

An important additional factor is that classes can be *first class types* in some object-oriented systems (e.g. Smalltalk-based systems). This means that a class is itself an instance of some other type (a *metaclass*) and may be treated as an object like any other. That is, it may be subject to operations such as creation, modification or deletion, or it may establish a relationship with another class. A class may even be passed as a parameter to an operation. Many semantic data models (e.g. TAXIS and SDM) have a similar concept to a metaclass. The metaclass provides object-oriented systems with a powerful tool for self description - a role normally played by a separate software subsystem, namely the data dictionary, in conventional database management systems.

3.7.2   Data integrity

As described in Chapter 1, relational systems require referential integrity to be enforced. Often this entire burden is placed on the applications developer. Some systems do offer facilities for the explicit specification of referential integrity constraints but even in these cases it is the responsibility of the database implementor to ensure that all such constraints are included. The system then assumes responsibility for enforcing the constraints at run-time, but this can be a significant overhead.

The relational model is incapable of expressing integrity constraints with greater semantic content than straightforward referential integrity. For example it is not possible to express the fact that a relationship is one-to-one or one-to-many. Such constraints must be built into the application code that manipulates the relational database. Since such code is not generally shared among all applications it is difficult to ensure that data will be updated consistently at all times. By contrast, in the object-oriented model a class defines a data abstraction and this abstraction includes a specification of the operations (methods) that can be applied to instances of the class. By defining the database in terms of such abstractions a high degree of data independence is achieved. That is, it is possible to alter the way in which a class is implemented without affecting other classes or transactions that make use of the abstraction. Also, a user can derive new classes from existing classes by supplying a specification, and an implementation for any new properties or operations. These properties and operations are implemented by means of a general-purpose programming language and so any feasible user-defined operation can be constructed and stored in the database. An operation on an object can take the place of many database operations and every transaction which invokes the operation uses exactly the same code - the procedure stored with the class definition. This has significant benefits for data integrity since consistency checks may be incorporated in the procedures. Also, by storing operations as part of the database a large part of the application code is under the control of the database administrator and can be managed by all of the usual database management utilities (i.e. facilities for concurrency control, recovery, version control and security).

Entity integrity is also handled rather differently in object-oriented systems. All objects (class instantiations) have a unique identity and other objects can refer to that identity. An object retains its identity through arbitrary changes to its own state. This is in contrast to the relational model where the properties of an entity must be sufficient to distinguish it from all other entities. That is, there must be an attribute or attributes whose values uniquely and immutably identify that entity. The properties of uniqueness and immutability are not always present in the real world and it is often necessary in relational databases to introduce artificial identifiers for entities.

3.7.3   Schema evolution

As described in Chapter 2, database systems tend to evolve around a number of fundamental object types which form the kernel of the system. As the system evolves, new views of the data are added by restricting or extending existing object descriptions, and new applications on these views are generated using existing code modules as a basis. Relational database management systems tend to offer very limited facilities for the expansion or modification of existing data structures. For example, commercial relational systems typically allow the dynamic creation and deletion of relations and the addition of new columns to a relation. Changes to domain types will usually involve the rewriting of the relations involved and changes to the applications that use them. This is largely due to the fact that the data structures comprising the database schema and the application programs are very loosely coupled.

    The tight coupling between applications and data in the object-oriented model offers considerably more scope for schema evolution through the extension and refinement of existing data structures and the effective reuse of applications code. The richness of the model permits the semantics of schema evolution to be rigidly defined and validated. The ORION system [Banerjee *et al.*, 1987] is perhaps the most sophisticated in this regard. This system provides the user with an extensive taxonomy for schema evolution which includes the following:

1. Changes to the contents of a class
    1.1   Changes to a property
         1.1.1   Add a new property to a class
         1.1.2   Drop an existing property from a class
         1.1.3   Change the name of a property
         1.1.4   Change the domain (type) of a property
         1.1.5   Change the default value of a property
    1.2   Changes to an operation
         1.2.1   Add a new operation to a class
         1.2.2   Drop an existing operation from a class
         1.2.3   Change the name of an operation
         1.2.4   Change the code of an operation
2. Changes in the class hierarchies
    2.1   Make a class S a superclass of a class C
    2.2   Remove a class S from the superclass list of a class C
3. Changes to the schema
    3.1   Add a new class
    3.2   Drop an existing class
    3.3   Change the name of a class

ORION provides a graphics-based schema editor to validate the semantics of changes in the schema. This validation is performed by means of a sophisticated framework which attaches invariants to the schema and provides a set of rules which maintains those invariants. The reader is referred to Banerjee *et al.* [1987] for a detailed description of the schema evolution framework.

3.8   SUMMARY

Object-oriented systems development is primarily a data abstraction technique, though it embellishes this technique with the notion of *inheritance*. In this chapter we discuss the relationship between data abstraction and object-oriented database design. We show that the extended entity-relationship approach, which includes the notions of generalization and subtyping, is a valuable first step towards an object-oriented data model.

In the object-oriented perspective every operation on the database must be associated with a particular object. Thus functions are grouped together if they operate on the same data abstraction. In this way, objects encapsulate both state and behaviour.

In this chapter we discuss five abstraction concepts which have emerged from studies in semantic data modelling and which form the fundamental basis of the object-oriented data model. These are the concepts of:

*   classification/instantiation

*   identification

*   aggregation

*   generalization/specialization

*   association

The object-oriented approach to database design is illustrated by two case studies for which both relational and object-oriented schemas are constructed. The extended entity-relationship model provides the conceptual basis for database design for both approaches. The object-oriented model is shown to possess significant benefits in the areas of semantic data modelling, data typing, integrity preservation and schema evolution.

3.9 BIBLIOGRAPHIC NOTES

Two general references for object-oriented databases are the books edited by Kim and Lochovsky [1989] and Zdonik and Maier [1990] each of which contains a collection of significant papers relating to object-oriented database systems and applications. There have been surprisingly few papers on object-oriented systems analysis or data modelling. Those which give some useful information on the subject include Booch [1986], Seidewitz and Stark [1987], Bailin [1989] and Ward [1989]. Smith and Zdonik [1987] give an interesting comparison of a relational and an object-oriented approach to implementing a large document retrieval database.

4

Classes and inheritance

4.1 INTRODUCTION

As we have seen in earlier chapters, a class is a type definition which
describes the state and behaviour of a group of similar objects. The state of
an object is described by the properties (sometimes called instance variables) of the class and its behaviour is defined by the operations (or methods) made available through the class interface. Even within these fundamental concepts, object-oriented languages and systems differ considerably, both with respect to philosophy and implementation detail.

The concept of inheritance was introduced by Simula [Dahl and
Nygaard, 1966] and has been widely imitated by other object-oriented programming languages and by object-oriented database management systems.
Inheritance permits new software modules or classes to be defined as
extensions, specializations or combinations of existing classes. As such it
is central to the object-oriented approach to software development in which
the reusability and extensibility of software components are principal goals.

Within a database framework, the fundamental idea of inheritance is
that new objects may be defined in a schema as extensions, specializations
or combinations of previously defined objects, which do not have to be
modified for the purpose. This facilitates not only extensions and modifications to the database schema but also the integration of different user
views of a system.

In this chapter we describe the facilities available in a variety of object-
oriented programming languages and systems for class definition and
inheritance. Many such languages have been designed and implemented
over the past ten years: Smalltalk [Goldberg and Robson, 1980] is perhaps
the best known and has its own unique style; C++ [Stroustrup, 1986] and
Objective-C™ [Cox, 1986] are object-oriented extensions of the C language; Eiffel [Meyer, 1988] is a strongly typed object-oriented language,

loosely based on Simula but offering much greater sophistication; Flavors [Moon, 1986] is an object-oriented extension to LISP; LOOPS [Bobrow *et al.*, 1986] and KEE™ [Fikes and Kaehler, 1985] are advanced object-oriented programming environments aimed at applications in artificial intelligence. In this chapter, we choose to illustrate typical mechanisms for class definition and inheritance through the languages Smalltalk, C++ and Eiffel. These languages provide three contrasting approaches to object-oriented programming and differ considerably in their basic philosophies. We justify this approach by noting that Smalltalk and C++ have each had considerable influence on the development of object-oriented database systems. GemStone and its associated language OPAL [Maier and Stein, 1987] are based on Smalltalk, while ODE [Agrawal and Gehani, 1988] and ONTOS [Ontologic Inc., 1989] have been strongly influenced by C++. Eiffel is a relatively new language, and does not yet have the widespread commercial support enjoyed by Smalltalk and C++, but it offers much in the areas of strong typing, genericity, inheritance and above all, the preservation of integrity.

In addition, by way of comparison, we look at the data description facilities offered by the object-oriented database system Vbase [Andrews and Harris, 1987]. Vbase has its own (very elegant) type definition language. Flavors and KEE™ will be studied in Chapter 9 when we consider the application of object-oriented techniques to knowledge based systems development.

4.2   SMALLTALK

Smalltalk[†] was developed at the Xerox Palo Alto Research Centre in the mid 1970s and is now marketed throughout the world by a subsidiary of Xerox called ParcPlace Systems. As mentioned above, the object-oriented database management system GemStone and its associated language OPAL are based very closely on Smalltalk. Many features of this system will be studied in subsequent chapters, but with regard to class definition and inheritance OPAL adds little to Smalltalk. For this reason we shall concentrate our attention on Smalltalk in the following discussion.

The original aim of the developers of Smalltalk was to produce an advanced personal programming environment. Although influenced by Simula, Smalltalk has a free, typeless style in which dynamic binding plays

---

[†] This discussion refers to Smalltalk-80. There have been other implementations of the language (e.g. Smalltalk/V) which differ in some respects from the system described here.

an important role. No static type checking is performed and so the binding of all structures takes place at run-time. For example, errors resulting from invoking an operation (*sending a message* in Smalltalk parlance) on an object that contains no such operation are only detected at run-time. In a statically typed language such errors are detected at compile time.

Everything in a Smalltalk program is an object, including every class. That is, every class is viewed as an instance of a higher level class called a metaclass. Thus a Smalltalk program can be described as a tree of objects where the root is a built-in superclass called *Object*. The root of the subtree containing only classes is a special built-in metaclass called *Class*.

Viewing a class as an instance of a more abstract metaclass makes it possible to define *class methods* which apply to the class itself rather than its instances. Such class methods can be used for example, to implement special cases of built-in operations, such as the *new* operation which generates instances of a class. Making classes part of the run-time environment facilitates the development of tools, such as symbolic debuggers, which require access to the class text at run-time.

In Smalltalk, even simple data elements such as integers are regarded as objects, with associated methods. For example the operation,

$$2 + 4$$

is interpreted as sending the '+' message with the argument '4' to the integer object '2'. The class 'Integer' has a method whose selector is '+' and this is inherited by the instance object '2' which performs the addition and returns the result to the sender. The Integer class is a subclass of Number which also has subclasses Float (for floating point numbers) and Fraction (for representation of rational numbers). Also the class Integer has subclasses for large and small integers. Each of the subclasses of Number inherit the '+' method although the implementation of the method may differ from class to class.

To illustrate class definition and inheritance in Smalltalk, consider the simple inheritance hierarchy involving bank accounts, illustrated in Figure 4.1. In this hierarchy the classes SAVINGS ACCOUNT and CURRENT ACCOUNT are subclasses of the superclass ACCOUNT. Properties associated with ACCOUNT objects are *owner* and *balance*, operations are *deposit* and *withdraw*. An instance of SAVINGS ACCOUNT inherits all the properties and operations of ACCOUNT but has the additional property of interest rate, and the additional operations *calculate interest* (over a specified period) and *add interest* (to the current balance). A CURRENT ACCOUNT (i.e. a cheque book account) has an extra property *overdraft limit* and an operation *pay standing order* which when called transfers an amount from the account to a specified payee.

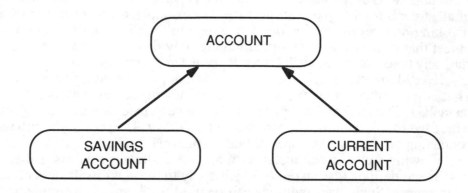

Figure 4.1   Inheritance hierarchy for bank accounts

A Smalltalk class definition takes two forms:

1.   A *protocol description* describes the functionality of the class, and consists of a list of messages with each message accompanied by a comment describing the operation that an instance will carry out when it receives that message.

2.   An *implementation description* shows how the functionality described in the protocol description is implemented. It consists of four parts:

    (i)   A class name.

    (ii)   An indication of the superclass for this class. Each class may have only one superclass.

    (iii) A declaration of the properties (called *instance variables* in Smalltalk) of the class.

    (iv)   A description of the methods (operations) used by instances of the class to respond to messages. Messages that invoke related operations may be grouped together in categories. The categories have names which indicate the common functionality of the messages.

Outline implementation descriptions for the classes Account, Savings Account and Current Account, illustrated in the hierarchy of Figure 4.1, might take the following form:

class name   Account
superclass   Object

instance variable names balance

instance methods

    open: theOwner
       owner <— theOwner
       ...

    balance
       ^balance

    deposit: amount
       balance <— balance + amount.

    withdraw: amount
       balance <— balance - amount

class name   SavingsAccount
superclass   Account

instance variable names interestRate

instance methods

    calculateInterest: period
       ...

    addInterest
       ...

class name   CurrentAccount
superclass   Account

Instance variable names overdraftLimit

instance methods

    payStandingOrder: amount   to: payee
       ...

Since each class in Smalltalk has only one superclass, only single inheritance may be modelled in the language. A subclass may introduce additional instance variables (properties) and methods may be added or redefined. That is, if the implementation description of a subclass contains a method with the same name (selector) as a method in its superclass, instances of the subclass will respond to messages with that selector by executing the method defined in the subclass. This is called *overriding* a method.

4.2.1   Messages

There are three principal forms of message in Smalltalk, corresponding to different forms of method. These are *unary*, *keyword* and *binary*. A method which has no parameters is invoked by a unary message, as in

```
myAccount balance
```

which sends the message *balance* to the object *myAccount*. The message is called unary because only one object, the receiver, is involved. A message may, as in this example, return values.

    Methods with arguments are invoked by keyword messages. For example,

```
myAccount open: thisPerson
mySavingsAccount deposit: 100
myCurrentAccount payStandingOrder : 200   to : otherAccount
```

The selector of a keyword message is composed of one or more keywords, one preceding each argument. A keyword is a simple identifier followed by a colon.

    Binary messages are composed of one or two non-alphanumeric characters (typically symbols such as +, -, <, <=, etc.), and are used primarily for arithmetic messages. Examples of binary messages are:

```
2 + 3
sum - 10
balance <= 100
```

Note that Smalltalk classes may only export methods. An instance variable (property) may only be exported by providing a method which gives access to its value. For example, in the method balance in the class account above, the upward arrow ^ means that the following expression is the value to be returned by the method to the sender of the corresponding message.

4.2.2   Collections

Smalltalk also provides a built-in class called *collection* that allows for subclasses that are collections (ordered or unordered) of other objects. This
provides the Smalltalk programmer with abstractions for sets, arrays,
strings, etc. A Smalltalk implementation also normally provides classes for
commonly used abstractions such as file streams, windows and graphic
images. There are also *Dictionaries* that associate pairs of objects.

The basic protocol for collections is specified by the superclass of all
collection classes called Collection which is a subclass of class Object. The
protocol provides categories for adding, removing and testing elements of
the collection.

Collection instance protocol

adding

add: newObject   Include the argument newObject
                          in the receiver collection.

addAll: aCollection   Include all the elements of the
                          collection argument aCollection in
                          the receiver collection.

removing

remove: oldObject   Remove the argument oldObject
                          from the receiver collection.

removeAll: aCollection   Remove each element of the
                          argument aCollection from the
                          receiver collection

testing

includes: anObject   Answer whether the argument
                          anObject is equal to one of the
                          receiver's elements.

isEmpty   Answer whether the receiver is
                          empty.

occurrencesOf: anObject   Answer how many of the
                          receiver's elements are equal to
                          the argument anObject.

4.2.3   The Smalltalk environment

Smalltalk is not just a programming language but a comprehensive, highly-interactive environment which provides many of the functions of an operating system. It is this environment and its distinctive user-friendly interface that has led to Smalltalk's popularity. This interface pioneered many of the features now common to other operating systems such as windows, icons, pull-down and pop-up menus, the use of a mouse for selecting and dragging, and the integration of text and graphics. Because of Smalltalk's pioneering role in this area, these features are often regarded as an essential aspect of object-oriented programming. However, from our point of view, these features are quite separate from the model. Also included in the environment is a powerful window-oriented tool called the browser. This allows users to retrieve classes and view them at different levels of abstraction (i.e. protocol or implementation descriptions, class hierarchies, etc.).

4.3   C++

C++ was developed by Stroustrup at AT&T and offers a number of object-oriented extensions to the popular systems programming language C. The additional facilities include a class construct with private, protected and public sections, and derived classes which provide an inheritance mechanism. The design of these features shows a clear Simula influence.

Class declarations in C++ consist of two parts: a specification and a body. The specification represents the user interface (or *signature*) of the class and contains descriptions of the properties and operations available to users of the class. The structure of a class specification in C++ is illustrated by the following template:

```
class <class_name>
{
    private:
        // The data items and operations declared here cannot be
        // accessed directly.

    protected:
        // The data items and operations declared here can only be
        // accessed by classes derived from this class.

    public:
        // The data items and methods declared here can be
        // accessed directly.
};
```

Now consider the example of a class representing the object type ACCOUNT from Figure 4.1.

```
class account
{
    private:
        person owns;
        int bal;

    public:
        account (person owner);  // The constructor

        person owner  ();

        int balance ();

        void deposit (int amount);

        void withdraw (int amount);
};
```

The private part of the class declaration contains the declarations of two variables: *own* and *bal*, representing respectively the owner and balance of the account.The public part of the class declaration contains the headings of member functions of the class interface, including the constructor function *account* (constructor functions in C++ normally have the same name as the class). The body of code of a constructor is executed when an object is declared to be of the given class. The implementations are defined separately in the class body.

Operator overloading in C++ makes it possible to use the same name for different functions, provided that each function is unique with respect either to the number or types of its arguments. For example, addition functions on a variety of data types (integers, reals, strings, vectors, matrices, etc.) may all use the '+' symbol. Another common use of overloading is to give the constructor function within a class the same name as the class.

4.3.1   Inheritance in C++

Single and multiple[†] inheritance are supported in C++ by means of *derived* classes. A derived class is declared by following its name with the name of its base classes as follows:

[†] Early implementations of C++ provided only single inheritance. Multiple inheritance is now provided by most commercially available C++ compilers.

```
class <derived class name> :
      {public | private <base class name>}
{
      // class body
}
```

A derived class may form a base class of another derived class permitting the construction of class hierarchies. The keyword **public** or **private** placed before each base class indicates the access control to be applied to the inherited members. **Public** means that the inherited members retain the status that they have in the base class, while **private** causes the inherited members to become private members of the derived class irrespective of their status in the base class.

A class definition for savings_account may take the following form:

```
class savings_account:
      public account
{
      private:
            int interest_rate;

      public:

            void savings_account (person owner);

            int calculate_interest (int no_of_days);

            void add_interest ();

};
```

The effect of this declaration is that class savings_account inherits all the public components of class account. Note that class account is specified as a *public* base class of savings_account. In this way, the class savings_account can access the public components of account as if they had been declared in its own public section.

Multiple inheritance [see Cardelli, 1984a] in C++ permits a new class to be derived from a number of other classes. Staying with our example of bank accounts, suppose that the bank introduces a new type of account, called a Premium account, which offers interest on current accounts provided a specified minimum balance is maintained. As shown in Figure 4.2, such an account can be considered both as a savings account and a current account since it offers features of both.

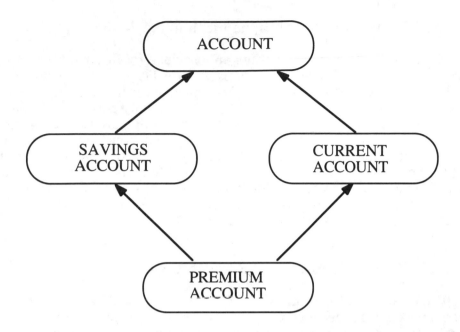

Figure 4.2   An example of multiple inheritance

A class definition for premium_account is shown below:

```
class premium_account:
     public savings_account, current_account
{
     private:

          int min_balance

     public:

          premium_account (...);  // The constructor

          minimum_balance (...);
               ...

};
```

If the base classes contain member functions with the same names, then ambiguities must be prevented by using explicit qualification (i.e. preceding the function name by the appropriate class name).

4.3.2   Polymorphism and dynamic binding in C++

Polymorphism and dynamic binding are provided for in C++ through the mechanism of *virtual member functions*. A virtual C++ routine is provided with a definition in its original class, but may be redefined in descendant classes. That is a virtual function may have different versions in different derived classes and it is the responsibility of the run-time system to find the appropriate version for each call of the virtual function. The requirement that functions may not be redefined unless specifically marked as virtual leads to easier implementation, since static binding may be used for non-virtual functions. A problem with this approach, however, is that it is the responsibility of the base class to decide which of its functions may be redefined. Ideally this should be left to derived classes.

4.3.3   ODE: A database extension to C++

ODE [Agrawal and Gehani, 1989] is an object-oriented database programming language and environment modelled closely on C++ but offering significant extensions to support database applications. It borrows the class definition facility of C++ but extends the language to provide:

- persistence;

- versioning;

- constraints and triggers;

- defining and iterating over sets;

- query processing constructs.

Many of these features are studied in other chapters.

4.4   EIFFEL

Eiffel is a strongly-typed, compiled language that supports most of the object-oriented concepts described in earlier chapters including data abstraction via classes, genericity, inheritance (single and multiple), dynamic binding (though this is carefully controlled), and polymorphism. In addition it provides a comprehensive programming support environment with an extensive library of classes, and support for garbage collection and automatic configuration management (these features of object-oriented systems will be described in detail in Chapter 8). The Eiffel environment is primarily geared for software engineering applications, rather than the database or artificial intelligence areas, and it has very limited support for persistent objects and as yet no facilities for modelling concurrent activities. (It is reported in Meyer [1988] that an effort to add concurrency to Eiffel is in progress.)

An Eiffel class describing the entity ACCOUNT might take the following form (text segments preceded by the symbol '--' are comments):

```
class ACCOUNT

export
      owner, balance, open, deposit, withdraw

feature
      owner : PERSON ;

      balance: INTEGER ;

      open (the_owner : PERSON) is
           do owner := the_owner end;

      deposit (amount : INTEGER) is
           do balance := balance + amount end;

      withdraw (amount : INTEGER) is
           do balance := balance - amount end;

   end -- class ACCOUNT
```

Eiffel provides an implementation for classes which closely mirrors the form used in this book for illustrative purposes. Features of a class may be **attributes** (i.e. properties) which denote data items associated with objects of the class, and **routines** which implement the operations. Routines may be either procedures or functions. The 'dot' notation (i.e. <class_name>. <feature_name>) is used to access features. Thus if my_account is an object of type ACCOUNT then the balance of my_account is denoted by

my_account.balance

Features listed in the **export** clause form the class interface. That is, such features are available to clients of the class. Features which are not exported are said to be secret and are available for use only within the class.

Every entity in an Eiffel program must have a type, which may either be a simple type (INTEGER, REAL, CHARACTER, BOOLEAN) or a class.

Commonly used aggregate types such as arrays and strings are implemented as system classes, while data structures such as linked lists and trees are provided through a class library.

4.4.1   Genericity in Eiffel

Classes in Eiffel may have generic parameters which represent types. As described in Chapter 2, generic classes may be used to represent general data structures that have the same structure and behaviour regardless of the type of elements that they contain. For example, the Eiffel class library provides generic classes of the following form:

    ARRAY [T]

    LIST [T]

    LINKED_LIST [T]

The first generic class represents a one-dimensional array whose components may be of any type T. An actual type for T is provided when the generic class is used in a declaration. The actual type may be either a simple type or a class. For example, we might have the following declarations:

    integer_array : ARRAY[INTEGER];

    accounts_list : LIST [ACCOUNT];

    structure : LINKED_LIST [ARRAY[INTEGER]]

Using this technique alone it is not possible to declare a list which can contain elements of more than one type, for example a list which can contain both integers and reals. However this restriction can be overcome using inheritance.

4.4.2   Inheritance in Eiffel

Eiffel provides both single and multiple inheritance, and also the ability to rename or redefine inherited features. To illustrate these features we consider an Eiffel class definition for SAVINGS_ACCOUNT of the following form:

    class SAVINGS_ACCOUNT

    export
            owner, balance, open, deposit, withdraw

```
inherit
        ACCOUNT redefine withdraw

feature
        withdraw (amount : INTEGER) is
                require
                        amount <= balance
                do
                        balance := balance - amount
                end;  -- withdraw

        end -- class SAVINGS_ACCOUNT
```

The class SAVINGS_ACCOUNT is defined as inheriting all the features of class ACCOUNT but with a redefinition of the withdraw operation. In this case the restriction on savings accounts that the amount withdrawn must not be greater than the balance is implemented as a **precondition** in the procedure withdraw. A precondition in Eiffel is introduced by the keyword **require** and expresses a condition that must be satisfied whenever a routine is called. Eiffel also offers explicit facilities for defining **postconditions** in routines and class **invariants**. Together these facilities provide very powerful facilities for ensuring the correctness of programs written in Eiffel.

Returning to the issue of inheritance, we have seen above how a class may redefine a routine which has been inherited. In some cases we may wish to force redefinition, i.e. force a subclass to provide an explicit implementation for an inherited routine. Eiffel provides for such a requirement by allowing routines to be deferred. For example, to defer the implementation of the withdraw routine we introduce it in the ACCOUNT class in the following way:

```
        withdraw (amount : INTEGER) is
                deferred
                end;
```

In this way the routine is known to the class in which it is deferred but implemented only in descendant classes. The parent class provides a complete specification, but a partial implementation of the corresponding abstract data type.

Eiffel also provides for multiple inheritance, in that a class may inherit the features of more than one parent class. Thus the class definition for PREMIUM_ACCOUNT (described in section 4.3.3) could take the following form:

```
class PREMIUM_ACCOUNT

export
        owner, balance, open, deposit, withdraw

inherit
        SAVINGS_ACCOUNT;
        CURRENT_ACCOUNT;

feature
        minimum_balance : real;

end -- class PREMIUM_ACCOUNT
```

In this case the **inherit** clause lists all the parents of the new class. That is, in this example all the features of savings accounts and current accounts are applicable to objects of type PREMIUM_ACCOUNT. No name conflict is permitted among inherited features. Name clashes resulting from multiple inheritance in Eiffel are resolved in the inheriting subclass using appropriate **rename** clauses, through which any of the features of a parent class may be given a new name. For example:

```
class A  export ...

inherit
        B rename x as xb, y as yb
        C rename x as xc, y as yc

feature              ...

end -- class A
```

In this case, unless the inherited features with the same names are renamed, the inherit clause is illegal.

4.5   VBASE

Vbase[†] [Andrews and Harris, 1987] is an integrated object-oriented systems development environment that incorporates a type definition language,

---

† Vbase is now a commercial product marketed under the name ONTOS™ by Ontologic Inc. ONTOS is modelled closely on C++ and differs considerably from the original Vbase system as described by Andrews and Harris.

an object-based processing language and an underlying persistent object management system. The language is strongly typed and is based on the abstract data type facility of the language CLU [Liskov *et al.*, 1981], rather than the object/message model of Smalltalk. The advantages of strong typing have already been alluded to in earlier chapters.

For database modelling the system provides direct support for the semantics of one-to-one, one-to-many and many-to-many relationships between objects. Triggered procedures and object clustering are also features of the system. Object identity (discussed in detail in Chapter 6) is provided by the system, which creates a unique internal identifier (called an OID) for each object.

The type definition language (TDL) is essentially a data description language which is used to define both simple data types (enumerated types, discriminated unions and variants) and also classes together with their properties and operations. Single inheritance is supported and inherited properties and operations may be redefined within a subtype. The TDL is used to construct an object-oriented schema for an application. The kernal of Vbase provides a library of system-defined types and classes which the user may incorporate into his schema. The user may also extend the type library with new types, which must be integrated into the existing type hierarchy. This hierarchy has as its root a built-in type called ENTITY of which every type is a subtype. An *aggregate* type is provided through which the user may define abstractions such as lists, sets, strings and arrays. Relationships among objects are represented via properties. That is, a property within a class can be used to relate it to another class. The value of such a property for an instance of the class is the OID of the related object.

The object processing language (called COP) is a vehicle for developing application code. It is a strict superset of C and a preprocessor for the language yields standard C code as its output. All possible type checking is performed by COP (with reference to the types in the TDL schema) at compile time. The operations (methods) in TDL class specifications are written in COP. A method is a class in its own right, and the same abstract operation may have different implementations in different classes.

4.5.1 Classes and inheritance in Vbase

Vbase incorporates most of the standard object-oriented language features described in the previous chapters. To illustrate the data modelling capabilities of the TDL we shall consider a Vbase implementation of an expanded version of our bank account example. In order to illustrate a larger subset of the data modelling features of Vbase we introduce two additional entities - an entity PERSON representing the owners of accounts and an entity BRANCH representing the branch offices where accounts are held. A partial TDL schema for this database is as follows.

define type Person

    supertypes = { Entity }

    properties =
        {   Name :   String;
               Address : String
               Sex :   (Male, Female);
               DOB :   Date;
               Owns :   optional distributed
                             Set[Account]
                             inverse Account$Owner
        };

    operations =
        {   Age (today : Date) : returns (Integer);
        };

end person;

define type Account

    supertypes = { Entity }

    properties =
        {   Held_at : Branch
                          inverse
                          Branch$Accounts_held;
               Owner :   Person
                          inverse Person$Owns;
               Balance : Integer;
        };

    operations =
        {   Open (owner : Person);
            ...
           Deposit (amount : Integer);
           ...
           Withdraw (amount : Integer);
        };

end Account;

```
define type Branch

    supertypes = { Entity }

    properties =
        {       Address :    String;
                Manager :    Employee;
                Accounts_held:   distributed Set[Account]
                                 inverse
                                 Account$Branch;
        };

end Branch;


define type Savings_Account

    supertypes = { Account }

    properties =
        {       interest_rate :      Integer;
        };

    operations =
        {       withdraw (amount : Integer)
        };

end Savings_Account;
```

Note that the main difference between the TDL definitions, and those in a conventional object-oriented programming language such as Eiffel, is that properties can have additional specifications which incorporate some of the additional semantics of entity-relationship models. These additional specifications include:

- Optional or mandatory membership (mandatory is the default).

- Single-valued or multi-valued (the term *distributed* is used to denote multi-valued).

- The *inverse* of the property may be specified in cases where the property represents a relationship with another entity.

- Inherited properties may be refined or constrained.

- The property may be protected against access or modification.

The support for inverse relationships is useful (as mentioned in Chapter 3). For example, Account contains a property Owner which has as its inverse the property Owns in the Person type. Whenever an instance is modified on one side of an inverse relationship, it is automatically modified on the other side. This feature of the system solves the problem of referential integrity which arises in relational databases. That is, one-to-one, one-to-many and many-to-many relationships can all be supported and maintained automatically using the inverse construct.

In Vbase a subtype inherits the properties and operations of its supertypes. It may define additional features of its own and may redefine any of the inherited features.

4.6   SUMMARY

In this chapter, we illustrate typical mechanisms for class definition and inheritance through the languages Smalltalk, C++ and Eiffel. These languages provide three contrasting approaches to object-oriented programming and differ considerably in their basic philosophies. Smalltalk and C++ have had considerable influence on the design and development of object-oriented database management systems. Eiffel offers a contrasting approach, providing sophisticated facilities for type definition, genericity, inheritance and integrity preservation within the framework of an elegant, strongly typed programming language.

In addition we study the facilities offered by the object-oriented database system Vbase. The type definition language of this system elegantly illustrates the additional language features necessary for modelling database applications. These include single-valued and multi-valued properties, optional and mandatory relationships and the ability to model inverse relationships explicitly.

4.7   BIBLIOGRAPHIC NOTES

A very lucid review of object-oriented programming languages is given by Wegner [1989]. A detailed description genericity and inheritance is given by Meyer [1986], and a comprehensive description of many of the programming language features discussed in this chapter can be found in Meyer [1988]. This latter reference also describes the Eiffel language in detail. An interesting discussion on encapsulation and inheritance in object-oriented programming languages is provided by Snyder [1986]. The papers by Agrawal and Gehani [1989] and Andrews and Harris [1987] give good descriptions of how to extend an object-oriented programming language to cope with database applications. A good overview of the message-passing paradigm within a database context is given by Maier and Stein [1987].

5

Object-oriented query processing

5.1 INTRODUCTION

As we have already seen, object-oriented database systems model every real-world entity as an object with a unique identity, where every object belongs to a class. The system must provide persistent storage for the class definitions (schema) and objects and furnish the user with an interface for creating, destroying, modifying and accessing classes and objects. In object-oriented programming languages such data manipulation is performed by sending messages to objects. However, in a database environment there is a need for a comprehensive, high-level query language which is flexible and easy to use and which adheres to the fundamental principles of the object-oriented model.

Relational database query languages provide notations for deriving information from the permanent relations in the database. There are many such languages available but most of them are based on one of two fundamental approaches, namely,

1. *Relational algebra*, in which specialized operators are applied to relations.

2. *Relational calculus*, which is based on first-order predicate calculus, and in which queries are expressed by specifying a predicate that tuples must satisfy.

SQL (Structured Query Language) [Chamberlin *et al.*, 1976] is based mainly on relational calculus, using English key words in place of the quantifiers and logical connectives. However, it also provides set operations which give it a flavour of relational algebra. SQL was developed by IBM in the 1970s as part of their experimental relational database system called 'System R'. It is rapidly becoming the internationally recognized standard relational database query language and, consequently, most currently available relational database systems provide an SQL interface.

Some object-oriented systems have a query language which might be described as an extended, and semantically enriched version of SQL. We shall study some aspects of these languages later in the chapter. In the next section we give a brief overview of the principal features of SQL.

5.2   AN OVERVIEW OF SQL

Implementations of SQL contain sophisticated features for retrieval, insertion, deletion and update as well as built-in functions for tailoring output. In the following sections we shall examine, by way of examples, only some of the principal features of the language.

5.2.1   Retrieval operations

To illustrate some of the basic features of SQL we shall give expressions for typical queries on the following relations, taken from a simplified version of the company database in Chapter 1.

DEPARTMENT (DNAME, MANAGER_EMP#)

EMPLOYEE (EMP#, ENAME, DNAME, FLOOR)

PROJECT (P#, PNAME, BUDGET)

WORKS_ON (EMP#, P#, ROLE)

Query 1: 'Retrieve the numbers and names of all employees in the planning department on floor 1.'

```
SELECT EMP#, ENAME
FROM   EMPLOYEE
WHERE DNAME = 'Planning'
AND FLOOR = 1 ;
```

This example presents the simplest form of the SELECT statement in SQL, whereby specified attributes (EMP# and ENAME) are selected from tuples in a specified relation (EMPLOYEE) for which some specified condition (FLOOR = 1) is satisfied. An important point to stress is that the result of a query in SQL is another relation - a relation derived from the permanent relations in the relational schema for the database.

SQL being an end-user language also includes facilities for tailoring the output of a query. For example, we may order the resulting tuples according to some sort criterion, by including an ORDER BY clause:

```
SELECT  EMP#, ENAME
FROM  EMPLOYEE
WHERE  FLOOR = 1
ORDER  BY  ENAME  ASC ;
```

The result of this query will be a relation containing the numbers and names of employees on floor 1, in ascending alphabetical order.

Query 2: 'Retrieve the numbers and names of employees who work on project 121.'

```
SELECT EMPLOYEE.EMP#, EMPLOYEE.ENAME
FROM EMPLOYEE, WORKS_ON
WHERE EMPLOYEE.EMP# = WORKS_ON.EMP#
AND WORKS_ON.P# = 121 ;
```

In this example, unlike the first query, we must qualify the attribute names with the names of the relations in order to avoid ambiguity.

This example shows how the SQL SELECT statement handles queries which would require join operations in relational algebra. An alternative solution to the above query in SQL is the following:

```
SELECT  EMP#, ENAME
FROM  EMPLOYEE
WHERE  EMP# IN
          (SELECT EMP#
         ' FROM  WORKS_ON
            WHERE  P# = 121 ) ;
```

Note here the use of a *nested* SELECT clause in conjunction with the IN operator. A nested SELECT clause denotes a set of tuples, i.e. an unnamed intermediate relation. In this example the inner SELECT clause retrieves the set of employee numbers, EMP#, from the WORKS_ON relation, where each of those employees takes project 121. The outer SELECT clause retrieves from the EMPLOYEE relation the name, ENAME, corresponding to each EMP# value in that set.

SELECT clauses can be nested to any depth, subject to restrictions imposed by specific implementations. The next example has three such clauses.

Query 3: 'Retrieve the numbers and names of employees who work on at least one of the projects with a budget of more than 10000.'

```
SELECT EMP#, ENAME
FROM  EMPLOYEE
```

```
WHERE EMP# IN
        (SELECT EMP#
         FROM WORKS_ON
         WHERE P# IN
                (SELECT P#
                 FROM PROJECT
                 WHERE BUDGET > 10000 ) ) ;
```

Alternatively, we could write:

```
SELECT  EMPLOYEE.EMP#, EMPLOYEE.ENAME
FROM  EMPLOYEE, WORKS_ON, PROJECT
WHERE  EMPLOYEE.EMP# = WORKS_ON.EMP#
AND  WORKS_ON.P# = PROJECT.P#
AND  PROJECT.BUDGET > 10000 ;
```

Whether one uses this form or the nested query form above is largely a matter of personal choice. Both forms are equally valid and ideally both should be equally efficient in any given implementation.

Query 4: 'Find all pairs of employee numbers such that the employees are in the same department.'

In SQL we may express this query in the following form:

```
SELECT  EMPLOYEE.EMP#, TEMP.EMP#
FROM  EMPLOYEE, EMPLOYEE TEMP
WHERE  EMPLOYEE.EMP# < TEMP.EMP#
AND  EMPLOYEE.DNAME = TEMP.DNAME ;
```

Here again we have introduced an alias relation called TEMP in the FROM clause, which is a logical copy of the EMPLOYEE relation. The first condition in the WHERE clause (EMPLOYEE.EMP# < TEMP.EMP#) ensures that a employee number does not appear in the result paired with itself, and that any given pair appears only once.

Query 5: 'Retrieve all details of those employees who do not work on project 121.'

In SQL this query may be expressed in the following way:

```
SELECT *
FROM  EMPLOYEE
WHERE NOT EXISTS
        ( SELECT *
          FROM WORKS_ON
          WHERE  WORKS_ON.EMP# = EMPLOYEE.EMP#
          AND  WORKS_ON.P# = 121 ) ;
```

This example firstly illustrates the use of the star symbol (*), which is a shorthand notation indicating that all the attributes of the relation (or relations) specified in the FROM clause are to be retrieved. Secondly we have used the SQL representation of the existential quantifier, EXISTS. In SQL the expression

```
EXISTS ( SELECT ... )
```

evaluates to true if the result of the enclosed SELECT expression is not empty. Thus the SQL solution to the above query is more easily understood if we reformulate the query as

'Retrieve all details of those employees such that there does not exist a tuple in the WORKS_ON relation connecting them with project 121.'

Actually, as the careful reader may have already realized, this query could have been expressed in a simpler form, without the use of the existential quantifier, i.e.

```
SELECT *
FROM  EMPLOYEE
WHERE  EMP# NOT IN
        ( SELECT EMP#
          FROM  WORKS_ON
          WHERE  WORKS_ON.P# = 121 ) ;
```

However there are certain classes of complex query which require the use of EXISTS, especially in its negated form. The next query illustrates such a situation.

Query 6: 'Retrieve the numbers of those employees who work on every project.'

To answer this query using relational calculus one may use the universal quantifier. SQL does not have an explicit equivalent to this quantifier but queries involving the universal quantifier can always be rewritten in terms of the existential quantifier in its negated form. Thus the above query may be re-expressed in the following form:

'Retrieve the numbers of those employees such that there does not exist a project on which they do not work.'

In SQL this may be expressed in the following form:

```
SELECT EMP#
FROM  EMPLOYEE
WHERE  NOT EXISTS
        ( SELECT *
          FROM  PROJECT
```

```
WHERE NOT EXISTS
    ( SELECT *
      FROM WORKS_ON
      WHERE EMP# = EMPLOYEE.EMP#
      AND P# = PROJECT.P# )) ;
```

Query 7: 'List the numbers of all those employees who are on floor 1 or who work on project 121.'

The SQL answer to this query illustrates the use of a set operator, namely that of set union.

```
(SELECT EMP#
 FROM EMPLOYEE
 WHERE FLOOR = 1)
UNION
(SELECT EMP#
 FROM WORKS_ON
 WHERE P# = 121) ;
```

The UNION operator in SQL merges the results of two subqueries and eliminates duplicate tuples.

Query 8: 'How many employees work on project 121 and what is their average salary?'

SQL being a practical end-user language, includes a variety of built-in functions to increase its retrieval capabilities. The most useful of these functions operate on the values of a single attribute of a relation (which may be a permanent relation or the result of a SELECT statement). These so-called *aggregate functions* may be described as follows:

(i)   COUNT: counts the number of values in a specified column.

(ii)   SUM: totals the values in a specified column containing numeric values.

(iii)   AVG: calculates the average of the values in a specified column which contains numeric values.

(iv)   MIN: returns the minimum value in a specified column.

(v)   MAX: returns the maximum value in a specified column.

Thus query 8 may be expressed in SQL by the following statement:

```
SELECT COUNT(*), AVG(SALARY)
FROM WORKS_ON, EMPLOYEE
WHERE WORKS_ON.EMP# = EMPLOYEE.EMP# AND P# = 121 ;
```

5.2.2   Update operations

We shall merely illustrate update operations in SQL with three simple examples.

Example 1:   Insert into the relation EMPLOYEE a new tuple with the following field values: EMP# = 867520, ENAME = 'James Smith', DNAME = 'Planning' and FLOOR = 2.

```
INSERT
INTO  EMPLOYEE
VALUES ( 867520, 'James Smith', 'Planning', 2) ;
```

Example 2:   Delete all employees on floor 3.

```
DELETE
FROM  EMPLOYEE
WHERE  FLOOR = 3 ;
```

All the tuples in the specified relation which satisfy the predicate in the WHERE clause are deleted.

Example 3:   Change the budget on project 251 from 10000 to 15000.

```
UPDATE  PROJECT
SET  BUDGET =  15000
WHERE  P# =  251 ;
```

All the tuples in the specified relation which satisfy the predicate in the WHERE clause are updated according to the assignments in the SET clause.

The popularity of SQL can be attributed to its flexibility, its ease-of-use and its availability on a wide range of relational systems. However, it is by no means without faults, and deficiencies in the language have been highlighted by several authors [e.g. Date, 1990].

5.3   FUNCTIONAL DATA MANIPULATION

The basic elements of the functional data model are described in Chapter 1. Since the object-oriented model has many similarities with the functional data model, it is instructive to study the basic techniques of data manipulation in functional databases. The data manipulation facilities of functional languages may be exemplified by the language DAPLEX [Shipman, 1981]. A DAPLEX schema for the database involving departments, employees and projects might take the following form:

```
DECLARE Department ()              —>> ENTITY
DECLARE Name (Department)          —>  String

DECLARE Employee ()                —>> ENTITY
DECLARE Number (Employee)          —>  INTEGER
DECLARE Name (Employee)            —>  STRING
DECLARE Department (Employee)      —>  Department
DECLARE Floor (Employee)           —>  INTEGER
DECLARE Project (Employee)         —>> Project
DECLARE Role (Employee, Project)   —>  STRING

DECLARE Project ()                 —>> ENTITY
DECLARE Number (Project)           —>  STRING
DECLARE Name (Project)             —>  STRING
DECLARE Budget (Project)           —>  INTEGER
DEFINE Team (Project)              —>  INVERSE OF
                                        Project (Employee)
```

Note the very elegant way in which the relationship WORKS_ON is represented in this schema, via the functions Project (Employee), which is multivalued, Role (Employee, Project), and the derived function Team (Project).

Consider again Query 3 from the previous section:

'Retrieve the numbers and names of employees who work on at least one of the projects with a budget of more than 10000.'

In DAPLEX we could write this query in the following form:

```
FOR EACH Employee SUCH THAT FOR SOME Project (Employee)
     Budget (Project (Employee))  > 10000
  PRINT Number (Employee), Name (Employee)
```

The FOR EACH statement iterates over the set of entities of type Employee, executing the PRINT statement for each member of that set for which the qualification specified in the SUCH THAT clause is satisfied.The SUCH THAT clause here contains a further quantification indicated by the phrase 'FOR SOME Project (Employee)'. This implies that if the following predicate is true for at least one of the Project entities returned by applying the Project function to the current Employee entity under consideration, then the Name of that Employee entity will be printed.

Note the use of nested function application and the absence of explicit looping variables. This gives the language a format which is closer to 'natural' language than, for example, many relational data languages.

Data entry and update in DAPLEX are illustrated by the following two examples:

1. *'Add a new employee named Joe Smith and assign him to the projects with numbers 121 and 137':*

```
FOR A NEW Employee
    BEGIN
        LET Name (Employee)  =  'Joe Smith'
        LET Number (Employee)  =  12345
        LET Department (Employee)  =  'Accounts'
        LET Floor (Employee)  =  1
        LET Project (Employee)  =
            (THE Project SUCH THAT Number (Project )  = 121,
             THE Project SUCH THAT Number (Project )  = 137 )
    END
```

2. *'Move the employee Tom Brown from project 147 to the project 156':*

```
FOR THE Employee SUCH THAT Name (Employee)  =  'Tom Brown'
    BEGIN
        EXCLUDE Project (Employee)  =
            THE Project SUCH THAT Number (Project)  = 147
        INCLUDE Project (Employee)  =
            THE Project SUCH THAT Number (Project)  = 156
    END
```

Like SQL, DAPLEX also provides aggregate functions such as AVERAGE, TOTAL, COUNT, MAXIMUM and MINIMUM.

5.4 OBJECT-ORIENTED DATA MANIPULATION

Data manipulation in an object-oriented database system is accomplished by means of the operations defined in the class interfaces and through the constructs provided by the programming language surrounding the class definitions. However, many object-oriented systems also provide high-level query language interfaces, mostly based on SQL. To illustrate the principles we shall make use of the object-oriented version of the department/employee/project database given below:

```
class Department

    properties
        name : String;
        manager : Employee;
```

operations
    create (...) —> Department;
    ...

end Department.

class Employee

properties
    number : Integer;
    name : String;
    department : Department;
    floor : 1..5;
    works_on : Set (Project)
                inverse is Project.team;

operations
    create (...) —> Employee;
    role (Employee, Project) —> RoleType;
    ...

end Employee.

class Project

properties
    number : Integer;
    name : String;
    budget : Integer;
    team : Set (Employee)
                inverse is Employee.works_on;

operations
    create (...) —> Project;
    ...

end Project.

In the above schema, the relationship WORKS_ON between employee and project is represented by the property Employee.works_on with inverse Project.team. The role played by an employee on a particular project is represented by the *operation* Employee.role.

The data manipulation facilities of Vbase [Andrews and Harris, 1987] are typical. As described in Chapter 4, a type definition language (TDL) is provided in this system for the definition of classes. Another language, called COP (C object processor), which is a superset of C, is used to implement the operations defined in class interfaces and to write application programs which access the object database. A COP program can create and destroy objects and can directly access named objects in the database. Operations are called from application programs by name and are passed an appropriate list of arguments.

A similar approach to data manipulation is taken in the ODE system [Agrawal and Gehani, 1989]. In this system both class definitions and data manipulation are performed through the medium of a procedural programming language called O, which is an extension of C++. From the point of view of object manipulation languages like COP and O provide programming constructs for iterating over sets or *clusters* of objects. These typically consist of *for* (or *forall*) loops of the general forms:

```
for <object variable> in <cluster> {, <object variable> in <cluster> }
[suchthat <Boolean expression>] do <statement sequence>
```

Note the similarity here to the functional data manipulation language described in the previous section. Also note that one can have multiple looping variables in a for statement. This permits the expression of operations with the functionality of the arbitrary relational join operation.

Referring to the object-oriented schema above, and using these constructs we may write statements of the form:

1.   for p in Project suchthat p.budget > 100000 do ...

2.   for e in Employee, p in Project
     suchthat (e.floor = 1 and p in e.works_on and p.number = 125) do ...

The first statement is accessing all projects which have a budget greater than 100000. The second is accessing all employees on the first floor who work on project 125. This is performing an operation that would require a join in the relational implementation of the database.

COP and ODE are highly procedural languages in which efficiency is largely in the hands of the programmer. In this respect their use might be compared with interacting with a relational database by means of a C interface. An important difference however is that in the object-oriented case there is a much stronger affinity between the programming language constructs and the objects in the database, and each object has a well-defined manipulation protocol. This avoids the so-called 'impedance mismatch' which occurs when SQL (or a similar query language) is embedded in a programming language and the objects manipulated by the query language statements are not subject to the type-checking constraints of the language. A fully-integrated, strongly-typed data manipulation language has significant implications for integrity preservation.

However, the notion of predetermining and pre-specifying all operations on objects by a fixed set of functions might be thought of as a rather rigid constraint which is contrary to the current trends in database technology, with its ad hoc query languages, natural language interfaces, application generators, etc. That is, not every user of an object-oriented database wants to interact with the system through a procedural programming language. There is clearly a need in most application areas for a high-level query language and tools such as report generators. As yet, there is no well-defined, widely accepted query language for object-oriented database systems which fulfils the general purpose role that SQL plays in the relational environment. Object-oriented extensions to SQL have been proposed but their use is somewhat difficult in that relational operations such as join must be carefully defined when the attributes to be joined over may themselves be complex data structures. Such object-oriented extensions to SQL are described below.

5.4.1   Object-oriented SQL

As well as a procedural data manipulation language, several object-oriented database management systems, including Vbase, provide a high-level query language called Object SQL (or OSQL). It employs the familiar syntactical form of SQL (SELECT ... FROM ... WHERE ...), but uses object names in the FROM clause and properties in the SELECT clause. Using the familiar 'dot' notation it is possible to retrieve information from related objects. The main differences between Object SQL and relational SQL are:

- Objects are referenced directly rather than via key values. Variables may be bound to objects on creation or retrieval and may then be used to refer to the objects in subsequent statements.

- Operations may appear in the SELECT and WHERE clauses.

For example, consider the following query on the department-employee-project object-oriented schema.

1. *Retrieve the the names of all the employees in the Planning department.*

```
SELECT     e.Name
FROM       e IN Employee
WHERE      e.department.name = 'Planning'
```

Note the use of the 'dot' notation to access information in other related objects. That is, the Employee property department is an object of type Department, and we access the name of that department through the expression Employee.department.name. Otherwise there is strong similarity to standard SQL.

2. *Retrieve the names and departments for all employees working on project 121 together with the roles they play.*

```
SELECT     e.name, e.department.name, e.role (e, p)
FROM       e IN Employee, p IN Project
WHERE      p.number =121
AND        p IN e.works_on
```

IRIS [Fishman *et al.*, 1989; Wilkinson *et al.*, 1990] also provides a query language which might be described as an object-oriented extension of SQL. In this case the query language has a strongly functional style which reflects the functional nature of the underlying IRIS data model. For example, the two queries above might be written as follows:

```
1.   SELECT     Name(e)
     FOR EACH   Employee e
     WHERE      Name (Department (e)) = 'Planning'
```

```
2.   SELECT     Name(e), Name(Department(e)), role(e, p)
     FOR EACH   Employee e, Project p
     WHERE      Number (p) = 121
     AND        p IN Works_on (e)
```

Note the similarity here to the functional data manipulation language DAPLEX described in Section 5.3. The nesting of function application can be to any depth, permitting the compact expression of very complex queries. That is, if class C_i has a property P_i which returns an object of type C_{i+1} (i = 1..n-1), then a valid function application is:

$$P_1 (P_2 (... P_n(p) ...)$$

5.4.2   The O_2 database programming language

The O_2 database programming language [Lecluse and Richard, 1989; Deux *et al.*, 1990] provides a procedural object-oriented data manipulation language. In this language a class is defined as a *tuple type*, as illustrated by the following schema definition commands which add the Employee and Project classes to the database:

```
add class Employee
     type tuple  ( number : integer,
                   name : string,
                   department : Department,
                   floor : integer)


add class Project
     type tuple  ( number : integer,
                   name : string,
                   budget : integer,
                   team : set(Employee))
```

A value of the Employee class might be:

```
Einstein:
tuple  ( number : 12345,
         name : "Albert Einstein",
         department : Mathematics,
         floor : 3)
```

and a value of the Project class is:

```
Relativity:
tuple (   number : 125,
          name "Relativity",
          budget : 12000,
          team : (Einstein, Minkowski, Lorenz)
```

The italicized names in the above value denote objects. The Employee object will always be accessible through the name Einstein, and the Project object through the name Relativity, during the lifetime of the system. Every named object or value is automatically persistent and every object or value which is part of another persistent object is itself persistent.

A method is added to a class by giving its *signature*, i.e. its name, the type or class of its arguments and the type or class of the result if any. For example:

```
add method move (new_floor : integer)
in class Employee
```

Methods may be private (i.e. only visible to that class) or public. Programming with methods is carried out using a standard programming language such as C, with access to and manipulation of objects and values being performed using features of O_2. Using CO_2 (the C interface to O_2) the code of the method 'move' defined above might take the form:

```
body move (new_floor : integer) in class Employee
    co2 { (*self).floor = new_floor; }
```

The chain brackets denote the CO_2 block of code. The value of an object is obtained using the dereferencing syntax of C, i.e. preceding the name by '*'. Thus self is the object and *self is the associated value. A method is applied to an object using a 'message-passing' syntax:

```
[<receiver> <selector> <argument list>]
```

For example:

```
[Einstein move (5)]
```

When this method is applied, the object 'Einstein' will take the place of the keyword self in the method code.

The language CO_2 also allows the construction of O_2 values using set, list and tuple constructors, and it provides an iterator to facilitate set and list manipulation. For example, the following code moves every employee on the 'Relativity' project to the 4th floor.

```
co2{  o2 Employee x;
      for (x in Relativity.team
      when (*x.floor <> 4))
      [x.move(4)];
   }
```

The O_2 system also provides a high-level query language [Deux *et al.*, 1990] with an SQL-like syntax, but a functional character (like the query language of IRIS). Consider the following query:

Retrieve the name of all employees on the 4th floor who work on a project with a budget greater than 10000.

In O_2 SQL we may write the following expression to evaluate this query:

```
select tuple (Employee: e.name)
from   e in Employee,
       p in Project
where e.floor = 4 and e in p.team and p.budget > 10000.
```

This query language can be used embedded in a programming language or in interactive mode for ad hoc queries. In the embedded mode it cannot violate encapsulation, i.e. it cannot access the value of an object except through its public methods. In interactive mode this restriction is relaxed and the query language can directly access the values of objects.

In common with some other object-oriented database systems, O_2 has a graphical user interface which allows a casual user to browse, edit and query the data without having to make use of the query language.

5.5   SUMMARY

In this chapter we give an overview of some of the basic approaches to object-oriented query processing. The close relationship of these approaches to SQL and to functional data manipulation languages is illustrated.

It is shown that despite the significant differences in the data models, object-oriented databases may be queried in a manner similar to relational systems. For example, the relational selection operation by which tuples satisfying some predicate are selected from a relation is equivalent to the retrieval of instances of a specified class. Also, the retrieval of an instance of a class C_1 which is the value of a property P of a class C_2 is equivalent to the familiar join operation of relational algebra. However, more complex queries, which, for example, involve join or set operations over nested classes, are not well defined for object-oriented databases.

Thus, despite the attempts that have been made to provide object-oriented extensions to SQL for specific systems, there still does not exist a well-defined query model for object-oriented databases which offers the power of relational database languages, while at the same time honouring the fundamental principles of the object-oriented data model [Kim, 1990]. Nevertheless, we cannot agree with criticisms of the object-oriented model [Date, 1990] which imply that current data manipulation techniques in the model amount to record-at-a-time, 'pointer chasing', as in old-fashioned network databases. One cannot compare a record with a complex object nor a linked list of records with a class hierarchy. To do so does great injustice to the object-oriented model and its sophisticated data abstraction mechanisms.

5.6   BIBLIOGRAPHIC NOTES

A detailed description of relational SQL may be found in Date [1990]. Descriptions of object-oriented extensions to SQL may be found in Vbase [Andrews and Harris, 1987], O_2 [Deux *et al*., 1990] and IRIS [Fishman *et al*., 1989]. Some other object-oriented query languages (for example, that of ORION) are based on those of the nested relational model. This model is described in Abiteboul and Bidoit [1984, 1986].

One of the few attempts at developing a comprehensive, well-defined query model for object-oriented systems is provided by Kim [1989].

6

Persistence

6.1 INTRODUCTION

Conventional programming languages concentrate on the provision of facilities for the definition and manipulation of data structures whose existence does not extend beyond the lifetime of the program in which they are created. If data is required to survive an activation of a program, then some file I/O system must be used. Often this file system is rather primitive and may sometimes be external to the built-in language features. For example, standard Pascal provides only sequential files, while the file-handling system of Modula-2 consists of an external, implementation-dependent Files module. This approach gives rise to two classes of data within an application program:

- *volatile* data, which is created and manipulated by the programming language facilities, resides in volatile memory, and whose existence ends with the termination of the program;

- *persistent* data, which resides in persistent (or permanent) store and must be transferred into the program's volatile memory space before it can be accessed or manipulated.

For example, consider a Pascal program which is concerned with objects of type car which is defined by the record structure:

```
type
    car = record
                registration : string;
                make : (Ford, Nissan, VW, ... );
                size : (compact, midsize, large);
                ...
          end;
```

We may declare variables c1 and c2 of type car in the following manner:

```
var c1, c2 : car;
```

The variables c1 and c2 are examples of volatile data. We may assign the fields of c1 and c2 to appropriate values and manipulate them within the program, but they do not exist outside of the program. If we require c1 and c2 to persist we must define and create an external file of car records and write c1 and c2 to this file.

```
var carfile : file of car;
begin
    ...
    c1.registration = 'ABC1' ;  c1.make := Ford;  c1.size := compact;
    c2.registration = 'ABC2' ;  c2.make := VW;  c2.size := midsize;
    rewrite (carfile, 'cars.dat');
    write (carfile, c1);  write (carfile, c2)
    ...
end.
```

An alternative approach, popular in commercial database application environments, is to embed statements from a data manipulation sublanguage, such as SQL, in a conventional programming language (typically COBOL, PL/1, FORTRAN, C or Pascal). In such systems SQL statements may be interspersed with the host language code in a manner that makes them recognizable by a precompiler that generates the appropriate external subroutine calls. Using the above example, we may embed SQL statements (distinguished by the prefix 'exec sql') in a Pascal program in order to permit the information represented by c1 and c2 to persist, in the following manner:

```
exec sql begin declare section
        reg, make, size : string;
exec sql end declare section;

begin
    ...
    registration = 'ABC1' ;  make := 'Ford';  size := 'compact';
    exec sql insert into cars(registration, make, size, ...)
                values (:registration, :make, :size, ...);
    ...
    registration = 'ABC2' ;  make := VW;  size := midsize;
    exec sql insert into cars(registration, make, size, ...)
                values (:registration, :make, :size, ...);
end.
```

where *cars* is a relation in the underlying database implementation. Communication between the host language and SQL is performed through a special class of variable (here prefixed by a ':' symbol). One problem that arises is that SQL queries generate arbitrarily large subsets of tuples and there is no general purpose data type available in the host language for representing such sets. In such cases a buffer variable or 'cursor' must be used to sequence through the tuples in a manner similar to scanning a sequential file.

This clear-cut distinction between volatile and persistent data has two major disadvantages. Firstly a considerable fraction of the code is devoted to performing the necessary mappings between volatile and persistent data structures. A figure of 30% of the code is often quoted [Atkinson *et al.*, 1983] but for many I/O intensive database applications the figure may be considerably higher. A second disadvantage is that there may be a significant mismatch between the data typing facilities offered by the programming language and those provided by the filing system or DBMS. For instance, in the example above which employs embedded SQL code, the underlying DBMS is unlikely to provide enumerated types and so values of make and size have to be mapped to strings of characters before they can be transmitted to the database. Thus the data protection offered within the program by the enumerated types is lost when the data is transferred to persistent store. In general data may only be conveyed from the programming language to the DBMS through variables of very simple data types such as integer, real and character string.

There have been numerous attempts in recent years to integrate the concept of persistence with well-structured, strongly typed programming languages and much of this work is of direct relevance to object-oriented database systems. Thus in the following sections we review some of these persistent database programming languages before studying the models of persistence required for object-oriented databases.

6.2   PERSISTENCE IN DATABASE PROGRAMMING LANGUAGES

In their efforts to provide a better framework for persistent data, database programming languages have typically adopted one of two contrasting approaches. The first approach, pioneered by the language Pascal/R [Schmidt, 1977], is to provide a tight integration of a database model (usually the relational model) with a conventional programming language. Variables of type relation may persist and additional control structures, based on the relational algebra or calculus, are added to the language for accessing and manipulating relations. Other languages falling into this category include Astral [Amble *et al.*, 1979], Rigel [Rowe and Shoens, 1979], Theseus [Shopiro, 1979], Plain [Wasserman *et al.*, 1979, 1980, 1981], Modula/R [Reimer, 1984], and RAPP [Hughes and Connolly, 1987]. In the following section we shall examine the persistent aspects of Pascal/R, these being fairly representative of this large group of languages.

A second group of languages adopts a more elaborate model of persistence in which *any* value may persist irrespective of its type, and persistent objects are subject to the same rigorous type checking as program variables. The languages PS-algol [Atkinson *et al.*, 1983] and Amber [Cardelli, 1984b] were the first to treat persistence in such a uniform manner. Poly [Matthews, 1985] and Galileo [Albano *et al.*, 1985] are also in this category. Below, for illustrative purposes, we shall study the model of persistence provided by PS-algol.

6.2.1   Persistence in Pascal/R

As mentioned above, the aim of Pascal/R is to integrate as closely as possible the relation data type with the existing data and control structures of Pascal. Consequently Pascal/R takes advantage of the similarity in structure between the tuples of a relation and the Pascal record type, and the relation type is introduced as a constructor similar to the existing set type. The definition of a relation type requires two parameters: a record type which defines the structure of the tuples of the relation, and the subset of the fields of the record which constitute the primary key. This second parameter effectively defines an integrity rule which imposes the constraint that no two tuples in an instance of this relation type may have the same values in all the key fields.

Databases are defined by means of the **database** constructor which is parameterized in a manner similar to the record type, except that all its components must be of type **relation**. A database variable may then be declared in the program and its persistence is ensured by including it in the program heading (cf. external file parameters in standard Pascal). Only variables of type **database** may persist. Variables of type **relation** declared outside of a database constructor are considered volatile and are typically used for holding the results of intermediate relational operations within the program.

The program fragment below shows a Pascal/R data definition for a simple library database consisting of relations for books, borrowers and loans.

```
TYPE
    string = packed array [1..30] of char;
    number  =  1..9999;

    BookRecord =       RECORD
                           catno : number;
                           title, author, publisher  :  string;
                       END;
    BorrowerRecord  =  RECORD
                           cardno  :  number;
                           name, address  :  string;
                           status  :  (staff, student, other)
                       END;
    LoanRecord  =      RECORD
                           catno : number;
                           cardno  :  number;
                           datedue : datetype
                       END;

    BookRel  =  RELATION <catno> OF BookRecord;
    BorrowerRel  =  RELATION <cardno> OF BorrowerRecord;
    LoanRel  =  RELATION <catno> OF LoanRecord;

VAR
    Library  :  DATABASE
                       Books        :  BookRel;
                       Borrowers    :  BorrowerRel;
                       Loans        :  LoanRel
              END;
```

Note that the structure of the database as expressed in Pascal/R is identical to its relational schema. Pascal/R adds little by way of semantics to the relational model and so, for example, neither referential integrity constraints nor inheritance semantics may be specified in the language. Also note that when defining the field types of a record structure which is to form the base type for a relation, one should be able to take advantage of whatever types are offered by the language, including enumerated types, sets, arrays, variant records (or ideally abstract data types). Pascal/R however, presumably for ease of implementation, restricts such field types to the simple numeric and character data types (packed arrays of characters are the only 'structured' types permitted).

Pascal/R provides specialized operations for accessing and manipulating relations which are based on the tuple-oriented relational calculus. Existential and universal quantifiers are provided, and, as a consequence, Boolean expressions of the power of first-order predicate calculus can be defined, and relational expressions can be formed to select tuples fulfilling some predicate. For example, the predicate

'Have all borrowers at least one book on loan?'

may be represented by the expression:

```
ALL b IN Borrowers : SOME l IN Loans : (b.cardno = l.cardno)
```

It is possible to iterate over relation elements (tuples) which satisfy some predicate, by means of the FOREACH statement. For example, to list the names of all borrowers who have not returned a book by the date due, we may write:

```
FOREACH b IN Borrowers : SOME l IN Loans :
    ((b.cardno = l.cardno) AND (l.datedue < CurrentDate)) DO
    WriteLn (b.name)
END ;
```

The assignment statement is applicable to relation variables and relational expressions. In addition to the normal assignment operator (:=), Pascal/R provides operations for insertion (:+), deletion (:-) and replacement (:&). For example, the following code selects all student borrowers and assigns them to a relation Students:

```
VAR  Students : BorrowerRel ;
BEGIN
    Students := [EACH b IN Borrowers : b.status = student] ;
END ;
```

To delete all the tuples in the Loans relation corresponding to books borrowed by Smith, we may write:

```
Loans :- [EACH l IN Loans : l.name = 'Smith'];
```

To insert a new record newbook into the Books relation requires the following code:

```
VAR
    newbook : BookRecord;
BEGIN
    ...
    { Read in book details and initialize newbook }
    ...
    Books :+ [newbook];
END;
```

Relation variables are fully integrated into the language. Not only can they be part of a permanent database, but they may be declared as local variables in procedures. In addition they may be used as both value and variable parameters in procedures.

6.2.2   Persistence in PS-algol

In PS-algol, persistence is an orthogonal property of data. That is, any data object, regardless of type, may exist beyond the lifetime of the program in which it is created. Unlike Pascal/R, PS-algol does not involve the addition of new data structures to a language, but rather provides persistence as a property applicable to all existing data structures.

As already outlined, one of the primary motivations for database programming languages is to relieve the database applications programmer of the considerable effort normally required to transfer data between the database storage system and the program. Languages like Pascal/R go some way towards alleviating the programmer's burden to provide this mapping code, in that they integrate the data type relation, which has the property of persistence, into the programming language. PS-algol adopts the principle of data type completeness, by which the rules governing the manipulation of all data objects should be consistent. Thus all data types in PS-algol have the property of persistence.

Consider the ER diagram shown in Figure 6.1.

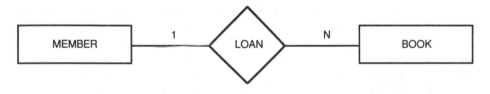

Figure 6.1   A simple library database

This consists of two entity types, BOOK and MEMBER, and a single 1:N relationship LOAN (only current loans are recorded).

A data structure in PS-algol for this database might be defined as follows.

```
structure date ( int day, month, year )
structure book ( int catno;          ! unique catalogue no.
                 string title,        ! title of book
                        author )      ! author of book
```

```
structure member ( int cardno;          ! unique id no.
                    string name;         ! member's name
                    string address )     ! member's address
structure loan ( pntr loaned;            ! to a book record
                 pntr borrower,          ! to a member record
                 pntr datedue )          ! to a date record
```

The **structure** construct defines a record class. **pntr** is a type which ranges over tokens for all the existing instances of those classes, together with the special token **nil**. Note that pointers are not constrained to a particular type (as in Pascal and Modula-2 for example), and thus it is necessary for the programmer to use comments to clarify their meaning. The absence of precision about pointer references can be exploited to write polymorphic functions. A dynamic type check is incurred when dereferencing fields of structures and thus the language can be regarded as strongly typed.

PS-algol was originally implemented as a number of functional extensions to S-algol [Morrison, 1982]. This language offers the following data typing facilities:

1. The scalar data types are integer, real, Boolean, string, picture and file.

2. For any data type T, *T is the data type of a vector with elements of type T.

3. The pointer data type comprises a structure with any number of fields, and any data type in each field.

Obviously, very complex data structures may be defined by the recursive application of rules 2 and 3.

The language itself does not change to accommodate persistence. The implementation takes care of storing and retrieving persistent data, and of checking type equivalence when data is reused in different programs. PS-algol provides a variety of procedures for managing persistence and also a set of procedures for manipulating indexes. Some of these are:

(i)   **procedure** open.database (**string** database.name, password,

                                        mode —> **pntr**)

This procedure attempts to open the database specified by database.name (the dot here is not an operator, but part of the identifier name) in the required mode (read or write). If it succeeds the result is a pointer to a table which contains a set of (name, value) pairs which are the roots of trees of persistent data.

(ii) **procedure** commit

This procedure commits the changes made so far to a database currently open for writing. Any data value reachable from the top level (i.e. the root) of a database is copied to persistent store when commit is called.

These procedures manage persistence, but in addition PS-algol provides a number of procedures to manipulate tables, including procedures to insert a (name, value) pair in a table, to provide for associative look-up of tables, and to provide iteration over the entries in a table. These table facilities effectively provide the equivalent of indexing in a conventional database system.

An important feature of PS-algol is that procedures are first class objects and can be manipulated like any other program object. Most importantly they may be stored as part of a database. This permits the modelling of abstract data types and what might be called 'active data', and thereby provides the language with some of the capabilities of object-oriented languages.

PS-algol, in common with the other languages in its group, does not support any formal data model. In fact, manipulating databases in PS-algol is reminiscent of the complex 'pointer-chasing' techniques associated with old-fashioned network and hierarchical databases. Also, in current implementations, none of these languages provide support for transaction concurrency and recovery. For these reasons, the persistence provided by these languages would seem to be rather weak from a database perspective [Khoshafian and Valduriez, 1987]. In fact, it is difficult to find good engineering techniques to support arbitrary persistent structures within the framework of large, multi-user database systems. Implementation mechanisms associated with relations are much better understood at present, largely due to the substantial research effort expended on relational technology over the past two decades.

Some of the above criticisms of persistent database programming languages (lack of a formal data model, pointer-oriented access paths) are sometimes levelled at object-oriented systems [Neuhold and Stonebraker, 1988]. However the class structure, associated with good semantic data modelling techniques, provides a sound framework for database design, while pointers in object-oriented systems tend to be rather less explicit than, for example, in PS-algol.

6.3   PERSISTENCE IN OBJECT-ORIENTED SYSTEMS

In an object-oriented environment we may visualize memory as consisting of two distinct parts: volatile memory and persistent store. Volatile objects are allocated in volatile memory, as is the case with normal program variables. They may be allocated on the program stack or on the heap and their lifetime is bounded by the lifetime of the program. An object-oriented database, however, is a collection of persistent objects, each identified by a unique identifier which may be visualized as a pointer to a persistent object. Persistent objects must be allocated in persistent (i.e. non-volatile) store and they exist beyond the lifetime of the program that created them. The media used for persistent store is, of course, implementation dependent and interaction with these objects is handled by an object store manager. In principle, accesses to persistent objects should be as fast as volatile object accesses, but in practice they are likely to be slower (for example, if persistent objects are stored on disk). An implementation may speed up access to persistent objects by caching them, but such implementation details should be transparent to the programmer.

In recent years a number of different approaches have been pursued with regard to the incorporation of persistence into an object-oriented framework. The simplest, but least transparent approach is to add a library of procedures and data structures to a language environment, which supports persistence. This imposes a considerable burden on the user to call appropriate procedures to map objects to and from persistent store. A better approach, but one which is more difficult to implement, is to add a transparent persistent capability to the language and its supporting environment. Recent developments in the area have also included the provision of hardware support for persistence [Harland, 1988], but this is, at this point in time, insufficiently mature to warrant a detailed discussion in this text.

When incorporating persistence in an object-oriented programming language the following principles should be adhered to:

- Persistence is a property of object instances and not of object types. That is, a given object type (or class) may have both persistent and volatile instances.

- Objects of any type, including arbitrarily complex user-defined types, may be allocated in either persistent or volatile store.

- Persistent and volatile objects should be accessed and manipulated in exactly the same way. That is, program code is expressed independently of the persistence of the objects that it accesses and manipulates. For example, if we have a function f with object type O as parameter, it should be possible to call f with both persistent and volatile instances of O as actual parameter. Also, there should be a simple mechanism for the movement of objects from persistent store to volatile store and vice versa.

An important property of an object which is central to any model of persistence is that of object *identity*. Identity is that property of an object which distinguishes it from all others. It is a concept which has been investigated almost independently in programming languages and database systems. For object-oriented database systems, which combine many aspects of these two themes, it is extremely important to adopt a uniform approach to object identity. Khoshafian and Copeland [1986] provide an in depth study of identity with regard to object-oriented systems, and show how the concept differs from the idea of address or key in conventional systems. The following discussion is largely based on their paper .

6.3.1   Object identity

Every database system must have some way of distinguishing one object from another. Programming languages typically use variable names to identify objects and a variable name is of course simply a representation of the *address* of the object in volatile memory. However, as we have already seen, the structures supported in the virtual address space of the program are not usually supported in persistent store. Also, the concepts of address and identity are quite different. The address of an object is external to the object, providing a mechanism for accessing the object within a particular environment. The address is therefore dependent upon the environment. Identity, on the other hand, is an intrinsic property of an object and is independent of how it is accessed.

Most database systems use keys (i.e. attributes whose values uniquely identify a tuple) to distinguish persistent objects, thereby using *content* rather than address for identity. Some of the problems associated with the use of keys to identify objects have already been discussed in Chapter 3. Recall that these include the problems of ensuring key uniqueness and referential integrity, and the need to use joins for data retrieval.

It is clear therefore that object-oriented database systems should maintain a separate and consistent notion of the identity of an object independent of its content, structure or location.

6.3.2   Implementing object identity

Implementing object identity in an object-oriented database system involves the provision of three kinds of independence:

* *Location independence* implies that an object's identity is preserved despite changes in its physical location, whether in volatile or persistent store.

- *Value independence* involves the preservation of object identity through changes in its value.

- *Structure independence* involves the preservation of object identity through changes in its structure.

With regard to location independence, it should be noted that in an object-oriented database environment the physical description of a conceptual object may not be stored at a single physical location. For example, an object may be physically partitioned, on the basis of frequency of use, in order to enhance performance. Also, as is common in many database management systems, a certain amount of controlled replication may be used in order to facilitate data recovery. Such replicas must be stored on separate media for maximum security. In providing location independence, such fragmentation and replication of objects must be transparent to the user.

Before describing a technique for implementing object identity which provides the three levels of independence above, it is useful to examine the shortcomings of the traditional approaches to object identity as provided by traditional programming languages and database systems.

Identity through address

Identity through physical address (either real or virtual), as provided by most conventional programming languages, does not allow an object to be moved and maintain its identity, and so offers no location independence. For example, in Pascal the identity of an object may be a pointer to the object which is implemented as a virtual heap address. The object cannot be moved without updating the pointer. (Experienced Pascal programmers will be well aware of the problems of 'dangling pointers'.) However, both real physical address and virtual address implementations provide value and structure independence, unless modifications to the structure cause the object to be moved within the address space due to changes in size.

In Smalltalk-80 [Goldberg and Robson, 1983] object identity is implemented by means of a pointer which is not the virtual address of the object but rather is an entry in an object table. This is equivalent to indirect addressing and has the advantage of allowing individual objects to move within a single address space without the necessity to change their identity. Full value and structure independence are also provided by this approach. However, since the pointers are not globally unique, the scheme does not permit the sharing of objects among multiple programs. In LOOM [Kaehler and Krasner, 1983], it is shown that the scheme can be extended to support objects resident on secondary storage, but a more elaborate system is required to support a large-scale, multi-user, persistent environment.

Identity through keys

In database management systems, identity is primarily implemented via identifier keys, which may be user-defined or generated internally by the system. Relations are stored as physical files and an auxiliary structure, such as a B-tree index, provides fast access to objects (tuples) on the basis of their key values. Such implementations offer full location independence since, if a tuple changes position in the file, only the index is updated and not the tuple's identity (key value). Little however is offered by way of value independence, since if a tuple changes its value its identity may change. Structure independence is not supported either, since key values are unique only within a given relation, and restructuring may involve for example the expansion of an attribute into a separate tuple, or the fragmentation of a tuple across several relations.

User-defined keys have additional problems which can have serious consequences with regard to the integrity of the database. If the user changes a key value for example he must ensure that referential integrity is preserved, i.e. that all instances of that key value in other relations are changed accordingly. User-defined keys are also subject to errors in data entry, leading to situations where relations contain references to non-existent entities and where joins on user keys yield incorrect or incomplete information. An additional problem is that in many situations users are compelled to invent artificial keys where no natural identifier for an object exists or where the key for an object is composite, i.e. involves a number of different attributes.

Identity through surrogates

A powerful technique for supporting identity is through the use of surrogates [Abrial, 1974; Hall *et al.*, 1976; Kent, 1978; Codd, 1979; Date, 1983]. Surrogates are system-generated, globally unique identifiers, independent of physical location. They therefore offer full location independence. Also, if a surrogate is associated with each *object*, regardless of its complexity (rather than with a tuple as in Codd's RM/T), then they provide full value and structure independence. Thus, each object of any type is assigned a globally unique surrogate at the time of instantiation, and this surrogate represents the identity of the object throughout its lifetime. The generated surrogate value is unique with respect to all surrogates that exist or have ever existed within a particular database. It is guaranteed never to change even if that object is removed from the database. In this way it will be possible to reinstate an object from archive storage without compromising the integrity of the database.

Users, of course, do not have any control over surrogates. They cannot access their values and in fact may not even be aware of their existence. This prevents a user from introducing object references which are outside the control of the system and therefore prone to the errors and ambiguities associated with user-defined keys. User-keys, however, are not necessarily made redundant by surrogates, and may still play a role in identifying objects at the user level, outside the internal database environment. Examples include account numbers, social security numbers, subject names, etc. However, such user-defined keys are considered merely as properties of an object and have no special status, as they have in relational databases. Within the object-oriented database system all object identification and object referencing is via surrogates.

6.4   MODELS OF PERSISTENCE

Object-oriented database languages and systems have taken several different approaches to providing persistence. In the following sections we study several contrasting techniques. The first is from GemStone [Maier and Stein, 1987] which, as previously described, is an object-oriented database system based on extensions to Smalltalk. The second technique is from ODE [Agrawal and Gehani, 1989] which has a persistent database programming language based on C++. Other approaches are described for the purposes of comparison.

6.4.1   Persistence in GemStone

GemStone is an object-oriented database management system based on Smalltalk-80 and, before considering its model of persistence, it is useful to give an overview of object management in Smalltalk.

Object management in Smalltalk-80
Smalltalk-80 is an object-oriented programming language and environment in which everything, including data and code, is regarded as an object. As described previously, every Smalltalk object has an associated unique identifier called its *oop* (object-oriented pointer). The size of an oop in any particular implementation (usually either 16 or 32 bits) determines the number of objects that can exist in the system. The object manager, which is the interface between the Smalltalk interpreter and the objects, uses an object table to translate an oop to a direct memory pointer. The memory pointer points to the object and the object contains the oop of its class and the oops of its instance variables, which describe the object's state. Thus for a given object the object manager can determine its class and can retrieve or set a given instance variable. To eliminate the indirection of the

object table, some implementations use actual memory addresses rather than identifiers for oops [Samples *et al.*, 1986; Caudill and Wirfs-Brock, 1986].

Smalltalk-80 is a single-user environment. At any time in a session a user may save his objects by writing a snap-shot of memory to disk. Upon restart, the interpreter can load this snap-shot back into memory. However, in order to share objects with another user, the objects must be explicitly written to external files using some agreed format.

Crash recovery in Smalltalk-80 is facilitated by automatic logging of changes to objects in an external file. Utilities are provided to redo some or all of the changes after a crash. During a session, users can rollback changes by quitting the interpreter without saving the changes. They can then return to the most recently saved snap-shot. In this way transactions can be simulated by saving a snap-shot of memory prior to commencement of the transaction, and then either quitting or doing another save depending on whether the transaction is to be aborted or committed.

Object management in GemStone

GemStone turns Smalltalk into a database system by adding facilities for persistent storage management, concurrency control, authorization, transactions, recovery and support for associative access via secondary indexes. It implements object identity through surrogates (oops), and maps an oop to a physical location by means of an object table. As described above, the object table approach allows objects to move around in physical storage, which is important when objects change size. An object may be stored separately from its sub-objects but the oops for the values of the instance variables within a given object are grouped together in the object table. Users can control the placement of objects in physical clusters (called segments) which are the unit of concurrency control in GemStone.

In GemStone a server stores the objects and runs a special implementation of Smalltalk-80. User programs, which can be written in either C or Smalltalk, run on separate machines and communicate with the server over a LAN or serial link. User programs can request copies of objects from the server, manipulate them and then commit the changes back to the server. A user program may also request the server itself to perform operations on objects stored in the server.

In the server, large objects are stored as tree structures spanning as many pages as are required. The pages of a given object need not be contiguous and so an object can grow and shrink without the need to copy the entire object. Also, parts of an object may be updated without bringing the whole object into main memory

All objects in GemStone may persist and four basic storage formats are supported for persistent objects:

- *self-identifying*, for objects of simple types such as integers, characters, Boolean, etc.;

- *byte*, for classes whose instances may be considered unstructured, as in a string of bits, e.g. character strings, floating point numbers, etc.;

- *pointer*, which supports references to other objects through their identity (an object-oriented pointer). Components of pointer objects are accessed via instance variable names or array indices.

- *non-sequenceable collection*, which is used for collection classes, such as Bag and Set, in which instance variables are anonymous. That is, members of such collections are not identified by name or index number, but a collection may be queried for membership and have members added, removed or enumerated.

6.4.2   Persistence in ODE

In the ODE system [Agrawal and Gehani, 1989], the database is defined, queried and manipulated via the database programming language O++, which extends the object-oriented facilities of C++. Facilities are provided for creating persistent and versioned objects. Persistence is a property of object instances, not types, and persistent objects are referenced by pointers which are local to the program in which they are declared. Persistent objects are allocated and deallocated in a manner similar to volatile objects through the provision of the operators pnew and pdelete, which are persistent versions of the familiar heap operators new and delete. If successful the operator pnew returns a pointer to the persistent object created by it. For example,

```
persistent item *pip ;
...
pip = pnew item ( ... ) ;
```

The declaration statement introduces the pointer variable pip as a pointer to a persistent object of type item. The variable pip is not itself persistent, but rather is allocated on the run-time stack for the program. The call to pnew allocates a new object of type item in persistent store and returns its identity in pip. Persistent objects may be mapped to volatile objects and vice versa using simple assignments. For example, the statement:

```
*ip = *pip ;
```

copies the object pointed to by pip from persistent store to the object pointed to by pip in volatile memory.

Sharing of persistent objects across multiple application programs is provided through the *cluster* mechanism. A cluster groups together all persistent objects of the same type, and the name of the cluster is the same as that of the corresponding type. Before creating a persistent object, the corresponding cluster must exist. A cluster is created by invoking the create macro in a program:

```
create (<type name>) ;
```

A corresponding destroy macro is available, whose effect is to destroy all objects in the specified cluster. Clusters may be partitioned into *subclusters* which group together objects within the cluster which have a common property. This may be useful both from the point of view of logical organization and also for reasons of efficiency.

6.4.3   Other approaches to persistence

There have been many diverse approaches to the issue of persistence reported in the literature. The following sections give brief descriptions of the models of persistence adopted in other object-oriented database systems.

EXODUS

A number of other systems provide persistence within an object-oriented framework. For example, a component of the EXODUS system [Carey *et al.* 1989] is the language E, an extension of C++ that provides for persistent class instances. In order to maintain compatibility with C++, types (including classes) are grouped into persistent and non-persistent categories. Syntactically, a persistent class is declared using the keyword **dbclass** and all data properties of a dbclass must themselves be dbclass objects. E provides a collection of built-in dbclasses which are the persistent equivalents of the normal C++ fundamental types. These include, for example, **dbint**, **dbfloat**, and **dbchar**. All the normal arithmetic operations are defined for these types, and assignment and coercion are defined between persistent types and their non-persistent equivalents (the pointer type is an exception to this rule).

For example, if we wish to store objects of type BOX (i.e. a rectangle defined by the coordinates of its upperleft andlower right corners) in the database, we may declare a persistent class in the following manner:

```
dbclass BOX
{
        // representation is upper left and lower right corners

        dbstruct { dbfloat x, y } upperleft, lowerright ;

public
        ...

};
```

Files, which are unordered collections of persistent objects, are introduced to E as another built-in class. A given file may contain only one type of object and that type must be a dbclass. Thus the declaration of a permanent file f takes the form:

```
persistent fileof [ <some dbclass> ] f;
```

A variety of operations are provided in the language for accessing and manipulating files.

This rather pragmatic approach to persistence has clear advantages from an implementation point of view, and is similar in many respects to the techniques used in conventional programming languages such as Pascal. An important difference of course is that, in E, files may contain objects of arbitrary complexity. However, it would appear that in developing applications in E, the programmer is still responsible for much of the mapping between persistent and volatile store.

ALLTALK

Alltalk [Straw *et al.*, 1989] extends Smalltalk-80 by providing object persistence but without the addition of a data manipulation sublanguage. Objects persist in a database and may be retrieved via a unique identifier (oop) or associatively, by specifying a query which provides values or ranges of values for instance variables. All objects have oops, so there is no distinction between volatile and persistent objects, and oops are managed in an object table. A buffer manager and a pool are used to manage memory-resident objects and the buffer manager uses a database access manager to map objects between persistent and volatile store. Objects which have been created or changed since the last commit are marked, and when the transaction manager performs a commit all new and modified objects are written to the database. Alltalk retains the semantics of Smalltalk with its free, typeless style and pointer-oriented database navigation.

POSTGRES

The POSTGRES database system [Rowe and Stonebraker, 1987] extends the relational model with mechanisms that include abstract data types for domains, and data of type procedure. Although not object-oriented in the strict sense, these mechanisms can be used to simulate a wide variety of semantic and object-oriented data modelling constructs including aggregation and generalization, and complex objects with shared sub-objects. The system also provides a form of inheritance by which relations may inherit the properties of other relations. The model of persistence in POSTGRES is relatively simple, being of course based on relations. For abstract data types, users must supply appropriate routines for converting between internal and external forms. Procedures which are used as data types or as operators in abstract data types have their object code stored in the system catalogs and this is dynamically loaded at run-time when the procedure is called by a query.

PGRAPHITE

PGRAPHITE [Wileden *et al.* 1988] is the prototype object management system of the Arcadia software environment research program [Taylor *et al.* 1988]. It currently provides a type definition mechanism with inbuilt persistence for only one class of object, namely directed graphs. The model of persistence provided by PGRAPHITE is quite similar to that of the language ODE described in the previous section. Persistent objects may be referenced by pointers generated at run-time called non-persistent references (NPRs), or by persistent identifiers (PIDs). Persistent store is modelled as a collection of *repositories*. Within a repository, the name of an object is guaranteed to be unique and unchanging. Two operations are associated with this persistent-object abstraction. The operation GetPID generates a PID for an object given an NPR. This has the side effect of indicating that the object is to persist. The second operation, GetNPR, generates an NPR to a persistent object given its PID. The PIDs of PGRAPHITE appear to be very similar to surrogates.

FAD

Another language which is worthy of mention, although not object-oriented, is FAD [Bancilhon, 1987]. FAD provides a model of persistence not unlike that of PS-algol, but supports object identity (implemented through surrogates) and concurrent transactions. The only types supported by the language are base atomic types, sets and tuples. There is no class concept.

Other object-oriented systems that include some form of persistence include Trellis/Owl [O'Brien *et al.*, 1986], O_2 [Bancilhon *et al.*, 1986;

Deux *et al.*, 1990], Ontos [Ontologic Inc., 1989], and ORION [Kim *et al.*, 1988, 1989, 1990]. Some features of these systems are described elsewhere in this text.

6.5   SUMMARY

There are two classes of data within an application program in a database environment: *volatile* data, which resides in volatile memory, and whose existence ends with the termination of the program; and *persistent* data, which resides in persistent (or permanent) store and must be transferred into the program's volatile memory space before it can be accessed or manipulated. There have been numerous attempts in recent years to integrate the concept of persistence with well-structured, strongly typed programming languages and much of this work is of direct relevance to object-oriented database systems.

When incorporating persistence in an object-oriented system the following principles should be adhered to:

- Persistence is a property of object instances and not of object types.

- Objects of any type may be allocated in either persistent or volatile store.

- Persistent and volatile objects should be accessed and manipulated in exactly the same way.

An important property of an object which is central to any model of persistence is that of object *identity*. Identity is that property of an object which distinguishes it from all others and which can be used to retrieve the object.

6.6   BIBLIOGRAPHIC NOTES

A comprehensive review of persistence in database programming languages is given by Atkinson and Buneman [1987]. The issue of object identity is lucidly described by Khoshafian and Copeland [1986]. A good overview of the issues relating to persistence in an object-oriented environment is provided by Agrawal and Gehani [1989].

7

Object-based concurrency, recovery and distribution

7.1 INTRODUCTION

The object-oriented approach to systems design closely matches our model of reality, whereas the traditional procedural or functional languages concentrate on operational and algorithmic abstractions of the problem. Since many real-world activities are inherently concurrent, object-oriented programming languages and systems that support concurrency would be more expressive. However, popular object-oriented languages such as Smalltalk, C++ and Eiffel concentrate on modularity and high reusability and provide no facilities for modelling concurrent activities. Examples of object-oriented languages that do support concurrency are Orient84/K [Ishikawa and Tokoro, 1986], ABCL/1 [Yonezawa *et al.*, 1986, 1987], Concurrent Smalltalk [Yokote and Tokoro, 1987] and SINA [Tripathi *et al.*, 1988].

Concurrent object-oriented programming languages typically model the real world with concurrently executable objects called processes. A process has an interface of executable operations and one or more threads of control which may be active or suspended at any given time. Processes engage in shared events by sending and receiving messages. A thread may be queued until a process is ready to execute it, and it can be suspended and reactivated according to the conditions prevailing in the program. Around these basic principles, several models of concurrency have been proposed for programming languages [Wegner, 1989]. The most conservative of these support *communicating sequential processes* [Hoare, 1978, 1985] in which a process has just one thread. In languages based on the *Actors* model [Hewitt, 1985; Agha, 1986] on the other hand, a process may have multiple active threads.

These models of concurrent programming are based on the fact that activities in the real world are inherently concurrent and therefore objects are themselves active. This approach places a considerable burden on the programmer since correct concurrent behaviour must be specified as combinations of interactions within a potentially large set of concurrent objects [Martin, 1988]. That is, correctness of concurrent behaviour is left to the programmer who must verify that the implementations of his objects and their associated threads of control do not produce undesirable interactions.

In a large, multi-user database environment this approach is clearly impractical and it is more appropriate to view objects as *data*, with concurrent access to objects from user programs being controlled by the underlying system according to some correctness criteria. In this model, a programmer need only consider the serial behaviour of an object in isolation and need not be concerned with how other concurrent activities might affect the object. Thus, preconditions, postconditions and other traditional program verification techniques may be used to verify the correctness of implementations of operations within a class. Correctness of interleaved executions of operations on the various object instances is left to the concurrency control system.

In this chapter we investigate the implications of concurrent access on object-oriented database systems. We begin with an overview of the various techniques used for transaction processing and concurrency control in conventional database systems and discuss their applicability to object-oriented environments. We then review some recently proposed models for object-based concurrency control and investigate the techniques employed in existing object-oriented DBMSs.

We also review the basic principles associated with recovery in both conventional and object-oriented databases. In the final section we study the advantages offered by the object-oriented model for distributed databases.

7.2   DATABASE TRANSACTIONS

In the context of a multi-user database system, database procedures are often called *transactions*. A transaction [Gray, 1978] is a unit of work which corresponds directly to a single activity of the enterprise which is modelled by the database. A given database system may have many different classes of transactions ranging from simple interactive updates to very large and complex programs involving perhaps thousands of database operations. The property that all transactions must have in common is that they must all preserve the consistency and correctness of the data stored in the database. That is, the operations performed by an updating transaction should transform the database from one consistent state to another. Intermediate states, which exist after individual statements of an updating transaction have been performed, may be inconsistent. Therefore, to guarantee the consistency of the database, it must be required that updating transactions be processed entirely or not at all (i.e. transactions are *atomic*). A transaction which does not complete, due possibly to a program or system failure, must be backed up to its initial state and any changes which it has written to the database must be undone.

When several transactions are executed concurrently on a shared database their executions must be synchronized. That is, the effect on the database of a transaction must be that which would be obtained if no other transaction were executing concurrently. The effect of executing several transactions concurrently, therefore, must be the same as if they had been executed serially in some order. If the sequence of operations of a set of concurrently executing transactions is such that this condition is satisfied, the sequence is said to be *serializable*. The problems associated with guaranteeing the serializability of transactions are discussed later in this section.

The need for concurrency control in a database system is illustrated by the following example (adapted from Amble *et al.*, 1976).

Example
Consider a database for an airline reservation system which contains an object class DEPARTURE which represents the departures of flights on specified dates. The definition of class DEPARTURE might be as follows:

>   **class** DEPARTURE
>
>   **properties**
>   flight_details : flight;
>   date_of_flight : date;
>   seats_left : integer;
>
>   **operations**
>   reserve_seat
>
>   **end** DEPARTURE

A particular transaction on this database may involve booking several connecting flights on a particular date for a customer travelling with his family. Only if sufficient seats are available on all the required departures are the bookings confirmed. Otherwise an alternative group of flights has to be considered.

Thus the transaction must do the following:

1. Read the date, flight numbers and the number of seats required.
2. Check if each of the specified flights on the given date has sufficient seats available.

3. If sufficient seats are available, then reserve the seats. Otherwise report the failure.

An algorithm for the transaction might take the following form:

```
BEGIN
    read  date_required, flights_required, no_seats_required ;
    failure := FALSE ;
    set F to first in flights_required ;
    WHILE NOT failure AND (not at end of flights_required list ) DO
        retrieve DEPARTURE instance, d, where
        (d.flight_details.flight_no = F) AND (d.date_of_flight = date_required) ;
        IF d.seats_left < no_seats_required
        THEN failure := TRUE
        ELSE set F to next in flights_required
        END
    END ;
    IF failure
    THEN
        WriteString (' Flight ', F,' has insufficient seats')
    ELSE
        FOR (each F in flights_required ) DO
            update DEPARTURE instance, d, where
        (d.flight_details.flight_no = F) AND (d.date_of_flight = date_required)
            with d.seats_left :=  d.seats_left - no_seats_required
        END ;
        WriteString (' Flights confirmed ')
    END
END ;
```

One difficulty with this transaction is that it is possible to complete the initial check for seats available successfully (i.e. with failure = FALSE) and yet overbook a flight. This could happen if another user updated one of the relevant DEPARTURE instances after the above transaction had performed the initial check, but before it had carried out its updates.

A second problem with this transaction would arise if a program or system failure occurred while it was performing its updates. Thus some of the DEPARTURE instances would have been updated but not others. Simply re-running the transaction is not the answer since this would result in the customer and his family being booked twice on some flights. To maintain the consistency of the database therefore, the effect of the failed transaction on the database must be undone and the transaction re-run in its entirety. The techniques for undoing, or redoing, transactions will be considered in more detail later in this chapter.

The airline reservation example above illustrates just one of a number of problems that can arise if we allow transactions write-access to a database concurrently without some form of control. (Note that if a database is read-only, then no concurrency control is required.) The problems that can arise may be described more generally as follows:

The lost update

Consider the following sequence of events, where transactions T_1 and T_2 are executing concurrently:

1. Transaction T_1 reads object O from the database.
2. Transaction T_2 reads object O from the database.
3. Transaction T_1 updates object O and writes it back to the database.
4. Transaction T_2 updates object O and writes it back to the database.

The result of these events is that the update performed by transaction T_1 has been lost.

The out-of-date retrieval

Consider the following sequence of events:

1. Transaction T_1 reads object O from the database with a view to updating its value.
2. Transaction T_2 reads object O for retrieval purposes.
3. Transaction T_1 modifies object O and writes it back to the database.

The result of these events is that transaction T_2 has retrieved an out-of-date value for object O.

An obvious solution to both of these problems would be to permit a transaction to *lock* an object during update, giving it exclusive access to that record while the update operation is in progress. However locking mechanisms can themselves give rise to serious problems in database systems and must therefore be carefully monitored and controlled. The following sections describe the typical locking mechanisms found in database management systems as well as some alternative strategies for concurrency control which have been proposed in the literature. The applicability of these concurrent features to object-oriented database systems is then discussed in detail, with reference to the models of object-based concurrency found in some existing systems.

7.2.1   Read- and write-locks

In order to prevent any transaction from reading or updating an object that is being updated by another transaction, or from updating an object that is currently being read by another transaction, we require a *locking* mechanism. A lock guarantees a transaction the appropriate mode of access to an object while the lock is in force. We can distinguish between two kinds of locks:

1. A *read-lock* which gives read-only access to an object and prevents any other transaction from updating the object. This kind of lock is often called *read-sharable* since any number of transactions may hold a read-lock on an object at the same time.

2. A *write-lock* which gives read/write access to an object and, while in force, prevents any other transaction from reading or writing to the object. This kind of lock is often called *write-exclusive* since it gives a transaction exclusive access to an object while the lock is in force.

The compatibility of read- and write-locks is summarized by the *compatibility matrix* shown in Figure 7.1. A lock of mode M_1 is said to be compatible with a lock of mode M_2 if a transaction T_1 can be granted a lock of mode M_1 on data item A while another transaction T_2 holds a lock of mode M_2 on A. Thus, a read-lock is compatible with a read-lock but not with a write-lock. A write-lock is compatible with neither a read-lock nor a write-lock.

	read-lock	write-lock
read-lock	Yes	No
write-lock	No	No

Figure 7.1 Compatibility matrix for read- and write-locks

Thus the problem of interfering transactions outlined in the example above, which could lead to overbooking a flight, is prevented if our transaction write-locks all the relevant instances of the DEPARTURE class when it retrieves them for inspection and (possible) update. That is, the transaction takes the following form:

```
BEGIN TRANSACTION
read  date_required, flights_required, no_seats_required ;
WRITE-LOCK all DEPARTURE instances, d, where
     (d.flight_details.flight_no in flights_required) AND
     (d.date_of_flight =  date_required) ;
```

... as before ...

END TRANSACTION;
Unlock DEPARTURE instances ;

Any other transaction which requires either read or write access to these DEPARTURE instances must wait until the write-locks are released.

A data item, of course, need not necessarily be locked for the entire duration of the transaction, and the level of concurrency could be increased by locking a data item only for the duration of the actual data access. However, narrowing the sequence of statements for which a data item is locked increases the possibility of *deadlock* occurring, and involves the system in rather complex recovery procedures if locks are released before a transaction terminates. These points are discussed in greater depth below.

7.2.2   Deadlock

A problem that can arise in a system which permits transactions to lock data items is a phenomenon known as *deadlock* or *deadly embrace*. This is best described by a simple example.

Example
Consider two transactions T_1 and T_2 executing concurrently, and the following sequence of events takes place:

1. T_1 write-locks object A.
2. T_2 write-locks object B.
3. T_1 requests a lock on object B but must wait since T_2 has locked B.
4. T_2 requests a lock on object A but must wait since T_1 has locked A.

At this point neither T_1 nor T_2 can proceed - they are deadlocked.

There are a number of strategies which can be adopted to prevent deadlock occurring. For example, one could insist that each transaction requests *all* its locks before it begins execution and allow it to proceed only if every lock can be granted (the *preclaim* strategy). Otherwise it is forced to wait. This strategy would clearly have a detrimental effect on the level of concurrency in the system since transactions may have to wait a long time before they can start. Also, in a database environment the resource needs of a transaction (and therefore its locking requirements) may be dependent on factors known only at run-time. That is, the set of objects to be locked by a transaction are generally determined dynamically by the logic of the transaction, its input data and the current state of the database.

Thus it is clear that deadlock-free locking protocols, which may be effective in other concurrent environments such as operating systems, are generally inapplicable to database systems. A more effective strategy in a database environment therefore may be to allow deadlocks to occur and to *detect* and *resolve* them when they do. To detect deadlock the system maintains a graph whose nodes consist of currently executing transactions and whose arcs are determined as follows: If transaction T_i requests a lock on an object that is locked by T_j, an arc is drawn from node T_i to node T_j. The arc is removed when T_j releases the lock. A deadlock situation is indicated by a cycle in this graph. This detection technique may be expensive if there is a high degree of granularity in the system.

Resolving deadlock involves choosing one of the deadlocked transactions and invoking a 'roll-back' procedure. The transaction is then restarted at some suitable later point in time. The roll-back procedure will involve the system in undoing any updates which the transaction has written to the database. Also, all the locks held by a transaction which is rolled back must be released, thereby allowing other deadlocked transactions to proceed.

A disadvantage of this strategy is that it involves costly run-time procedures for acquiring and releasing locks, testing for the disjointness of data objects, and implementing roll-back operations. However, roll-back is a procedure which may also be required for crash-recovery in database management systems and the subject will be discussed in more detail later in this chapter.

7.2.3   Serializability and the two-phase protocol

As stated earlier, the effect of executing several transactions concurrently must be the same as if they had been executed serially in some order. That is, if two transactions T_1 and T_2 are executed in parallel their effect on the database must be equivalent to $T_1;T_2$ (i.e. T_1 followed sequentially by T_2), or $T_2;T_1$. The following simple example shows that, if no restrictions are placed on the way in which transactions are scheduled, serializability is easily violated.

Consider the following two transactions which update an object A.

```
T₁ :    BEGIN
            read(A) ;  A := A + 1 ;  write(A)
        END ;

T₂ :    BEGIN
            read(A) ;  A := A - 1 ;  write(A)
        END ;
```

Clearly the effect of running these transactions serially in any order will be to leave the value of A unchanged. However, suppose the transactions are executed concurrently and the steps of each transaction are carried out in the following order:

T_1:   read(A)
T_1:   A := A + 1
T_2:   read(A)
T_1:   write(A)
T_2:   A := A - 1
T_2:   write(A)

The effect of this schedule of steps is to leave the value of A in the database decremented by 1. Obviously we could solve this problem for this simple example by allowing T_1 to write-lock object A while it carries out its update. Transaction T_2 would then be required to wait until T_1 had written its updated value of A back to the database. However a locking mechanism is not in itself sufficient to guarantee serializability.

A fundamental theorem of transaction scheduling [Eswaran *et al.*, 1976] states that concurrent transactions can be guaranteed serializable if, in any transaction, all locks precede all unlocks. Transactions obeying this protocol are said to be *two-phase* (or equivalently, to obey the *two-phase locking protocol*), in the sense that locks and unlocks take place in two separate phases during the transaction. If all transactions are two-phase, then all concurrent executions of those transactions are serializable.

We may test for the serializability of a given schedule of transactions with the following algorithm [Eswaran *et al.*, 1976; Ullman, 1982].

Algorithm
Construct a directed graph (called a precedence graph), with transactions as nodes, whose arcs are determined by the following rules (an arc from T_i to T_j implies that in any equivalent serial schedule T_i must precede T_j.):

1. If transaction T_i read-locks object A and transaction T_j is the next transaction (if any) to write-lock A, then draw an arc from T_i to T_j.

2. If transaction T_i write-locks an object A and T_j is the next transaction (if any) to write-lock A, then draw an arc from T_i to T_j.

3. If transaction T_k read-locks A between the write-locks of T_i and T_j then draw an arc from T_i to T_k. If transaction T_j does not exist (i.e. there are no further write-locks on A) then T_k is any transaction to read-lock A after T_i releases its write-lock.

If the precedence graph, constructed using the above rules, has a cycle then the schedule is not serializable. If the graph has no cycles then the schedule is serializable and any *topological sort* of the precedence graph yields an equivalent serial schedule. (A topological sort reduces a directed graph to a serial order of nodes such that if there is an arc from T_i to T_j in the graph then T_i will precede T_j in the serial order.)

An algorithm which performs a topological sort is as follows:

```
BEGIN
    Find the set S of nodes with no predecessors (i.e. no incoming
      arcs);
    WHILE (S is not empty) DO
        Remove a node T from S;
        Remove T and its outgoing arcs from the graph ;
        Add any new members to S;
        {i.e. any nodes which have no predecessors
          following the removal of T}
    END;
END;
```

Example

Consider a schedule S of three concurrently executing transactions T_1, T_2 and T_3, consisting of the following steps listed in chronological order of their execution on the database:

1.	T_1 :	write-lock (A) ;
2.	T_2 :	write-lock (B) ;
3.	T_1 :	unlock (A) ;
4.	T_2 :	unlock (B) ;
5.	T_1 :	write-lock (B) ;
6.	T_3 :	read-lock (A) ;
7.	T_1 :	unlock (B) ;
8.	T_3 :	unlock (A) ;
9.	T_2 :	write-lock (A) ;
10.	T_3 :	read-lock (B) ;
11.	T_2 :	unlock (A) ;
12.	T_3 :	unlock (B) ;

Using the rules given above we may construct a precedence graph for this schedule as illustrated in Figure 7.2.

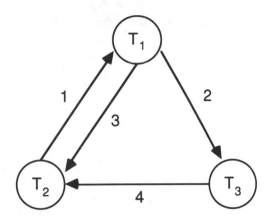

Figure 7.2 A precedence graph

In this graph the arcs 1 to 4 are due to the following rules:

Arc 1: Rule 2 and steps 2 and 5 of the schedule;
Arc 2: Rule 3 and steps 1, 6 and 9 or steps 5 and 10;
Arc 3: Rule 2 and steps 1 and 9;
Arc 4: Rule 1 and steps 6 and 9.

Since the precedence graph has cycles, the schedule is not serializable.

Proof of the two-phase locking protocol
We are now in a position to prove that the two-phase locking protocol guarantees serializability. Recall that the theorem states that any schedule S of concurrent transactions can be guaranteed serializable if, in any transaction, all locks precede all unlocks.

Suppose that S is not serializable. Then the precedence graph for S will contain a cycle of the form:

$$T_i \longrightarrow T_j \longrightarrow T_k \longrightarrow \ldots \longrightarrow T_i$$

Thus from the rules for constructing arcs, a lock in T_j must follow an unlock in T_i, a lock in T_k must follow an unlock in T_j, and so on. Finally therefore we see that a lock in T_i must follow an unlock in T_i, which violates our assertion that the transactions are two-phase.

7.2.4   Granularity of locks

The size of items that may be locked in a database system is referred to as the *degree of granularity*. In a relational database system for example, an item to be locked could be any one of the following:

- The entire database
- A relation
- A physical disk block
- A tuple
- An attribute value

If the items are large (coarse granularity) the system overheads for concurrency control are small, but the degree of concurrency is low. For example if locks are at the level of entire relations then the number of locks generated will be relatively small and the system does not have much work to do in maintaining those locks. However, a transaction which requires read/write access to just a small number of tuples in a relation will prevent every other transaction from accessing the entire relation. With finer granularity (e.g. tuple-level or attribute-level locking), a high degree of concurrency is possible but at the cost of high system overheads in maintaining the large number of locks which are generated by transactions.

Items for concurrency control may be any composite collection of one or more of the abstract elements of the database. The only requirements are that they must not overlap (with respect to constituent data elements), and the collection of items must form a partition of the entire database. The fundamental motivation in choosing the degree of granularity must be to minimize the number of locks to be set by transactions but at the same time achieve a satisfactory level of concurrency. In an object-oriented database, the obvious choice for a lockable data item is an object. However, when a transaction wishes to access most of the instances of a class, it makes sense to set one lock for the entire class, rather than a separate lock for each instance. A shared or exclusive lock on a class will imply a lock of the same type on every instance of the class. When only a few instances of a class need to be accessed by a transaction, it is better to lock the instances individually so that other concurrent transactions may access other instances.

The locking process in object-oriented database systems is complicated by the concepts of inheritance and generalization hierarchies. Recall that a class may inherit properties and operations from its superclasses which in turn may inherit from their own superclasses. Thus, for example, when a class definition or its instances are being accessed by a transaction the DBMS must ensure that the definitions of that class's superclasses (and their superclasses, etc.) are not modified. We can minimize the number of locks that must be set in such a class hierarchy by using the process of *multiple granularity locking* [Gray, 1978; Garza and Kim, 1988].

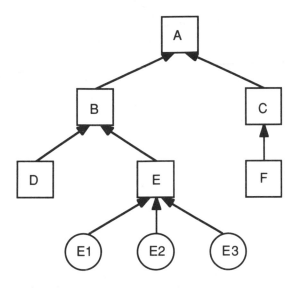

Figure 7.3   A granularity hierarchy

Consider the hierarchy shown in Figure 7.3 in which A, B, C, D and E are classes and E1, E2 and E3 are instances of E. A node in such a granularity hierarchy may be locked in one of a number of possible lock modes. Instances are always locked in either shared (S) or exclusive (X) mode depending on whether they are to be read or updated. The semantics of the S and X lock modes are as described earlier for read-locks and write-locks respectively. However, classes may be locked in one of five possible modes:

(i)   IS: An IS (Intention Share) lock on a class implies that specific instances of the class will be locked by the transaction as necessary.

(ii)   IX: An IX (Intention Exclusive) lock on a class means that specific instances of the class will be locked in either S or X mode as required.

(iii)   S: An S (Shared) lock on a class means that the class definition is locked in S mode and all instances of the class are implicitly locked in S mode.

(iv)   SIX: An SIX (Shared Intention Exclusive) lock on a class implies that the class definition and all its instances are locked in S mode and specific instances which are to be updated will be explicitly locked by the transaction.

(v)   X: An X (Exclusive) lock on a class means that the class definition and all its instances are locked in X mode.

Note that the only lock mode which permits a transaction to update a class definition is mode (v), an X lock on the class which implicitly locks all its instances in X mode. The compatibility matrix for these lock modes is given in Figure 7.4.

	IS	IX	S	SIX	X
IS	Yes	Yes	Yes	Yes	No
IX	Yes	Yes	No	No	No
S	Yes	No	Yes	No	No
SIX	Yes	No	No	No	No
X	No	No	No	No	No

Figure 7.4   Compatibility matrix for granularity locking

A multiple granularity locking protocol which guarantees serializability is as follows:

1.   The compatibility matrix of Figure 7.4 must be observed.

2.   To set an S or IS lock on a node P, a transaction must first lock the parent of P in either IX or IS mode.

3.   To set an X, SIX or IX lock on a node P, a transaction must first lock the parent of P in either IX or SIX mode.

4.   All transactions must be two-phase, i.e. they cannot lock a node if they have previously unlocked any node.

5.   A transaction can unlock a node P only if none of the children of P are currently locked by the transaction.

Note that in this protocol, rules 2 and 3 require locks to be acquired in root-to-leaf order, while rule 5 requires locks to be released in leaf-to-root order.

To illustrate the protocol, consider the class hierarchy of Figure 7.3 and suppose that a transaction requires write access to instance E3. To obtain exclusive access to E3 it must lock classes A, B and E (in that order) in either IX or SIX mode, and then lock E3 in X mode. The locks must be released in the order E3 followed by E, B and finally A.

The above protocol can be extended to the case of a class lattice, in which a node may have more than one parent (cf. multiple inheritance). This situation has been investigated thoroughly in the ORION system [Garza and Kim, 1988] and the interested reader is referred to that paper.

7.3   OPTIMISTIC SCHEDULING

In many multi-user database environments, the system overheads incurred through lock management may be considerable, and not worth their expense if the competition for exclusive access to data objects is low. In such circumstances, it may be better to take an optimistic approach to scheduling [Kung and Robinson, 1981], which does not involve any locking at all, and thereby removes the possibility of deadlock occurring.

In this optimistic approach transactions are allowed free access to data objects but any updates are assigned to local copies or 'shadows' of the data objects. Also, details of all read and write accesses by a transaction are recorded by the system. These are referred to respectively as the read and write sets of the transaction. Before any updates, carried out by a transaction on its local data objects, are committed to the database, the transaction is put through a validation test. This test checks whether there has been any unserializable interaction with other concurrently executing transactions which may have already committed their changes to the database. If so, the transaction is rolled back[†] and restarted. Otherwise its changes are committed to the database. The roll-back procedure is simplified by the fact that changes were made to local copies of data objects and not to the actual database.

As transactions reach the validation phase they are sequentially assigned serialization numbers. The validation test for a transaction T must then verify that at least one of the following criteria holds for every transaction T_i which precedes T in the serialization order:

1. T_i committed before T started.
2. The write set of T_i does not overlap with the read set of T and T_i

---

[†] Transaction roll-back is a technique commonly used in database recovery. The process is described in greater detail later in the chapter.

completes its commitment before T starts to commit.
3. The write set of T_i does not overlap with the read set or the write set of T.

Any one of these criteria ensures serializability.

Overheads for optimistic scheduling

The processing time overhead for optimistic scheduling is incurred in maintaining the read and write sets and shadow copies for each transaction, carrying out the validation phase, and finally committing those transactions which pass the validation test. The magnitude of these activities clearly depends on the degree of concurrency in the system and on the characteristics of the transactions. Aborting a transaction and restarting it in an optimistic environment are relatively simple in view of the use of shadow copies.

In terms of storage space, the overhead is incurred in storing the read and write sets for each transaction together with the shadow copies of updated objects. These shadow copies may be discarded after the transaction has committed. However, for the validation phase the read and write sets must be retained for all transactions which completed after any currently running transaction began. In a highly concurrent database environment this could be a very large amount of information to store.

7.4   TIMESTAMPING

A third technique for dealing with concurrent transactions in a database system is timestamping [Bernstein and Goodman, 1980]. The technique was originally proposed for dealing with concurrency control in distributed databases, but it appears to be applicable to centralized systems also. With this method, each transaction is assigned a unique *timestamp* which is some identification of the place the transaction occupies in a serialization of the concurrently executing transactions. In the case of a single-processor system, the timestamp could simply be the time at which each transaction started. Clearly the clock used must be sufficiently fine-grained to ensure that timestamps will be unique.

The concurrency control system guarantees serializability by ensuring that all read and write operations are performed in timestamp order. Thus the equivalent serial schedule is the chronological order of the commencement of each transaction. A read or write request by a transaction with a timestamp t_1 will not be granted if the data object concerned has been written by a transaction with a timestamp t_2, where $t_2 > t_1$. Similarly a write request will be rejected if the data object has been read by a transaction with a higher timestamp. (These rules correspond to those defined in Section 7.2.3 for guaranteeing serializability in a locking environment.) When a transaction experiences a rejected request to read or write an object, it is rolled back and restarted with a new, higher timestamp. Thus any potential deadlock situations are avoided. However, rolling back a transaction every time a conflict occurs is likely to be more expensive than allowing it to wait until it can proceed (as is the case with locking).

Implementation of the method requires the system to maintain read and write timestamps with each object. These hold the timestamps of the transactions which last performed the corresponding operation on the object. The processing overheads are very low since it is only necessary to check and update the timestamps each time an object is accessed.

7.5   CONCURRENCY IN OBJECT-ORIENTED SYSTEMS

As we have already seen, serializability is the usual correctness criterion for concurrency control algorithms in database environments. Therefore, in an object-oriented database the concurrent execution of transactions applying operations on the objects of the database is correct if it is equivalent to some serial execution of the transactions. Transactions may thus be viewed as temporal modules in that they represent indivisible temporal units of execution. Concurrent object-oriented database systems must therefore be able to deal with not only spatial modularity (atomic objects) but also temporal modularity (atomic actions).

The main difference between object-based concurrency control and concurrency control in conventional database management systems is that the units of concurrency, namely object instances, may be very large. This permits us to consider a number of alternative interaction schemes for transactions running on the database. Some possible strategies are:

1.   A *pre-claim strategy* in which transactions must acquire all the (large) objects that they need before they are allowed to execute on the database. Objects may be acquired in either shared or exclusive mode and are released only when the transaction terminates. A transaction is aborted (or put onto a waiting queue) if some of its required objects are locked by another transaction. As described in Section 7.2.2 this scheme will prevent deadlock, and it will also guarantee serializability since transactions obey a two-phase locking protocol. It is only feasible when transactions typically require access to only a small number of large objects and the identities of these objects are

known before the transactions start executing. Such conditions commonly prevail in CAD/CAM databases and consequently this scheme is sometimes used in such systems. A typical CAD/CAM scenario involves transactions explicitly *checking out* objects from the database, in either shared or exclusive mode. The objects are then manipulated on a local workstation and when all the required updates have been performed they are checked back into the database through a transaction. To preserve the atomicity and serializability of transactions all updated objects must be checked back at the same time before any of the exclusive locks on them are released.

2.   An optimistic strategy (based on that described in Section 7.3) in which each transaction manipulates a shadow copy of the database in its own workspace and then submits a commit request. The system will either reject the request due to conflicts with other transactions, or accept it, in which case the transaction will be committed. This scheme is employed in the GemStone object-oriented DBMS [Maier and Stein, 1986] and is described in greater detail below.

7.5.1   Concurrency in GemStone

GemStone supports concurrency by providing each user session with a workspace that contains a shadow copy of the most recently committed object table. (Actually, object tables are represented as B-trees and so for a shadow copy only the root node of the committed object table need be copied.) A session refers to the duration that a user is logged into the database management system, and during this session the user may submit one or more transactions. Whenever a user modifies an object a new copy of that object is created and the shadow copy of the object table is updated so that the object's pointer (oop) references the new copy. This new copy is inaccessible to other concurrent users.

An optimistic concurrency control scheme is applied. That is, access conflicts are checked at commit time rather than prevented from occurring through a locking mechanism. Thus, as described in Section 7.2.4 Gem-Stone keeps a record of which objects each transaction has read or written to and at commit time it checks that serializability will not be violated if the transaction's updates are applied to the database. That is, a transaction T must not have read or written to any object which has been modified by a transaction which has committed since T began. If a transaction does not pass this validation phase the changes recorded in its shadow object table are discarded. If a transaction is permitted to commit, its updates are transmitted to the database simply by replacing the root of the shared object table by the root of the shadow object table for that transaction. This guarantees the atomicity of the transaction since all its updates are performed at once.

This optimistic scheme has the advantage of ensuring that read-only transactions do not conflict with any other transaction. Such transactions are provided with a shadow copy of the database representing a consistent state at the time the transaction began. Also, deadlock cannot occur since transactions do not compete for access to objects. The most serious drawback of the scheme is that a user session that modifies a significant number of objects in the database may fail to commit any transactions for an arbitrarily long period of time. This is due to the high probability that the read-set or write-set of such transactions will conflict with the write-set of another concurrently executing transaction. Thus in practice a user may do a lot of interactive work, attempt a commit, and then be told that the commit cannot be accepted due to conflicts with other transactions.

A second problem with this optimistic scheme, as already mentioned in Section 7.3, is that the list of shadow objects that a session reads or updates can become very large. Part of the problem is that single objects, i.e. class instances, provide too fine a granularity for efficient implementation of optimistic concurrency control in a large multi-user database environment. GemStone attempts to alleviate this difficulty by introducing *segments* as the unit of concurrency control. Segments are logical groupings of objects similar to the object *clusters* found in other object-oriented systems. For each transaction, GemStone keeps a list of the segments which have been read or updated rather than the individual objects. A segment may contain any number of objects and users may control the placement of objects in segments in order to reduce the likely conflict between competing concurrent transactions. For example, immutable objects may be grouped into a single segment and the system need record only a single segment entry for a transaction no matter how many of these objects it accesses.

7.5.2   Non-serializable approaches to object-based concurrency

As previously described serializability is the traditional correctness criterion applied to database transactions. However many applications in CAD/CAM, software engineering and office information systems (OIS) require more concurrency than is allowed in a serializable system [Bernstein, 1987; Garcia-Molina and Salem, 1987]. The two-phase locking protocol for example will considerably reduce concurrency if transactions are long-lived since objects will be locked for unacceptably long periods of time. In a software engineering environment for example, a programmer may be locked out from editing a source file because some other programmer has previously edited the same file but has not yet completed his changes to other files. Moreover, in view of the multiple granularity locking protocol, transactions may have to lock an unreasonably large amount of data in order to preserve global consistency. Another problem is that in a serializable system, if a transaction aborts before committing all the changes made by that transaction will be discarded. This would be unacceptable if, for example, transactions were long-lived interactive user sessions. Also, atomicity and serializability require that transactions appear to be isolated units of work, and so do not permit *cooperative* applications in which transactions may interact concurrently not only with the database but also with each other. Such cooperative transaction environments are commonplace in the OIS (Office Information Systems), CAD and software engineering areas.

The problem is that the conventional transaction model is often too conservative for typical object-oriented applications. Data objects are often large, nested and closely interrelated. Applications are often decomposed into simpler, parallel subtasks that may be distributed among people and machines to reduce complexity. These subtasks are often interdependent with respect to data. Transactions corresponding to such subtasks cannot execute in parallel if serializability is to be maintained. The optimistic approach to concurrency control, exemplified by GemStone, goes some way towards alleviating this problem, but has its own fairly significant drawbacks as described in the previous section. Thus, a number of new correctness criteria have been proposed in the literature which allow more concurrency than serializability but still manage concurrent activities at a high level of abstraction. Such correctness criteria are often referred to as *non-serializable*. They constrain the legal sequences of operations within transactions and their behaviour, and specify requirements that must be met by a transaction before it can commit. Some of these proposed correctness criteria are discussed below in relation to object-oriented database systems. A comparison of the criteria is given by Langworthy [1988].

Linearizability

Within an object-oriented framework, linearizability [Herlihy and Wing, 1987, 1988] is a correctness criterion which requires transactions to be single operations on single objects which do not generate any further operations. Thus, complex tasks must be decomposed into a number of such transactions. In these circumstances a concurrent computation is said to be linearizable if it is equivalent to a legal sequential computation that satisfies the following two requirements:

(i)   Each operation must appear to take effect instantaneously;

(ii)   The order of non-concurrent operations must be preserved.

Informally, linearizability provides the illusion that each operation applied to an object by a transaction takes place instantaneously at some point between its invocation and its response, and that the order of invocations appears to be the order of operations. Thus the effects of an object's operations may still be specified using pre- and post-conditions but the specification of a class permits only linearizable interleavings of operations. To decide whether the concurrent history of an object is acceptable it is necessary to take into account the object's intended semantics. Thus linearizability might be called a 'local' correctness criterion as opposed to a global criterion such as serializability because it governs the correctness of a single object rather than the entire database system. This allows a higher degree of concurrency to be achieved than is possible with serializability, but of course tasks involving multiple transactions are not atomic and may conflict. It is the programmer's responsibility to ensure that such conflicts do not violate the integrity of the database. For some applications the enhanced level of concurrency that linearizability permits may justify placing this additional burden on the programmer.

Commit-serializability
Commit-serializability [Pu *et al.*, 1988; Kaiser, 1988] is a correctness criterion that requires all transactions to commit in a serializable manner but these transactions need not directly correspond to the transactions that were originally initiated. A transaction may be split by partitioning its read- and write-sets (i.e. the sets of objects that it requires either to read- or write-lock) and passing the subsets to the new transactions.

For example, consider two concurrent transactions T_1 and T_2. T_1 may be divided either by the system or by the user into T_3 and T_4, and sometime later T_3 may commit while T_4 continues. If T_2 is still operating it may view the committed updates of T_3, some of which may have been made by T_1 before the division. If T_2 then commits, T_4 may view the committed updates of T_2 before committing itself. Thus T_2, T_3 and T_4 are serializable (equivalent serial order is T_3; T_2; T_4) but the original transactions T_1 and T_2 are not.

Splitting transactions in this way clearly increases the level of concurrency in the system. However, if dependencies exist among the read- and write-sets passed to new transactions, then such transactions must commit together, atomically. Otherwise, inconsistent data may enter the system. By definition, two transactions cannot commit together atomically and so we must have an inverse *join-transaction* operation which merges two transactions into a single transaction so that their results may be committed together.

Nested Transactions

The nested transaction model [Moss, 1981, 1985] allows a transaction to spawn concurrent child transactions whose interactions are governed by the same correctness criterion as the parent transaction, namely serializability. Thus a transaction may spawn a hierarchy of nested transactions and transactions with the same parent must be serializable. A transaction may commit only when its parent commits and thus modifications are transmitted to the database only on commitment of the top-level transaction, the root of the transaction tree. Nested transactions allow for additional concurrency but sibling transactions must still be atomic and serializable. Thus the model does not permit cooperating transactions.

An alternative, three-level nested transaction model has been proposed by Korth *et al*. [1988] for CAD applications. In this model transactions may be nested but different correctness criteria may be applied at each level. There are three distinct types of transaction:

- Designer's Transactions which, at the simplest level, are atomic updates;

- Cooperating Transactions which consist of many designer's transactions. Serializability is not enforced at this level.

- Project Transactions which are composed of many cooperating transactions and are governed by traditional serializability.

This model allows increased concurrency and cooperation within project transactions but conflicts may arise at the levels of designer and cooperating transactions since these are not governed by serializability. As in the case of optimistic concurrency control, the system must ensure that such conflicts do not lead to inconsistent data being transmitted to the database.

7.6   RECOVERY

A database management system must provide the software tools necessary to implement recovery in the event of an *inconsistent state* arising in a database system. In a large multi-user database system inconsistent states may arise from a variety of diverse sources. For example:

1.   Failure of an updating transaction before it has completed its update but

after it has written some changes to the database.

2. A software failure in the operating system or database management system which causes some or all transactions executing at the time of the failure to abort.

3. A power failure which brings all transactions currently active to a halt and loses the contents of main memory.

4. A media failure, such as corruption of a disk. A portion, or possibly all of the data on the disk may be lost.

5. Corruption of the database by a faulty transaction, i.e. a transaction with faulty logic which writes incorrect or inconsistent data to the database.

System software failures or power failures which do not result in physical damage to the database are often known as *soft crashes*. Media failures are termed *hard crashes*.

Maintaining consistency must be the responsibility of the database administrator and many modern database management systems provide a variety of facilities for protecting against inconsistent states, or for resolving inconsistencies when they arise. Some of these facilities are discussed below.

7.6.1   Back-up copies and snap-shots

Taking back-up copies of a large database system is an expensive and time-consuming operation, and can only be taken as frequently as is cost-effective. Obviously it is important that the copy represents a consistent state, so in general no updating transaction must be in progress at the same time as the copying utility (the copying utility read-locks the database). In a highly volatile environment (i.e. one in which the information in the database is constantly being updated), frequent 'snap-shots' of highly active areas of the database are desirable.

7.6.2   The log file

Many database management systems maintain a transaction logging file (or journal file), which records a history of every transaction which has updated the database since the last back-up copy was made. Entries for each transaction in the log file typically consist of the following:

1. A unique transaction identifier.

2. The address of every object updated (or created) by the transaction together with the old value of the object (preimage) and its new value (postimage).

3. Key points in the progress of transactions, such as their start and end times. It is particularly useful if the log file records the point at which a transaction *commits*, i.e. when it has successfully recorded in the log file *all* its changes to objects in the database.

To facilitate recovery, transactions typically record their updates in the log *prior* to them being written to the database. This technique is often referred to as *write ahead logging*. In these circumstances the following restriction on transactions greatly facilitates recovery in the event of a crash.

The updates of a transaction cannot be committed to the database until it has recorded all those updates in the log file.

This important protocol is often called *deferred update*. Thus an updating transaction has two phases, as illustrated in Figure 7.5.

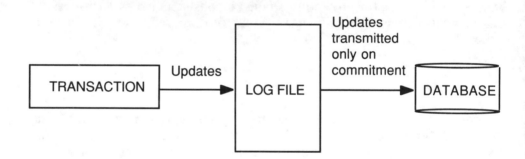

Figure 7.5 Write ahead logging and deferred update

Phase 1
The transaction writes to the log file details of changes which it is necessary to make to objects in the database. When all such changes have been recorded in the log, the transaction issues a COMMIT message.

Phase 2
The database management system transmits the changes from the log to the database.

If transactions do not obey this policy, but are instead permitted to write directly to the database before committing, then in the event of a transaction failure or system crash, recovery is difficult for two reasons:

1. A transaction which is uncommitted when it fails, or when a crash occurs, must have any updates which it has written to the database undone. The action of undoing the effects of a transaction is called *roll-back*.

2. Any transaction which has read a value which was updated by a transaction that is rolled back, must also be rolled back. Clearly, this effect can propagate, causing a large number of transactions to be undone. This phenomenon is sometimes called cascading roll-back.

Note that recovery in these circumstances requires that the log records the identity of every object *read* by each transaction, as well as those updated.

7.6.3   Recovery from inconsistent states

Recovering from an inconsistent state may involve either undoing the changes made by transactions, or redoing the updates of committed transactions (sometimes called *roll-forward*). If write ahead logging is in operation, then rolling back an uncommitted transaction simply involves discarding its changes from the log file, since those changes have not been transmitted to the database. As described above, if a committed transaction is rolled back it will be necessary to undo other transactions which read a value written by the rolled-back transaction.

   Most recovery strategies require the log to record *checkpoints*. These are simple records written to the log indicating a point in time to which the system can return and be consistent. This usually means a point in time at which no updating transactions are being committed to the database. All transactions which are recorded as committed in the log have had their updates transmitted to the database prior to the checkpoint. A checkpoint record contains a list of the identities of all transactions active at the time of the checkpoint.

   In the event of a soft crash, we must identify using the log those transactions which must be rolled forward (the REDO list) and those which must be rolled back (the UNDO list). The following procedure is required to effect recovery:

1. Go back to the most recent checkpoint and add all the transactions active at that time to the UNDO list. The REDO list is initialized to be empty.

2. Search forward chronologically through the log.

3. If we encounter a new transaction T starting, add T to the UNDO list.

4. If we encounter a COMMIT entry in the log for a transaction T, move T from the UNDO list to the REDO list.

5. Continue until the end of the log (the point of the crash) is reached.

Finally, transactions in the UNDO list are removed from the log and must be restarted. Transactions in the REDO list are rolled forward. Only then may normal processing resume.

In the event of a hard crash, which causes data to be lost or destroyed, it will normally be necessary to revert to a back-up copy of the database and roll forward all transactions which had committed prior to the crash.

7.6.4   Shadow paging

Shadow paging is a recovery technique that does not strictly require the use of a log file (though logging may be required for concurrency control). The technique views the database, not as files and records, but as a collection of fixed length pages (or blocks). A page table is maintained which is simply an index in which the ith entry points to the ith page of the database on disk. In a transaction processing environment this page table may be copied into main memory, if size permits, and all read and write accesses to the database from transactions go through the page table. When a transaction begins execution a copy of the current page table is copied into a *shadow page table*. This represents the (consistent) state of the database prior to the execution of this transaction and thus defines a state to which the database can return should the transaction fail. The shadow page table is thus saved on disk and is not modified by the transaction. All updates by the transaction are performed via the current page table.

When the transaction modifies an object in the database the page containing that object is not over-written. Rather a new page on a free portion of the disk is allocated and the modified page is written to this new area. The current page table is then updated to point to this new page while the shadow page table remains unchanged and thus still points to the old, unmodified page. Recovery from a transaction failure then involves the following steps:

1. Free the modified database pages for subsequent reuse.

2. Reinstate the shadow page table as the current page table.

This restores the database to its state prior to execution of the transaction. On the other hand, if a transaction successfully terminates and we wish to commit its changes then all that we need do is simply discard the shadow page table.

The clear advantages of shadow paging are that it greatly simplifies the processes of undoing and committing transactions. However, committing transactions will incur significant overheads if the page table is very large. Also, the process of writing a new page on a separate area of the disk every time an object on the page is updated will lead to the data becoming very fragmented. Without constant reorganization it will be difficult to keep related pages together (e.g. those containing tuples of the same relation or instances of the same class).

The shadow paging technique has been successfully extended to object-oriented systems with pages being replaced by objects and the page table by the object table (an index relating object identities to their position on disk).

7.6.5   Recovery in optimistic schemes

Recall that in object-oriented optimistic concurrency control each transaction gets a shadow copy of the shared object table. All updates are carried out on the shadow copy and these changes are invisible to other concurrently executing transactions. On committing a transaction, the shared table is simply replaced by the shadow copy of that transaction. Thus, if a transaction aborts before committing its shadow copy is simply discarded and the database is unaffected. Transactions can be rolled forward provided their shadow copies are saved after commitment and retained between back-ups of the entire database. No additional logging is required since this is already performed by the concurrency control mechanism.

7.7   DISTRIBUTED DATABASES

7.7.1   Fundamentals

In a distributed database the data are held on a network of computers across different sites (or nodes) which are geographically remote from each other. Each site holds a partition of the database and these partitions may overlap, i.e. some objects or even parts of objects may be replicated at different sites. Typically, each site runs its own version of the database management system which is responsible for handling the necessary communications across the network. In fact the local DBMSs could be different systems leading to what is known as a *heterogeneous* distributed system. We shall consider such systems presently.

Ideally, a distributed database management system should absolve the user of the responsibility for dealing with the significant additional problems which arise due to distribution. That is, the location and replication of data should be transparent to the user [Ceri *et al.*, 1984].

Location transparency absolves the user of the responsibility of knowing at which site a particular object is stored. Thus he may retrieve data from multiple sites simultaneously without restrictions. Obviously, due to the relative slowness of communication links, response times for accessing data stored at remote sites may be much greater than for accesses to locally held data. Except for this difference however, it should appear to the user that the entire database (or at least his view of it) is stored at his location. The provision of location transparency presents the system with the very considerable problem of devising and implementing efficient query processing strategies. If the objects are very large then transferring one of them in its entirety from one site to another, in order to compute a query at a single site, may result in significant delay. This delay will of course depend on the bandwidth of the communication links, but might often be larger than the computation time required to perform the query.

In providing replication transparency the system takes responsibility for maintaining duplicate copies of objects which are held at multiple sites to facilitate query processing. This means that updates to replicated data must be propagated automatically (and transparently to the user) to secondary copies, ideally at the same time as the primary update. If updates are delayed then out-of-date retrievals may result, leading to inconsistent states. Problems obviously arise if a site holding a copy of an updated object is temporarily unavailable. One possible strategy would be to reject any update operation on an object which cannot be broadcast immediately to all copies of that object. However this leads to a loss of local autonomy since transactions are rejected due to non-local factors. Also the probability of an update transaction failing may be quite high if there is a lot of replication across many sites. A better strategy is to leave pending (at some available site) any updates which cannot be applied immediately. A restart procedure for a site is then responsible for applying any pending updates to its local data upon reconnection to the network.

Data replication also has significant consequences for concurrency control in a distributed system. As shown by Traiger *et al.* [1979], a distributed system with data replication which enforces the following protocol will be guaranteed serializability:

1. Before reading an object a transaction must acquire a (shared) read-lock on *at least one* copy of the object .

2. Before updating a data object a transaction must acquire an (exclusive) write-lock on *every* copy of the object .

3. Once a transaction has acquired a lock (of either kind) it must not release that lock until it has *committed*.

This protocol may be regarded as a distributed version of the two-phase locking protocol described in Section 7.2. However complications arise if a write-lock cannot be granted because a site containing a copy of the relevant object is unavailable.

Also note that the commitment of a transaction in the distributed case requires that *all* sites have recorded the updates of that transaction relevant to their local data objects. That is, either all sites accept the transaction or they all reject it. It must not be possible for some sites to record the updates of a transaction and others not, since this would violate the atomicity of the transaction. This leads to an important elaboration on the normal commit/roll-back concept called *two-phase commit*. This works in the following way:

1. A centralized system component called the *Coordinator* asks each local recovery manager if it is able to commit the updates of the transaction.

2. If, and only if, all recovery managers reply 'OK' then the Coordinator tells each site to commit the updates of the transaction to its local data. If one or more recovery managers reply negatively, then all sites are told to roll-back the transaction.

A problem with locking in a distributed environment is that it may considerably reduce response time in view of the amount of message traffic it generates on the network (e.g. lock and unlock requests, lock and unlock grants, commit messages, etc.). There is also the problem of *global deadlock* arising, i.e. deadlock involving more than one site. It may be impossible for a single site to detect such deadlock since it does not have all the relevant information available locally. Thus detection and resolution of global deadlock can generate further message traffic. In many distributed systems therefore, deadlock is detected by a timeout mechanism, by which a transaction is aborted if it exceeds some specified waiting time. Timestamping in a distributed environment avoids deadlock and incurs less communication overheads. However this technique tends to provide a lesser degree of concurrency than locking.

7.7.2   Heterogeneous distributed databases

The proliferation of large, diverse computer-based information systems, particularly in the business and engineering fields, has led to a growing need for centralized management of pre-existing heterogeneous databases. That is, there is clearly a need in many application areas to view in an integrated way, data residing in separately developed applications, connected by some communication channel (i.e. local or wide area networks). In large corporations such systems are often required to span not only diverse applications, but organizational boundaries and geographical distribution.

A distributed database system may be viewed as a set of autonomous, heterogeneous information sources and their associated database management systems which comprise the sites of a communication network. The information sources have typically been designed and developed independently and hence may be inconsistent. Also, they are:

(i)   supported by heterogeneous database management systems;

(ii)   are completely autonomous, i.e. no system assumes authority over another.

The major concern lies in supporting cooperative behaviour, or *interoperability*, between these databases in a secure and efficient manner. The aim is to reconcile any semantic conflicts and establish a well-defined form of cooperation between the different sites in a transparent manner, so that users get the impression of a single integrated application. The need for close cooperation arises from the fact that each individual database models only a portion of the corporate application, and they need to exchange messages and data to contribute collectively to the solution of a common problem domain.

Existing heterogeneous distributed database systems can be classified in terms of the type of control used for processing queries involving the retrieval of data from more than one site. If control is exercised centrally then the architecture can be characterized as *logically centralized* [Smith, 1981]; otherwise, if control is decentralized the architecture is called *decentralized* or *federated* [McLeod and Heimbinger, 1985]. The type of architecture employed affects the degree of local autonomy and the degree and nature of coupling between the schemas of the various databases.

Both logically centralized and federated databases have several stringent limitations. At the one extreme the logically centralized databases require the existence of a single global schema, thus sacrificing some measure of local autonomy. Also, the use of a global data manager to implement the global schema leads to performance bottlenecks as the complexity of the distributed query processing increases. Integration in logically centralized databases may also go too far in trying to couple tightly aggregates of data that should retain some degree of individuality. At the other extreme, federated databases adhere strictly to retaining local autonomy, thus making it difficult to exercise global control. Information available to each individual site from the rest of the corporate domain is confined to that which conforms to that site's perception of the world. Moreover, this view may be inconsistent with the views of other databases in the network.

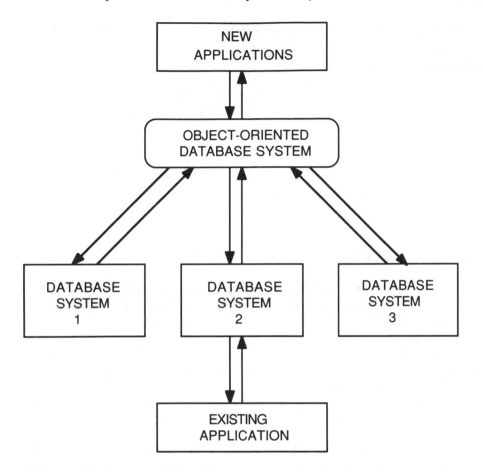

Figure 7.6 Interoperability of heterogeneous distributed database systems

Accordingly, host schema changes or integrity constraints can be enforced locally but are unable to span sites - a fact that represents a source of potential conflicts in corporate database applications.

In summary, none of the above architectural frameworks supports the advanced forms of interoperability whereby database systems are required to develop and analyse different, and possibly conflicting views of parts of the corporate domain. There can be differences in the underlying data models of the participating systems, differences in the languages used for developing applications, and differences in the underlying operating systems.

The object-oriented model can address some of the issues associated with the interoperability of heterogeneous distributed database systems. The powerful data modelling and data abstraction mechanisms that are embodied in the object-oriented model can be used to provide higher level abstractions of widely different applications interacting with a variety of database systems (Figure 7.6).

In effect, a pre-existing data storage system becomes the physical realization of the abstract data types in the global model. The user sees only the abstract data types, and when an operation is invoked on a type the system transforms it into an equivalent operation on the appropriate physical representation. An advantage of this approach is that existing application programs could continue to access the original database which is unaffected by the superimposition of the global object-oriented model. However, new applications would interact directly with the abstract data types.

7.8   SUMMARY

In a large multi-user database environment, objects are viewed as data items with concurrent access to objects from user programs being controlled by the underlying system according to some correctness criteria. Serializability is the usual correctness criterion for concurrency control algorithms in conventional database environments. However, a number of alternative strategies have been considered for object-oriented systems. All of these techniques attempt to increase the level of concurrency in a system by exploiting some of the application-specific semantics inherent in the model to relax the traditional constraints of atomicity and serializability on transactions. However, relaxing these constraints introduces additional complexity for the concurrency control system in that it must monitor the conflicts that arise among non-serializable transactions and protect the database from the consequences of such conflicts. This increased complexity may be acceptable if the application domain demands a level of concurrency and cooperation among transactions that cannot be achieved in the normal serializable environment. This is often the case with object-oriented database systems.

The object-oriented approach adds significant additional complexity to transaction management. In this chapter we have described some of the principal techniques employed in object-oriented database systems for concurrency control and recovery. However, the area is still the subject of considerable research.

We have also shown in this chapter that the object-oriented model can address some of the issues associated with the interoperability of heterogeneous distributed database systems. The powerful data modelling and data abstraction mechanisms that are embodied in the object-oriented model can be used to provide higher level abstractions of differing applications.

7.9   BIBLIOGRAPHIC NOTES

A comprehensive description of concurrency control and recovery in conventional database systems can be found in Bernstein *et al.* [1987]. Papadimitriou [1986] covers the theoretical aspects of concurrency control. Object-based concurrency, from the programming language point of view, is described in detail in Yonezawa *et al.* [1989]. Concurrency control for abstract data types is described by Schwartz and Spector [1984] and Herlihy [1986], the latter dealing with the optimistic approach. Garza and Kim [1988] provide a good general discussion of many of the issues associated with transaction management in an object-oriented database system.

8

Object-oriented database implementation

8.1 INTRODUCTION

Applications in engineering design, manufacturing, real-time systems and software engineering demand high performance object management systems. These applications utilize the sophisticated structural and behavioural interrelationships and inheritance mechanisms provided by object-oriented systems to model complex environments effectively. The fundamental object-oriented concepts have been further enhanced in object-oriented database management systems to support persistence, complex objects, versioning (the ability to create and access multiple versions of an object) and clustering (the process of grouping together related objects). The issue of persistence was studied in detail in Chapter 6. In this chapter we look at these other implementation issues.

8.2 STORAGE STRATEGIES FOR OBJECTS

Most object-oriented database management systems comprise two major subsystems, an *interpreter* and an *object storage manager*. The storage manager is concerned with the allocation and clustering of objects on secondary store, and the movement of data between this store and main memory. Thus, the interpreter relies on the storage manager for physical data access and manipulation. One of the major issues is how much of the semantics of the data model should be incorporated in the storage manager. Some object-oriented systems (e.g. IRIS [Wilkinson *et al.*, 1990]), have simply used a relational storage subsystem as the storage manager, while others have tailored their storage strategies to reflect concepts such as inheritance and class hierarchies.

The efficient storage and retrieval of complex objects on secondary storage presents some challenging problems, especially if we require objects and types to be free to change their structure, or we wish to support free-format portions of an object state. Additional problems are posed by objects whose property values are longer than a page, such as long textual documents or images stored as large bitmaps.

As an example, consider a complex object Employee defined by the following class:

```
class Employee

    properties
        Number : Integer;
        Name : NameType;
        DOB : DateType;
        Dept : DeptType;
        Salary : Real;

    operations
        ...

end Employee.
```

The properties Name, DOB and Dept are themselves objects, with types defined by other classes. One method for storing employee objects is to decompose them into their constituent fields and store each field in a binary relation containing the surrogate for the object and the value of the field. Thus, as shown in Figure 8.1, we have one relation storing employee surrogates and their numbers, another storing employee surrogates and their names, and so on. Actually, since Name is a complex object, a surrogate will be stored for the Name value in the appropriate binary relation. This will also be the case for the properties DOB and Dept. Each of these complex properties will have their own binary relations relating surrogates to field values. The disadvantages of this method are that it introduces a great deal of redundancy at the physical level, and, more importantly, an object is fragmented across many binary relations.

An alternative method for storing objects is the *object-based* approach in which all the fields of each object are grouped together on disk. A typical storage format [Kim *et al.*, 1988] is shown in Figure 8.2. In this format the object's surrogate is followed by its storage length in bytes and a count of the number of fields (properties) for which explicit values are stored. A vector containing the names of the fields follows. The field count and field name vector could be omitted if the object contained a reference to its class and a standard convention was used for storing objects of the same class.

Employee Surrogate	Number
......	......

Employee Surrogate	Name Surrogate
......	......

Employee Surrogate	DOB Surrogate
......	......

Employee Surrogate	Dept Surrogate
......	......

Employee Surrogate	Salary
......	......

Figure 8.1   Storage format based on binary relations

Surrogate	object length	property count	property name vector	values offset vector	values

Figure 8.2   Object-based storage format

The values offset vector gives the starting position of each field value as an offset from the start of the record. The values of properties which are themselves complex objects are generally represented by their surrogates since, clearly, uncontrolled duplication of such objects within employee objects would introduce a host of problems with regard to integrity control when updating the database. However, in some circumstances it may be desirable to store sub-objects with their parent objects in order to enhance performance. An example of such a situation is that in which the sub-object *is a part of* the parent object [Kim *et al.*, 1988]. (Recall from Chapter 3 that the IS_PART_OF relationship is, together with the IS_A relationship, one of the fundamental semantic data modelling concepts.)

Objects of the same type (i.e. all instances of the same class) may be stored in clusters on disk to facilitate query processing. One difficulty with this approach is that complex objects, even of the same type, may be highly variable in length (for example, properties may have linked-list representations). This causes problems when mapping such objects onto conventional file management systems based on fixed length pages. Each object is stored as a sequence of linked pages, often in a B-tree structure, and if the object increases in size, a new page can be acquired and linked.

The EXODUS storage mechanism [Carey *et al.*, 1986] is typical in this respect. Small objects are classified as those which fitted on to a single disk page while large objects are those which require more than one disk page. To simplify the storage mechanism, page sharing is restricted to versions of the same object. Each object has an object identifier (OID) in the form of a page number and a slot number. For small objects the OID points directly to the object on disk, while for large objects the OID points to a header record. This header contains pointers to the disk pages on which the large object is stored. Large objects are held as B+ trees and algorithms are provided for the efficient growing, shrinking and rebalancing of the trees. The tree structure is not the most efficient for updates, however it is the best method for holding large relatively static objects which have been built as a series of appends and are rarely updated on an ad hoc basis.

Comparing the binary relation and the object-based representations from the point of view of data retrieval, the binary relation approach is generally better for associative access [Copeland and Khoshafian, 1985]. For example, if we want to find all the employees in the 'Hardware' department, the system must determine the surrogate for this department (by looking up an object table for example) and then scan the employee-Dept binary relation to find the surrogates of those employees. Obviously, conventional indexing techniques may be employed to speed up the table lookup and the scan of the binary relation. However, the binary relation approach is not very good for queries which require all, or even several, fields for a particular instance of an object type, since those fields are dispersed across many disk blocks. Storing objects in their entirety on disk can deal with such a query very easily. However, to find all the employees in the Hardware department the system must scan a large cluster of employee objects. Once again, such a scan could be facilitated by indexing the cluster on Dept surrogates.

One storage representation is not obviously better than the other and in practice a hybrid approach, in conjunction with good indexing techniques, may be the most appropriate. In many applications of object-oriented databases the majority of queries have an *associative access phase*, where a few object references are retrieved on the basis of some selection criteria, followed by a *computation phase* where these objects are manipulated. Thus we might use binary relations on disk to speed up associative access, and an object-based approach in main memory where we have more flexibility with regard to storage allocation. On the other hand, for applications in which entire complex objects are typically retrieved (e.g. complex drawings in computer-aided design), the object-based approach may be more appropriate in both secondary storage and main memory. The time taken to reconstruct such large objects from fragmented binary relations may be significantly greater than that gained through faster associative access.

8.2.1   Storage strategies for class hierarchies

Additional storage issues must be addressed when considering the storage of objects which belong to a class hierarchy. Recall that in such a hierarchy a class may inherit properties and operations from superclasses, and we must decide where the values of inherited properties are to be physically stored. The code for an inherited operation is invariably stored with the description of the class in which the operation is first defined, but there are a variety of possible strategies for storing property values. A property value could be stored as far down the hierarchy as possible, in the class instance to which the value directly belongs. Alternatively, a property value could stored high in the hierarchy, in the class instance where the property is first declared.

To illustrate the variety of alternatives for storing object hierarchies, we shall consider a sample database which is an instance of the class hierarchy shown in Figure 8.3. In this hierarchy, a PERSON is a MAMMAL and a MAMMAL is a CREATURE. A BAT is a MAMMAL and also a WINGED-CREATURE, both of which are descendants of CREATURE. Each of the entities inherit the properties (and operations) of their ancestors but have additional properties of their own.

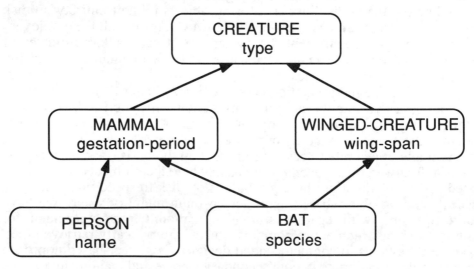

Figure 8.3   A sample class hierarchy

A logical view of a portion of this sample database is shown in Figure 8.4. Every instance has a unique identifier, or object-oriented pointer (oop) and the duplication of instances in the logical view represents the concept that an instance belongs to a class and to all superclasses of that class.

We could of course decide to implement this logical view directly in physical storage. However this strategy leads to excessive duplication of data which, while simplifying retrieval of a single instance, causes considerable complications for update operations. For example, updating an instance requires changes to be propagated throughout the hierarchy, and this clearly has implications for integrity preservation. Insertion and deletion of an instance also require multiple operations.

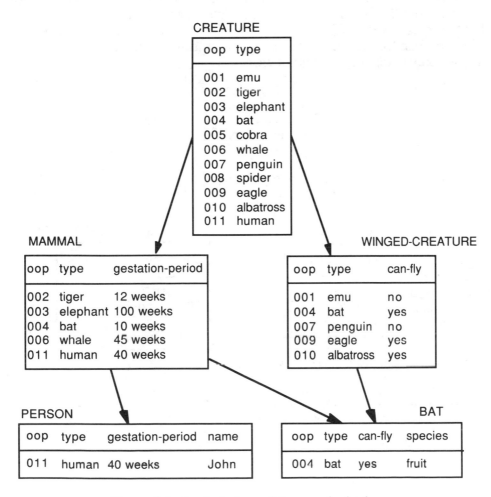

Figure 8.4 Logical view of the sample database

A more practical strategy is one in which an instance is stored at the lowest level possible in the class hierarchy, in the class to which it most specifically belongs. This model is employed in ORION [Banerjee *et al.*, 1987, 1988]. The storage of our sample database using this strategy is shown in Figure 8.5.

It can be seen that this model involves no duplication, so the update problems described above are avoided. Any updates to an instance will affect only the one occurrence of that instance, and so there is no need to propagate changes throughout the hierarchy. Retrieval of a single instance is also straightforward since all the relevant property values are stored with each instance. However, when retrieving instances of a class we must decide whether we require all instances (SELECT-ALL), which includes instances of all subclasses, or only those instances that are explicitly stored for that class (SELECT-ONLY). A SELECT-ALL operation will be less efficient than for the previous storage structure since all subclass instances are no longer stored in the parent class.

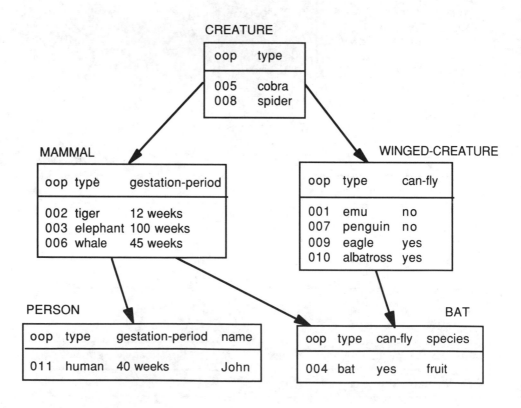

Figure 8.5   A storage strategy with no duplication

A third possible storage structure is shown in Figure 8.6. This approach is used in the IRIS system [Fishman *et al*., 1987]. For each instance of a class the oop is stored, together with the values of those properties which are peculiar to that class. That is, inherited property values are stored as high as possible in the hierarchy and are not duplicated at the lower levels. (This approach is similar to the strategy outlined in Chapter 1 for representing type hierarchies in the relational model. That is, each instance of a subtype contains only a key value and the values of those attributes peculiar to the subtype.) This model offers minimal storage overhead since only the oop is duplicated. However, retrieval of an instance requires multiple 'join' operations in order to reconstruct the instance from the various classes.

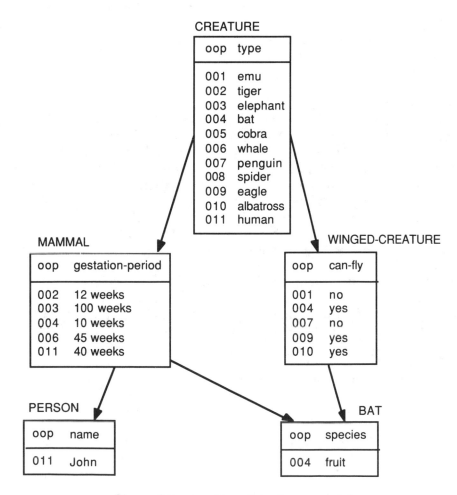

Figure 8.6 An alternative storage model

Updating a property value of a specified class instance requires only one write operation, since that value is stored only once. However in order to find the appropriate instance to update it may be necessary to access other instances higher up in the hierarchy. For example, consider the following update operation:

```
UPDATE Creature
WHERE type = human AND name ='John'
SET name = 'George'
```

Since the instance of Creature referred to in this update operation is spread over several classes (Creature, Mammal, Person) it is necessary to access the parent classes Creature and Mammal before updating the appropriate instance in class Person. Insertion and deletion of an instance clearly require multiple operations due to the fragmentation of instances across multiple classes.

Class-hierarchy indexing

The class hierarchy structure of object-oriented databases has important implications for secondary indexing [Kim *et al.*, 1989, 1990]. In relational database systems a secondary index is associated with an attribute (or group of attributes) of a single relation. When a query is posed involving an attribute in a specified relation, only that relation needs to be searched. However, in an object-oriented database a class inherits the attributes of its superclasses, and so a class and all its direct and indirect subclasses share the same attributes. As described above, the access scope of a query (or update) in an object-oriented database may be a class hierarchy. To support such queries we therefore need to maintain secondary indexes for every class in the hierarchy. There are two methods for doing this:

1. *Single-class indexing*, in which a separate index is maintained on an attribute for each class in the hierarchy;

2. *Class-hierarchy indexing*, in which a single index is maintained on an attribute for the entire class hierarchy.

A detailed analysis [Kim *et al.*, 1989] has shown that in class hierarchy indexing the number of index pages to be fetched is smaller in general than for single-class indexing. However, class hierarchy indexing will generally be less efficient for queries which are targetted at a single subclass rather than a hierarchy. A class-hierarchy index is also more complex, and therefore more difficult to maintain, than single-class indexes.

ORION supports class-hierarchy indexing with the structure of an index being similar to that of a B+ tree. Indexed attributes may have primitive types (e.g. integer, string) or be instances of user-defined classes. Thus the 'key value' in an index can be a primitive value or set of such values, the unique object identifier of some instance of the domain class, or a set of such object identifiers. The O_2 system also implements class-hierarchy indexing. It overcomes the disadvantages of the method in dealing with queries on a single subclass by structuring the index in such a way that all objects of a subclass are retrieved in a single block [Deux *et al.*, 1990].

8.2.2   Mapping objects from disk to memory

Conventional database management systems have a *buffer manager* that maintains a buffer of page frames and attempts to keep in that buffer data that is likely to be accessed again soon [Traiger, 1982]. Transactions must issue a request to the buffer managing subsystem to load an item of data into the buffer before the transaction can access it. When the transaction is finished with the data it informs the buffer manager that the space occupied in the buffer by that data may be overwritten. A data item is thus guaranteed to remain in the buffer while it is in use. Buffer managers typically use some form of LRU (least recently used) replacement algorithm [Chou and DeWitt, 1985] by which the choice of data to be overwritten in the buffer is that which has been unused for the longest period of time. The buffer manager maintains a *page table* which records information on each page of the buffer.

Buffer management is inherently more difficult for object-oriented systems than in conventional database/programming language interfaces. One reason for this is the variability of object sizes. Placement in memory of a retrieved object is a non-trivial task, since either a free chunk of memory with at least the size of the object must be found, or the object must be fragmented across the available free space. Fragmentation becomes severe as objects of different sizes are swapped in and out of memory and time-consuming *garbage-collection* may frequently be required.

Moving complex, variably-sized objects between secondary storage and program memory has many additional problems. Since we are moving from a storage system which has primitive types to the typing system of a programming language, a *type mapping* facility is required. That is, when an object is moved from program memory to persistent store, it must be 'unbound' from the run-time system and a description of how to generate its storage representation must be available. Similarly, when the object is retrieved by a program, the object must be recreated according to some predefined procedure. In languages such as Smalltalk, which allow application programs to determine information about an object's type at runtime, the mapping between an arbitrary object in main memory and its external storage representation can be determined dynamically. This permits the construction and use of a single, general-purpose mapping operation that may be applied to objects of any type.

Many statically typed languages, however, provide no facilities for making use of an object's type at run-time, and thus it is not possible to provide a single mechanism for the mapping of persistent objects of arbitrary types to and from secondary storage. In such languages therefore, the responsibility for the mapping must reside with each class definition. That is, each class is responsible for the storage of its own instances and must provide the necessary operations for moving instances to and from persistent store. Despite the obvious drawbacks of having to supply such operations with every class definition, this latter approach has a number of advantages. First, it is consistent with the concept of information hiding which is central to data abstraction and modularity. That is, only each individual class is aware of its internal and external representations and this information is hidden from the surrounding environment. Second, this approach offers more scope for optimization since the storage strategy for each class of object is tailored specifically to that object.

Object buffering

To solve some of the problems described above some object-oriented database management systems, such as ORION and GemStone, adopt a dual buffer management scheme [Kim *et al.*, 1988], in which a conventional page buffer and a separate object buffer are maintained. To access an object, the page that contains the object is brought into the page buffer. The object is then located, retrieved and placed in the object buffer. The page buffer manager performs the same functions as the buffer manager in a conventional database management system.

When an object is larger than a page it is typically broken up into sections and stored as a tree spanning several pages. A large object can be accessed and updated without the need to bring all its pages into the object buffer. The tree structure makes it possible to update portions of an object without rewriting the entire object. Since using the tree structure means that the pages of a large object need not be contiguous in secondary storage, such objects can increase or decrease in size without the need to copy the entire object.

The object buffer is essentially a workspace for transactions currently in progress. That is, unlike the page buffer the object buffer is directly accessible to transactions and the database management system supports data structures for the efficient management of objects in this buffer. The system maintains database consistency (concurrency control and crash recovery) for objects in the object buffer.

Memory management

An important issue that must be addressed by any object-oriented system is how to reclaim the memory space occupied by objects that are no longer required. This issue is certainly not unique to database applications but rather must be addressed by any programming system that permits dynamic creation of objects (e.g. conventional programming languages such as Pascal, C, Modula-2, Ada). For this reason the problems associated with this issue and the various solutions are discussed in depth by other authors (see Meyer [1988] for a particularly lucid description). We shall present here only a brief overview of the strategies typically adopted in object-oriented systems.

There are three possible strategies:

1. *Do nothing.*

   That is, allow programs to create objects as they please and simply ignore dead objects (i.e. objects that are no longer reachable) in the hope that main memory will not be exhausted. The increasing availability of very large main memory systems and the rapidly decreasing cost of memory means that this approach is not as unattractive as it may first appear. As well as a large main memory one may also have virtual memory. In a system providing virtual memory dead objects will tend to be 'paged out' to secondary storage as time proceeds, leaving more main memory for objects that are frequently referenced. Another important point to note is that in some object-oriented database environments the 'do nothing' approach may be appropriate if there are typically a large number of small, short-lived transactions running on the system rather than many long-lived transactions (such as those found in many CAD application areas). Small transactions do not create many objects in main memory and any that they do create are flushed out when the transaction terminates.

2. *Make memory reclamation the responsibility of the programmer.*

   This approach is adopted by many conventional (non-object-oriented) programming languages, which permit the dynamic creation of data objects (such as Pascal, C, PL/1 and Modula-2). That is, a procedure is provided by the language which is called when the programmer wants to dispose of an object that is no longer required, and reclaim its memory space. This approach obviously imposes a burden on the programmer which is hardly appropriate for large-scale database applications.

3. *Automatic garbage collection*

The third approach is of course to leave the responsibility of reclaiming memory from dead objects to the underlying system. In this case a garbage collector will typically only be activated whenever memory is running low. Its responsibility is to traverse the object structure in main memory and to reclaim the memory used by dead objects. The detailed mechanisms of such automatic garbage collection are beyond the scope of this book. The main issue from the point of view of a database applications programmer is whether the overheads associated with an automatic garbage collector will have a significant effect on the performance of the system.

8.3   CLUSTERING

Clustering refers to the process of grouping together related objects, whether at the conceptual level, in main memory, or in secondary storage. The primary motivation for clustering is to increase the probability that when an object is accessed by a user program, objects that it references or are related to it can be accessed quickly by virtue of being on the same or a neighbouring physical storage page. The concept of clustering has been studied from different standpoints in a number of research areas including artificial intelligence (AI), conventional database technology and object-oriented database systems.

AI research on clustering is focused at the conceptual level, and the objective of this research is to devise strategies for forming clusters of entities which can be interpreted conceptually. Simplicity is taken as the criteria for clustering [Stepp and Michalski, 1986]. That is, conceptual clustering is based on the assumption that entities should be arranged into clusters that represent simple concepts, rather than on a basis of some predefined measure of similarity. An important aspect of this research is that emphasis is placed on the role of background knowledge for constructing meaningful and useful clusters. This background knowledge consists of inference rules and heuristics. Stepp and Michalski's work is important in AI, for it was the first time the problems of classification and clustering were studied independently in the AI community, and it is important in clustering research because a sound mechanism for incorporating semantics into clustering was proposed.

In conventional database technology (i.e. relational, network and hierarchical systems), clustering is studied as a method for improving the performance of the database system, based on the observation that locality of reference is a basic feature of most transactions and queries. In this area, most clustering research has been concerned with the physical storage level, since the basic objective of clustering is to place frequently co-referenced objects near each other, both in main memory and in external storage. Physical storage units such as pages or cylinders are usually specified as the containers for clusters and the parameters of these containers specify the limits on the sizes of clusters. The specific objective of clustering is to reduce the number of I/O operations required for query processing, since I/O operations are typically expensive in comparison with the time spent on processing. The basic idea is that if related data (data which are usually co-referenced) are stored in one page or cylinder, or in a sequence of such storage units, then more useful data can be obtained from one I/O operation or one sequence of I/O operations. The transfer time as well as the search time (which is required for external storage devices) is diminished. Clustering systems can be constructed as part of a database design tool which facilitates the design of an efficient database system irrespective of the management system employed [Bell *et al.*, 1987]. This work is concerned with physical level clustering in relational databases, i.e. the storage in close proximity of tuples which are frequently co-referenced. Experimental results are presented showing the differences between clustering methods and it has been shown that a simple graph-collapse algorithm is generally the best approach. It has been shown that the problem of finding the best clustering is an NP-complete problem, so it makes no sense to try to find an algorithm which can always generate the best clustering for an arbitrary clustering base. What we should and can do is to search for algorithms which can derive a clustering strategy that is good enough for the required purpose.

An attractive feature of the research described above is that experiments have been carried out to compare alternative clustering strategies and to determine the influence of the parameters of the entities to be clustered. Few such experiments have been performed for object-oriented database systems.

8.3.1 Conceptual clustering

As described above, clustering research in database technology has been largely confined to the physical level. Recently however, some consideration has been given to *conceptual clustering*, namely the incorporation into the clustering process of semantic information. With conceptual clustering, a collection of objects having some common semantic properties are viewed at a higher level of abstraction as a single entity. Entities to be clustered may include complex objects and so the semantics to be considered include structural information and knowledge concerning the decomposition of complex objects. The storage unit for clustering, often called a *segment*, is a variable-sized group of physical pages which contains a cluster of related objects on disk. The segment is the unit of transfer from secondary storage to the object buffer. Options for clustering include the following [Hornick and Zdonik, 1987]:

- *One object per segment*: This is suitable for large objects which tend to be accessed on an individual basis and are expensive to transfer.

- *Storing an object with all its sub-objects*: This approach is appropriate for a group of closely inter-related objects that are almost always accessed together.

- *Storing all instances of a type together*: This is suitable for situations in which queries are frequently posed requiring a search of all objects of the type.

- *Clustering objects on the basis of certain property values*: This approach is similar to indexing in that it facilitates retrieval of objects that satisfy user-specified criteria. For example, all objects with property value 'red', or all objects having a property value in the range 1 to 10, might be stored together.

Thus, clustering research in the object-oriented area falls somewhere between the work in AI and that in database technology. The primary aim of object-oriented clustering research is the same as that in conventional database technology (i.e. performance enhancement) but more semantic information can be included. In practice such semantic information is most often provided in the form of 'user hints' which are specified at the time of class definition or object creation. For example, in O_2 clustering of objects depends on control information given by the database administrator [Deux *et al.*, 1990]. This information, which is called a *placement tree*, expresses the way in which a complex object and its components will be clustered together.

However, in semantically-rich applications where an object-oriented approach is appropriate, *dynamic* clustering, in which clusters adapt to changes in the content of the database, becomes more important. The CACTIS system [Hudson and King, 1990] for example, gathers statistics on traversals between objects and attempts to move objects around so that objects used together frequently are stored together. Dynamic clustering may degrade the response time of transactions that update the database but this can be offset by significant improvements of readers' response times. Thus, dynamic clustering becomes attractive in situations where reads dominate writes. However, much work remains to be done with regard to devising optimal dynamic clustering strategies for objects. In addition, since object-oriented systems provide for a more active environment than conventional database technology, external and internal storage are more tightly integrated, and buffering and clustering must be considered jointly. In the work of Chang and Katz [1989], inheritance and structural semantics are exploited to investigate improved strategies for dynamic clustering and buffering. Many parameters which influence the effectiveness of clustering are tested through extensive experiments. The main conclusion of this work is that structural relationships (i.e. IS-PART-OF relationships) and inheritance should be used as the basis for clustering, but more research is required on the physical representation of such relationships, and on the access patterns of object-oriented applications.

8.3.2   Clustering in practice

Most object-oriented database management systems provide some mechanism for clustering and it is instructive to study the different approaches. Besides a strategy for clustering and the ability to create and name clusters, some other operations are required for clustered objects:

1. *Adding objects to clusters*
   After clusters have been defined and created, objects should be added into one of the established clusters, normally at the time of creation. However, at the conceptual level, it is quite often the case that an object should be added to a cluster at a later stage. Thus, an operation is necessary for explicitly adding an object to a cluster.

2. *Object migration*
   There may be many reasons during the lifetime of a database system why an object in one cluster should be moved to another and it is obvious that migration is essential if dynamic clustering is employed. The main difficulty with object migration is ensuring the consistency of references to the migrating object.

3. *Reclustering*
   The most likely reason for reclustering is that some significant changes take place in the criteria used for clustering. It is possible that the changes can be incorporated satisfactorily by objects migrating among clusters, but it might still be the case that some splitting or merging of clusters, or even complete re-clustering is required.

Most of the object-oriented database management systems whose implementations have been reported in the literature employ a static clustering strategy in which the user controls the placement of an object at the time of creation. None of the systems as yet take advantage of structural or inheritance semantics for automatic clustering. Nor do they permit reclustering when object structures change.

The Encore/Observer system [Hornick and Zdonik, 1987] provides the user with a visible unit of clustering called the segment into which user programs explicitly place objects according to whatever criteria the user desires. When one object in the segment is retrieved, the entire segment is loaded into the object buffer. GemStone [Maier and Stein, 1987] also provides for logical groupings of objects called segments which are visible from within its associated programming language (OPAL) through the class *Segment*. Users can control placement of objects within segments. In Vbase [Andrews and Harris, 1987] segments are once again the unit for clustering, and the unit of transfer from and to secondary storage. Every create operation allows the user to specify a previously-existing clustering object. The new object is then clustered in the same segment as the specified clustering object.

In ODE [Agrawal and Gehani, 1989] a different approach is adopted, in that clusters are *type extents*. That is, all persistent objects of the same type are grouped together into a cluster which must be explicitly created by means of the create macro:

```
int create (<type name>) ;
```

Additional control over clustering can be effected by means of *subclusters*. Subclusters can be used to partition a cluster into groups according to the property values of objects. For example, we might wish to partition an employee cluster into groups corresponding to the department in which they work. This can be performed by the following code:

```
create (employee :: "Computer Science") ;
create (employee :: "Mathematics") ;
...
```

Employee objects are specified as belonging to a particular subcluster when they are allocated in persistent store. For example, to allocate a new employee object to the Computer Science subcluster we may write:

```
emp = pnew employee ("John Smith") :: "Computer Science" ;
```

The query language in ODE provides constructs for iterating over clusters and subclusters as described in Chapter 5.

8.4 VERSIONING

Many database applications require the capability to create and access multiple versions of an object. Examples of this are to be found in historical databases, such as those used widely in business and commerce for maintaining multiple versions of legal or financial documents. Other important uses of versioning are to be found in databases underlying tools for Computer Aided Software Engineering (CASE), and computer-aided design (CAD). It is widely recognized that version control is one of the most important functions in environments in which users need to generate and experiment with multiple versions of an object before selecting one that satisfies their needs. The issue of versioning in engineering design (e.g. CAD) applications has been studied by several authors [Attwood, 1985; Chou and Kim, 1986; Katz *et al.*, 1986]. The basic requirements of a system that supports versioning are:

- Versioning is applied to objects, not classes (although in a system such as Smalltalk in which classes may be viewed as objects, classes might also have versions).
- All persistent objects can have versions and there should (in theory) be no predefined limit on the number of versions an object should have.
- Applications should be able to access either the current version (which should be the default) or any specified version. Only the current version of an object can be updated. Access to older versions should normally be read-only.

Versioning has been implemented in a number of object-oriented database systems, including ORION [Banerjee *et al.*, 1987] and ODE [Agrawal Gehani, 1989]. Some of the basic techniques used in these implementations are described in the following subsections.

8.4.1 Versioning in ORION

The object-oriented database system ORION distinguishes between two types of versions depending on the types of operations that are allowed on them. They call these *transient* versions and *working* versions. A transient version has the following characteristics:

(i) It can be updated or deleted by the user who created it.

(ii) A new transient version can be derived from an existing transient version. The existing transient version then becomes a working version.

The promotion of a transient version to a working version may be explicit (i.e. specified by the user), or implicit (determined by the underlying system).

A working version is characterized by the fact that it cannot be updated, but may be deleted by the user who created it. Since it cannot be updated a working version is considered stable. Transient versions may be derived from it if updating is necessary.

We must *bind* an object to its versions in the same way that we have to bind an object to its class definition. The issues of static and dynamic binding were discussed in detail in Chapter 2 with regard to instances and types, and similar approaches may be adopted with versions. In static binding of versions, any reference to an object instance must include the object identifier and the version number. In dynamic binding any reference to an object needs to specify only the object identifier and the system assumes responsibility for selecting the appropriate version number at run-time. Clearly, dynamic binding has the advantage that new versions of an object may be created without the need to alter references to that object. In most implementations which incorporate dynamic binding the version that is selected by default is the *most recent* version. ORION adopts a more elaborate scheme in which the user may select as the default version, any particular version from the version derivation hierarchy. In the absence of such a selection, the system will select that version which has the most recent timestamp.

In order to facilitate the implementation of versions, ORION requires application systems to identify those classes that are *versionable*, i.e. those classes whose objects may have versions. When an instance of a version-able class is generated a generic object for that instance is created and the instance is designated as the first version. The generic object acts as a template for the version-derivation hierarchy and consists of the following system-specified properties:

(i)   the object identifier;

(ii)   the default version number;

(iii)   the next version number in the hierarchy;

(iv)   a version count; and

(v)   a set of version descriptors, one for each version on the version-derivation hierarchy.

The object identifier and the default version number are used in dynamic binding to determine which version is to be selected when a reference is made to the object. The next version number field is used to hold the version number that is to be assigned to the next version that is created. It is updated after each creation of a version. The version descriptors include the following information:

(i)   the object identifier;

(ii)   the version number of that version;

(iii)   the version number of its parent (i.e. the version from which it was generated);

Versions are managed and manipulated in ORION by a series of special commands:

* *Create*
  A versionable object is created initially by the *create* command which generates the appropriate generic object data structure for the object.

* *Derive*
  A *derive* command is used to generate a new transient version, and in the process allocate a new version number for it. If the parent is a transient version it is automatically converted into a working version.

* *Replace*
  The *replace* operation causes the contents of a transient version to be replaced by a working copy specified by the user.

* *Promote*
  A transient object may be explicitly promoted to a working version by the user via the *promote* command.

* *Delete*
  The user may *delete* a specified version or the entire version hierarchy with the delete command. If the argument specified in the delete operation is a generic object (which has its own object identifier) then every version of the instance related to that generic object is deleted.

* *Set_default*
  The user calls the *set_default* operation to specify the default version from the version derivation hierarchy. The parameter here may be a specific version number or the keyword *most_recent*.

8.4.2   Versioning in ODE

ODE adopts a fairly simple approach to versioning in which references to an object can be associated with its current version or with any specified previous version. In ODE an object and all its versions are regarded as one logical object with one object identifier (oop). By default the oop for an object refers to the current version. Therefore, when an object is updated and a new version created there is no necessity to update references to that object. To refer to a specific version, the applications programmer must use *version pointers* (i.e. pointers to versions of persistent objects). Version pointers are declared in ODE using a clause of the following form:

```
persistent vers <class name> *<variable name>
```

For example, the following version pointer definition

```
persistent vers document *vp
```

defines vp to be a version pointer that points to persistent objects of type document. Updating an updating does not automatically create a new version (this is desirable since an update may be a correction or amendment and the user may not always wish to retain the older, incorrect version). Thus, a new version must be explicitly created by a call to the macro:

```
newversion (<object identifier>)
```

As already indicated, following such a call the object identifier refers to the new version. Earlier versions are accessed using the macro previous which takes as its arguments a pointer to a persistent object and a non-negative integer n, and returns the nth previous version. If there is no such version, then the null pointer is returned. As an example, the following segment of code (taken from Agrawal and Gehani [1989]) computes the total salary of an employee over the past five years:

```
persistent Employee *e;
persistent vers Employee *ve;
...
for ( i = 0; i < 5; i++)
        if ((ve = previous (e, i)  == NULL)
        error("%s has not been with the company for 5 years\n", e–>name);
        total += ve –> salary;
}
```

8.5   SUMMARY

This chapter covers some of the major issues in object-oriented database implementation, namely object storage, clustering and versioning. The efficient storage and retrieval of complex objects on secondary storage presents some challenging problems which have yet to be completely solved. Only through the use of efficient storage strategies coupled with appropriate indexing and clustering strategies will object-oriented systems achieve a level of performance acceptable in commercial and industrial environments.

8.6   BIBLIOGRAPHIC NOTES

The papers by Kim *et al.* [1990], Stonebraker *et al.* [1990], Wilkinson *et al.* [1990], and Deux *et al.* [1990] (which are all published in a special issue of *IEEE Transactions on Knowledge and Data Engineering*) contain descriptions of many of the implementation issues associated with specific object-oriented database systems.

A very lucid description of conceptual clustering is provided by Stepp and Michalski [1986]. Implementation aspects of clustering in conventional databases are discussed in Bell *et al.* [1987].

The issue of versioning in engineering design applications (e.g. CAD) has been studied by several authors [Attwood, 1985; Chou and Kim, 1986; Katz *et al.*, 1986]. A comprehensive description of versioning in object-oriented systems is provided by Banerjee *et al.* [1987] in relation to the ORION system.

9

Object-oriented knowledge bases

9.1   INTRODUCTION

As databases and data models have evolved over the past decade there has been a steady, but slow movement towards the development of 'intelligent' databases. Such databases manage information in a natural and user-friendly way, making the information easy to store, access and use. They encompass not merely the traditional commercial data processing applications of databases, but applications such as knowledge based systems, CAD/CAM and image processing applications. There are a number of aspects of intelligent databases where object-oriented data modelling techniques are beginning to make a significant impact. One of the most important of these is the area of knowledge representation and manipulation.

The problems encountered in artificial intelligence (AI) are typically 'difficult problems'. In order to solve these problems, mechanisms must be provided to represent and to reason with knowledge at a high level of abstraction. Many methods have been proposed in the literature, from many different viewpoints and the area is still the subject of considerable research. The role of the object-oriented model has not yet been fully investigated but there is little doubt that it offers considerable promise for the future.

In this chapter we examine the subject of knowledge based systems from an object-oriented point of view. The advantages of the object-oriented approach to structured knowledge representation are investigated. and facilities offered by some existing systems are described. However, it must be borne in mind that applications of AI in real-world situations are considerably less mature than those of database technology. The primary purpose of the chapter is to draw the reader's attention to some aspects of current research in object-oriented knowledge based systems and to some of the issues still to be resolved.

9.2 KNOWLEDGE REPRESENTATION SCHEMES

Database systems can be thought of as large collections of complex, inter-related data structures that are organized for the primary purpose of providing efficient retrieval of information. The data objects represent typically, explicit factual information about the real-world application. A small number of *rules* may be incorporated into a database system, for example in the form of integrity constraints, but in general there is no provision for the *explicit* storage of rules concerning the application. As a simple example, consider a database which records information on a group of school children and their hobbies. In a relational model we might use a binary relation of the following form to represent the relationship between the entities child and hobby:

> *likes (child, hobby)*

A tuple $<c, h>$ in this relation records the explicit fact that child c likes hobby h. However, suppose we wish to record in the database a general rule such as

> *All boys like football*

or

> *If a child likes tennis then he/she also likes badminton*

Conventional database technology, whether relational or object-oriented, provides no facilities explicitly to record such general information. The fact that all boys like football would have to be recorded in a relational database by storing a separate tuple $<b, \text{football}>$ for all boys b in the database. If a new boy is inserted into the database a new tuple must be added to the *likes* relation to record the fact that he likes football. We may be able to enforce this using a triggered procedure or an integrity rule if the system permits. The second rule would require us to ensure that every time a tuple of the form $<c, \text{tennis}>$ was inserted into the *likes* relation, a tuple of the form $<c, \text{badminton}>$ was also inserted.

Knowledge bases allow for the *explicit* storage of rule-based information, and have an associated processing facility or *inference engine*, that can manipulate and interpret this information. For example the rule that *all boys like football* may be expressed in first order predicate calculus as

> $\forall x \, \{male(x) \implies likes \, (x, football)\}$

which states that, for all x, if x is male then x likes football. Using the same notation, the second rule above may be written in the form,

> *likes (x, tennis)* $\implies$ *likes (x, badminton)*

In the knowledge base approach a rule may be expressed in a single state-ment, rather than as multiple facts, and is in a form that is understandable and easily modified if necessary. Simple facts can of course also be added to a knowledge base, such as

> *male(john)*
> *female(mary)*
> *likes (john, baseball)*
> *likes (mary, tennis)*

A crucial difference between rules and the 'if-then-else' statements found in many conventional programming languages is that in a knowledge based system rules may be combined dynamically together into chains. This is done by the inference engine matching the premise of one rule to the con-clusion of another rule or matching the conclusion of one rule to the premise of another. There are two ways in which the inference engine may do this. In *backward chaining* (also called goal-driven reasoning) it attempts to establish the conclusion of a rule (a goal) by checking if the conditions of the rule can be established by facts within the system or by triggering other rules. In *forward chaining* (also called data-driven reason-ing) the inference engine starts with a set of facts and matches these to the conditions of a rule. If the conditions are satisfied then the conclusion of the rule is added to the knowledge base and may be used to prove other rules.

The knowledge based approach is best suited to applications in which it is required to capture the problem-solving expertise of a human being in a small, well-defined area (the *problem domain*), and where conventional algorithmic methods are inadequate for finding the best solution. In build-ing a knowledge base, one must select the significant objects and relations in the problem domain and transform these into a formal knowledge repre-sentation language. Over the years, numerous knowledge representation schemes have been proposed and implemented. These may be classified into the following categories [Mylopoulos and Levesque, 1984]:

1. *Logical knowledge representation schemes*

   In this scheme the knowledge base is represented by expressions in formal logic. Inference rules apply this knowledge to the solution of specific problems. The most commonly used logical representation scheme is first-order predicate calculus. The programming language Prolog is based on this calculus and is widely employed for imple-menting knowledge bases using logical representation schemes.

2. *Network knowledge representation schemes*

   Network schemes represent knowledge by a graph in which the nodes represent objects or concepts from the problem domain and the arcs represent relations between them. Semantic networks are an example of a commonly used network representation scheme.

3. *Procedural knowledge representation schemes*

Procedural schemes represent knowledge in the form of procedures or sets of instructions for solving specific problems. Such schemes view a knowledge base as a collection of active agents or processes. Most procedural schemes have been heavily influenced by Lisp. Production systems are examples of procedural schemes in which the knowledge base is a collection of production rules and a global database. Procedural schemes have the advantage of allowing the specification of direct interactions between facts, thereby eliminating the need for time-consuming searching. On the other hand, a procedural knowledge base, such as a large Lisp program can be difficult to understand and to modify.

4. *Structured knowledge representation schemes*

The contribution of structured representation schemes was to enhance network schemes by allowing nodes to be complex data structures consisting of named *slots* with attached values. These values may be simple data values, pointers to other complex structures or possibly procedures for executing some particular task. Frame-based knowledge representation schemes are typical of the structured approach. Not surprisingly, the object-oriented approach to knowledge representation and manipulation is closely related to frames.

The major advantages of logic representations are that they are capable of representing many different kinds of knowledge. They provide simple, but powerful reasoning mechanisms and thus offer a natural way to represent and reason with knowledge. All of these properties are desirable for a knowledge based system. However, logic representations also have some severe disadvantages. First, the structures for representing knowledge in logic systems are too small. Second, they lack the flexibility to represent changes in the problem domains, especially dynamic or nonmonotonic changes. Third, it is very difficult to incorporate additional control information in these representations and so the straightforward, uniform reasoning approaches tend to lead to combinatorial explosion when the knowledge base is large.

Of course, there are no restrictions in logic methods that prohibit the use of highly-structured, complex objects. However, in most logic systems it is very difficult to deal with complex problems in which it is necessary to adapt dynamically in order to respond to new information. The fault is not due to logic methods intrinsically, but to the way in which the representations of knowledge are constructed in logic-based systems, i.e. separating structural information on objects from behavioural information about how those objects act and how they interact with others. These disadvantages exclude logic from being a practical method for representing complex problems.

At the present time however, such disadvantages are present to different degrees in each of the knowledge representation methods outlined above. With the object-oriented approach on the other hand, knowledge can be handled at a high level of abstraction with the result that a number of significant advantages accrue. First, with the facilities of encapsulation and inheritance, representations can be constructed at different levels of abstraction. At the higher level, the objects can encapsulate very complex behaviour and the details are transparent to the representation at that level. Second, related information is structured and kept together, allowing changes in a problem situation to be easily transmitted to the representation. Third, by the very nature of the object-oriented approach, there is no distinction between the objects and their behaviour, so flexibility of control can be achieved.

The object-oriented approach to knowledge representation and manipulation has evolved from the structured approaches described above. For this reason we shall concentrate our attention on these structured techniques in the following sections.

9.3   STRUCTURED KNOWLEDGE REPRESENTATION

9.3.1   Semantic networks

As in database applications, many problem domains in artificial intelligence are concerned with large amounts of highly structured inter-related knowledge. To represent this knowledge adequately it is not sufficient simply to describe objects by listing their component parts; a valid description must include information on the roles played by those component parts, the way in which they are combined to make up the object, and the interactions that take place among them. This *semantic* information is essential to a wide range of situations involving taxonomic information such as the relationships among members of a family tree, the classification of species of plants or animals, or the description of a complex object in terms of its component parts. While all such information can be represented by collections of facts and rules, some higher level concept of structure is desirable when dealing with complex situations.

As a simple example, suppose we are required to represent the following information:

A whale is a large fish-eating mammal living in the ocean, and a mammal is a warm-blooded vertebrate.

(Actually many whales eat crustaceans or cephalopods but this is a simplified example.) This information could be represented by a collection of predicates:

size (whale, large)
eats (whale, fish)
isa (whale, mammal)
habitat (whale, ocean)
blood (mammal, warm-blooded)
isa (mammal, vertebrate)

The same information can also be represented schematically in a *semantic network*, as shown in Figure 9.1. In such a network the nodes represent data objects or concepts and their interrelationships are denoted by arcs. A system which is required to reason over this information deduces associations by following the arcs.

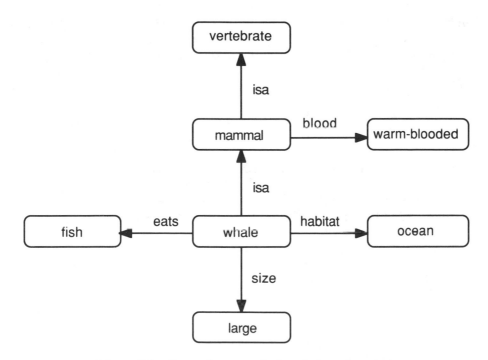

Figure 9.1   Semantic network description of a whale

In order to deduce that a whale is a vertebrate, it is necessary to follow the two arcs labelled *isa* in the network. In the representation above involving a collection of predicates, it would be necessary to search the database of predicates of the form *isa(X, Y)* in order to deduce the same information. The two representations, i.e. logical predicates and semantic networks, are reminiscent of the relational and network data models, and have similar associated advantages and disadvantages. An important advantage of the semantic network approach, however, is that it incorporates the notion of inheritance. That is, an object which is related to a higher level object via an *isa* relationship can inherit the properties of that object. This affords us the advantage of being able to represent knowledge at the highest level of abstraction, and helps to maintain the consistency of the knowledge base when adding new objects or concepts.

9.3.2   Frame-based knowledge representation

Using semantic networks we represent knowledge using explicit links to represent the associations among objects. As in network databases, this approach is somewhat inflexible and can lead to considerable complexity when the knowledge base is large. Thus the arguments for additional structure in knowledge representation schemes are very similar to those used throughout this text for justifying the object-oriented approach to data management over conventional record-based techniques, as epitomized by the network and relational models. The notion of a frame in artificial intelligence goes some way towards providing additional structure for knowledge representation.

Minsky describes the essence of frame theory as follows [Minsky, 1975]:

> *When one encounters a new situation (or makes a substantial change in one's view of a problem) one selects from memory a structure called a 'frame'. This is a remembered framework to be adapted to fit reality by changing details as necessary.*

Thus, in artificial intelligence frames are *static* data structures used to represent well-understood situations which have been encountered in past experiences. They provide a framework for representing *new* situations in that existing frame structures may be adapted to incorporate the individual characteristics of an environment which is similar to, but different from, a situation encountered in the past.

For example, when one encounters a new model of a car it is not an entirely new experience. One expects a car to have a bodywork, wheels, an engine, doors, etc. The specific details of the new model are added to this existing framework in our minds: colour and shape of bodywork, size of engine, number of doors and so on. That is, we do not have to start from scratch when we are faced with the situation of assimilating the details of a new model of car. Rather we have a generic structure for a car in our minds, and this structure may be adapted and extended when the details associated with an individual car are supplied.

Thus a frame represents a generic physical object or concept about which we have some knowledge, and that knowledge has some underlying structure. A frame consists of named slots with attached values or facts. For example, consider a company car about which we wish to store information on its use, size, number of doors, engine and service record. Figure 9.2 shows how such information might be represented in a frame-based approach. A company car is a specialization of the generic object car. Some of the values incorporated in the frame represent default assumptions about company cars: for example, size is assumed to be medium and the number of doors to be four. Specific instances of company cars may or may not have these values.

FRAME COMPANY CAR

superclass	car
use	business
size	medium
doors	4
engine	(frame car engine)
service	Major services at 12000 mile intervals Interim service at 6000 mile intervals Fluid renewal at 2 year intervals etc.

Figure 9.2 Frame-based representation of a company car

FRAME CAR ENGINE

superclass	engine
capacity	1.8
cylinders	4
fuel	unleaded

Figure 9.3   Frame-based representation of car engine

Note that slot values may be:

*   a simple data value or a set of values;
*   pointers to other frames, representing the fact that a relationship exists between frames. For example, a company car has a car engine - the car engine may be regarded as a separate frame which in turn could inherit the properties of a generic frame engine, illustrated in Figure 9.3.
*   procedural representations of knowledge, such as servicing the car.

Semantic integrity may be provided for in the frame-based approach by allowing slots to have subcomponents or *facets* into which one may place additional information concerning the slot value such as type specifications, constraints or *demons*. Demons are analogous to triggered procedures as discussed in Chapter 3. That is, they are procedures which are automatically activated when some specified condition becomes true. They are useful for consistency checking and for simulation (e.g. reacting to user-interface devices such as push buttons and switches). Typical demons found in frame-based systems are:

*   *on-insertion do <action>*:   Activated whenever a new value is added to the slot
*   *on-modification do <action>*:   Activated whenever a value in a slot is modified
*   *on-deletion do <action>*:   Activated whenever the value for a slot is deleted

These demons cannot be activated directly by the user but rather are automatically invoked by the system when the specified operations are carried out on slot values.

Figure 9.4 illustrates the kinds of facets that may be incorporated into the frame for company car.

FRAME COMPANY CAR

superclass	car
slot default value minimum number of values maximum number of values type	use business 1 3 (business, pleasure, sport)
slot default value minimum number of values maximum number of values type	size medium 1 1 (compact, medium, large)
slot default value: minimum number of values maximum number of values type	doors 4 1 1 2..5
slot minimum number of values maximum number of values instance of	engine 1 1 (frame car engine)
slot demon	service on-insertion, on-modification do check-service-schedule

Figure 9.4   Frame for company car, with facets.

The slots use, size, doors, engine and service have multiple facets. These facets are bound to the frame and apply to each instance of the frame that is created or modified. Typical facets include minimum and maximum cardinalities, default values, explicit type specifications and demons to be performed in some specified circumstances. Thus the facets for the slot use restrict its value to the values business or pleasure, or both, with a default value of business. The facets for the slot size restrict its value to exactly one of (compact, medium, large) with a default value of medium. The number of doors is restricted to one value in the range 2..5, while the engine slot references exactly one instance of the frame car engine.

The slot service has a demon which checks the service schedule whenever a new service record is entered, or the existing record is modified. This illustrates an important function of demons, namely consistency checking when an instance is created or modified; other uses include the implementation of side effects on other objects in the knowledge base.

9.4   OBJECT-ORIENTED APPROACHES

Although frame-based knowledge representation schemes provide ways of attaching procedural information to slots, they offer no specific facilities for declaratively describing the behaviour of the object represented by the frame structure. Thus, frames are *passive* data structures, which may be manipulated by procedures which are external to their structure. These procedures must be retrieved and invoked by some agent other than the frame. This signifies an important difference between frames and the objects in object-oriented systems, which encapsulate both state and behaviour and execute operations in direct response to messages received. That is, the objects are themselves active in the sense that the operations or methods are bound to the object itself, rather than existing as separate procedures for the manipulation of the data structure.

There is little doubt that knowledge representation and manipulation are the core problems in artificial intelligence. Thus, the concepts underlying the object-oriented paradigm, which permit the construction of objects with complex structure and behaviour, should have significant application potential in AI. To quote Minsky [Minsky, 1975]:

> *'... the ingredients of most theories (in artificial intelligence) have been on the whole too minute, local, and unstructured to account for sense or thought. The 'chunks' of reasoning, language, memory, and perception ought to be larger and more structured, and their factual and procedural contents must be more intimately connected in order to explain the apparent power and speed of mental activities.'*

Actually, one might expect to read such statements in the object-oriented literature as well. It seems that when he wrote these words the picture of the 'chunks' in Minsky's mind was not very clear. His theory of chunks revolved around frames and he was disappointed to note that the the theory had many deficiencies. However the object concept provides a more suitable theory. Intuitively we know that the 'chunks' might be objects, or, at least, should be very similar to objects.

There have been several attempts to provide object-oriented programming environments for AI, most notably FLAVORS [Moon, 1986], Common LOOPS [Bobrow *et al.*, 1983] and KEE (Knowledge Engineering Environment™) [Fikes and Kaehler, 1985]. In the following sections, we describe some aspects of FLAVORS, an extended AI programming language, and KEE, which is a sophisticated environment for knowledge based systems development. Our intention is to illustrate that many aspects of object-oriented programming offer desirable facilities in AI application areas.

9.4.1   Object-oriented programming in FLAVORS

All of the languages that we studied in previous chapters were either imperative (e.g. C++, Eiffel) or based on a message-passing system (Smalltalk). However, it is possible to design an object-oriented language which is applicative, i.e. based on the application of functions. The advantage of this approach is that the semantics of applicative languages are much better understood than those of imperative languages, and can be modelled more precisely in mathematical terms. In addition, it has been shown that object-oriented features are natural extensions of applicative languages, and within this context do not require the implementation of message-passing primitives. Perhaps the best known example of an applicative language is Lisp [McCarthy, 1960], and in recent years there have been a number of attempts to make Lisp object-oriented.

One such system is FLAVORS [Moon, 1986], which may be described as an object-oriented extension to Lisp designed for applications in artificial intelligence. FLAVORS is widely available for Lisp environments and has played an important role in AI implementations. Other Lisp-based object-oriented languages include OakLisp [Lang and Pearlmutter, 1986] and Common LOOPS [Bobrow *et al.*, 1986]. The Common Lisp Object System (CLOS) represents an attempt to provide a standard object-oriented system for Common Lisp (for a description of CLOS see for example, Hasemer and Domingue [1989]).

In the FLAVORS system new classes, which are called *flavors*, are created via the defflavor function. The terminology closely mirrors that of

Smalltalk: generic operations are called *messages*, and an object reacts to a message according to its *method* for that message.

To illustrate the basic principles, suppose we are required to implement using FLAVORS, the hierarchy shown in Figure 9.5 which contains a class student, a subclass graduate_student and an instance of graduate_student (Paul).

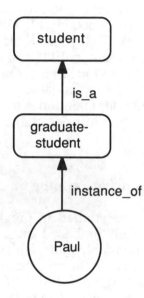

Figure 9.5 A simple hierarchy

Suppose that we wish to associate the following information with the classes and instance defined in this hierarchy:

* Each student has a property entryyear, giving the year of entry to the university;
* The level of a student may be computed by subtracting the value of entryyear from the value of the current year;
* Graduate students are distinguished by the fact that the property status has the value graduate;
* Paul is a graduate student whose year of entry was 1984.

We define a flavor for student in the following way:

```
(defflavor student (entryyear) ( ) )
```

The first argument to defflavor is student, the name of the flavor. The second argument is a list of properties (or *instance variables* in Smalltalk parlance) whose values define the state of instances of the flavor. Finally we define a list of superclasses for the flavor (FLAVORS permits multiple inheritance). For the case of the student flavor, this list is empty. A method to compute the level of a student, given the current year, can be defined as follows:

```
(defmethod (student :level) (currentyear)
     (- currentyear entryyear))
```

The definition of the flavor for graduatestudent takes the following form:

```
(defflavor graduatestudent ((status 'graduate'))
     (student)
     :gettable-instance-variables)
```

In this definition there is one property, namely status, which has the value graduate for all instances of this flavor. In this case the third argument is not empty but contains the name of the superclass for this flavor, student. The optional argument, :gettable-instance-variables, means that a method will be automatically generated by the system to retrieve the value of the instance variable status. Instances of a flavor are generated via the make-instance function. Thus, to create a new instance of graduatestudent and bind a variable Paul to this instance, requires the following code:

```
(setq Paul (make-instance 'graduatestudent : entryyear 1984))
     -> #<graduatestudent 192837465>
```

This new object is an instance of graduatestudent and will automatically inherit the properties and methods associated with the class person. The property entryyear, inherited from person, is initialized to the value 1984 at the time of creation. The object Paul also inherits from person a method to evaluate level. Sending an appropriate message to Paul will activate that method:

```
(send Paul :level 1990)
     -> 6
```

The presence of the option :gettable-instance-variables in the definition of graduatestudent means that we can also send the message :status to Paul:

```
(send Paul : level)
     -> graduate
```

9.4.2   Knowledge Engineering Environment™

Developed by Intellicorp Inc., KEE [Fikes and Kaehler, 1985] is a hybrid system incorporating a wide range of AI problem-solving techniques including functional programming, frames, rules and explanation facilities. The object-oriented programming facilities in the system are in the message-passing style of Smalltalk but the system is built upon the programming language Lisp. It includes a sophisticated graphical user-interface that facilitates the knowledge base development process.

The basic building block within the KEE environment is the *Unit*, which is roughly comparable to the concept of a class. A KEE unit can inherit properties and methods from units at higher levels, permitting multiple inheritance paths.

Like a frame, a KEE Unit consists of slots which store the attributes of the unit. Slots may contain simple numerical or textual data, but they can also store complex data structures such as tables or graphs. They can also store rules and, very importantly, methods. Each slot has its own attributes, called facets. As described previously, facets may contain additional information concerning the slot value, such as type specifications, constraints or demons. An important use for facets in KEE is the control of inheritance. Facets provide a mechanism for establishing the inheritance rules that govern the manner in which a property or method is derived from the multiple ancestors of a unit.

The methods within the slots of a unit are written in Lisp and these methods are initiated on receipt of a message. Units may send and receive messages and a message can be sent through the mouse-driven menu interface of KEE or from within a program. The value of a method slot in a unit must either be a function name or an actual piece of Lisp code (called a *lambda body* in KEE terminology). Methods may have any number of arguments.

Like any other type of slot, method slots may be inherited down a unit hierarchy. Inherited method slots can have inherited values or can be over-written by local values. This means that different units in a hierarchy can respond in their own way to the same message, an important advantage of the object-oriented style of programming. The value of an inherited method can be changed locally either by completely replacing the inherited value with a new one, or by adding so-called *wrapper code* to the inherited method. When adding wrapper code the inherited method acts as a core. The programmer can add a *before wrapper*, which is code to be executed before the core is executed, or an *after wrapper*, which is executed after the core.

An interesting recent addition to the KEE suite of utilities is KEE CONNECTION™ which provides a software bridge between SQL-compatible relational database management systems and knowledge bases developed within the KEE environment. Under the control of the application developer, this product will extract data from the database and transform the data into slot values within KEE Units. While this facility is very useful for many practical applications, the mechanism has all the disadvantages, described in previous chapters, which arise due to the 'impedance mismatch' between the programming environment (KEE) and the database system. The ideal solution of course is a fully integrated object-oriented knowledge based management system which is capable of handling efficiently large volumes of persistent complex objects on secondary storage.

9.4.3   Other applications of object-oriented techniques in AI

We finish this section with a brief look at some other potential applications of object-oriented techniques in artificial intelligence. We mention two specific areas, namely *evidential reasoning* and *explanation*. Both of these research areas are still in their infancy but we believe that object-oriented techniques will play an important role in their future development.

Evidential reasoning
Reasoning, as a mechanism for manipulating knowledge, is typically very complicated. Some aspects of reasoning are well understood (e.g. in mathematical logic) but other aspects are still the subject of intensive research (e.g. nonmonotonic reasoning, probability, uncertainty, inductive reasoning, etc.). Imprecision, uncertainty and probability are very important aspects of reasoning both in human beings and in knowledge based systems. Many mechanisms have been proposed in the literature for incorporating these factors into reasoning, but in real knowledge based systems, the mechanisms are greatly simplified to ease implementation. Usually, some kind of 'belief of conjecture' is stored with the rules, and the evidence accumulation process proceeds in parallel with the reasoning process. This mechanism has three faults. First, it complicates the reasoning process since evidence accumulation tends to frustrate the main line of the reasoning. Second, it makes a full and efficient implementation of the reasoning mechanism extremely difficult. Third, the result generated by the system is imprecise whereas a precise decision is normally required.

The faults mentioned above could be resolved by noting that inference and evidence accumulation are different, though interrelated, aspects of reasoning and belong to different levels. The evidence accumulation is really a level underlying the inference mechanisms. With object-oriented techniques, we can separate these different levels of concern but retain their inter-relationships.

Explanation

Most knowledge based systems need intermediate interaction with human beings. The motivation for interaction can be viewed from two different aspects. For complex problems, additional information during processing is desirable because users can often provide some heuristic information to benefit the performance of the knowledge based system. More importantly, users can provide some complementary knowledge when needed in cases where the built-in knowledge is incomplete. For a complex problem such lack of knowledge will almost certainly arise. From another point of view, users will not be willing to accept the solution to a complex problem without knowing something about the behaviour of the system, i.e. knowing something about how the system achieved the result. Thus the ability of knowledge based systems to explain their reasoning is essential.

In order for an knowledge based system to explain its own behaviour to human users, some mechanisms must be provided which allow the system to keep historical information and to express that information in a way which can be easily understood by users. The techniques provided in object-oriented programming offer a basis for all of these requirements. Knowledge representation with objects is natural and easy to human beings. In addition, with the persistence property of objects, a continuous and consistent notion of identity throughout the lifetime of an object is provided. A temporal model can be formed in which one can preserve the history of objects as 'versions', and this can provide a convenient way to preserve and retrieve historical information about the behaviour of the system.

9.5   SUMMARY

In this chapter we examine the application of object-oriented techniques to the design and development of knowledge based systems. The advantages of the object-oriented approach to structured knowledge representation are demonstrated and the facilities offered by some existing systems are described.

It is shown that although frame-based knowledge representation schemes provide ways of attaching procedural information to slots, they offer no specific facilities for declaratively describing the behaviour of the object represented by the frame structure. Thus, frames are *passive* data structures, which may be manipulated by procedures which are external to their structure. These procedures must be retrieved and invoked by some agent other than the frame. This signifies an important difference between frames and the objects in object-oriented systems, which encapsulate both state and behaviour and execute operations in direct response to messages received. That is, the objects are themselves active in the sense that the operations or methods are bound to the object itself, rather than existing as separate procedures for the manipulation of the data structure.

Finally, we draw the reader's attention to some aspects of current research in object-oriented knowledge based systems and to some of the important issues still to be resolved.

9.6   BIBLIOGRAPHIC NOTES

The relationship between logic programming and databases is explored in Gray [1984]. A good overview of knowledge representation is given by Mylopoulos and Levesque [1984]. There are a number of commercial expert system shells and knowledge based development systems that include object-oriented programming techniques as part of a hybrid environment. Some of these are reviewed in Harmon *et al.* [1988]. The book by Luger and Stubblefield [1989] provides a good introduction to artificial intelligence and knowledge based systems and includes a section on object-oriented techniques. The paper by Stefik and Bobrow [1986] is a good overview of the application of object-oriented programming in artificial intelligence.

References

Abiteboul, S. and Bidoit, N. [1984] Non First Normal Form Relations to Represent Hierarchically Organized Data, *Proc. ACM Symp. on Principles of Database Systems*, Waterloo, Canada.

Abiteboul, S. and Bitoit, N. [1986] Non First Normal Form Relations: An Algebra Allowing Data Restructuring, *J. of Computer and System Sciences*, **33**, 361–393.

Abrial, J.R. [1974] Data Semantics, in *Data Base Management* (eds J.W. Klimbie and K.L. Koffeman), North–Holland Publishing Co., New York.

Agha, G. [1986] *Actors: A Model of Concurrent Computation in Distributed Systems*, MIT Press, Cambridge, MA.

Agrawal, R. and Gehani, N. [1989] ODE: The Language and the Data Model, *Proc. ACM SIGMOD Conf. on the Management of Data*, Portland, OR.

Albano, A., Cardelli, L. and Orsini, R. [1985] Galileo: A Strongly-Typed Interactive Conceptual Language, *ACM Trans. on Database Systems* **10**, 230–260

Amble, T., Bratbergsengen, K. and Risnes, O. [1976] ASTRAL: A Structured and Unified Approach to Database Design and Manipulation, *Proc. Database Architecture Conference Venice*, 257–274.

Andrews, T. and Harris, C. [1987] Combining Language and Database Advances in an Object-Oriented Database Environment, *Proc. ACM Conf. Object-Oriented Programming Systems, Languages and Applications (OOPSLA)*, Orlando, FL.

Atkinson, M. and Buneman, O.P. [1987] Types and Persistence in Database Programming Languages, *ACM Computing Surveys* **19**, No. 2.

Atkinson, M.P. and Kulkarni, K.G. [1984] Experimenting with the Functional Data Model, in *Databases: Role and Structure* (ed. P.M. Stocker), Cambridge University Press.

Atkinson, M.P., Bailey, P.J., Chisholm, K.J., Cockshott, W.P. and Morrison, R. [1983] An Approach to Persistent Programming, *Computer J.* **26**, No. 4.

Attwood, T. [1985] An Object-Oriented DBMS for Design Support Applications, *Proc. IEEE COMPINT Conf.*, Montreal, Canada.

Bailin, S.C. [1989] An Object-Oriented Requirements Specification Method, *Comm. ACM* **32**, No. 5, 608–623.

Bancilhon, F. *et al.* [1986] The Design and Implementation of O_2, an Object-Oriented Database System, *Proc. 2nd Int'l Workshop on Object-Oriented Databases* (ed. K. Dittrich), Springer–Verlag Lecture Notes in Computer Science **334**.

Bancilhon, F., Briggs, T., Khoshafian, S.N. and Valduriez, P. [1987] FAD, A Powerful and Simple Database Language, *Proc. XIII Int'l Conf. Very Large Data Bases*, Brighton, England.

Banerjee, J., Chou, H.–T., Garza, J., Kim, W., Woelk, D., Ballou, N. and Kim, H. [1987] Data Model Issues for Object-Oriented Applications, *ACM Trans. Office Inform. Syst.* **5**, No. 1, 3–26.

Bell, D.A., McErlane, F., Stewart, P. and Arbuckle, W. [1987] Clustering Related Tuples in Databases, *Computer Journal* **31**, No. 4, 253–257.

Bernstein, P.A. [1987] Database System Support for Software Engineering, *Proc. 9th Int'l Conf. on Software Engineering Computing*.

Bernstein, P.A. and Goodman, N. [1980] Timestamp-based Algorithms for Concurrency Control in Distributed Database Systems, *Proc. Int'l Conf. on Very Large Databases*, 285–300.

Bernstein, P.A., Hadzilacos, V. and Goodman, N. [1987] *Concurrency Control and Recovery in Database Systems*, Addison–Wesley Publishing Co., Reading, MA.

Bobrow, D. *et al.* [1986] CommonLOOPS: Merging Lisp and Object-Oriented Programming, *Proc. ACM Conf. Object-Oriented Programming Systems, Languages and Applications (OOPSLA)*, Portland, OR.

Booch, G. [1986] Object-Oriented Development, *IEEE Trans. on Software Engineering* **SE-12**, No. 2.

Brady, J. [1977] *The Theory of Computer Science: A Programming Approach*, Chapman & Hall, London.

Bretl, R., Maier, D., Otis, A., Penney, J., Schuchardt, B., Stein, J., Williams, E.H. and Williams, M. [1989] The GemStone Data Management System, in *Object-oriented Concepts, Databases and Applications* (eds W. Kim and F.H. Lochovsky), Addison–Wesley Publishing Co., Reading, MA.

Brinch-Hansen, P. [1977] *The Architecture of Concurrent Programs*, Prentice Hall International, Englewood Cliffs, 1977.

Brodie, M.L., Mylopoulos, J. and Schmidt, J.W. (eds) [1984] *On Conceptual Modelling: Perspectives from Artificial Intelligence, Databases and Programming Languages*, Springer–Verlag, New York.

Buneman, O.P. and Frankel, R.E. [1979] FQL - A Functional Query Language, *Proc. ACM SIGMOD Int'l Conf. on the Management of Data*, Boston, MA.

Cardelli, L. [1984a] A Semantics of Multiple Inheritance, *Information and Computation* **26**, 138–164.

Cardelli, L. [1984b] *Amber Technical Report*, AT&T Bell Labs, Murray Hill, NJ.

Cardelli, L. and Wegner, P. [1985] On Understanding Types, Data Abstraction and Polymorphism, *Computing Surveys* **17**, No. 4, 471–522.

Carey, M.J., DeWitt, D.J., Richardson, J.E. and Shekita, E.J. [1989] Storage Management for Objects in EXODUS, in *Object-oriented Concepts, Databases and Applications* (eds W. Kim and F.H. Lochovsky), Addison–Wesley Publishing Co., Reading, MA.

Caudill, P. and Wirfs–Brock, A. [1986] A Third Generation Smalltalk-80 Implementation, *Proc. ACM Conf. Object-Oriented Programming Systems, Languages and Applications (OOPSLA)*, Portland, OR.

Ceri, S., Pernici, B. and Wiederhold, G. [1984] An Overview of Research in the Design of Distributed Systems, *IEEE Database Engineering Bulletin* **7**, 46–51.

Chamberlin, D.D. *et al.* [1976] SEQUEL 2: A Unified Approach to Data Definition, Manipulation and Control, *IBM J. R&D* **20**, No. 6.

Chang, E.E. and Katz, R.H. [1989] *SIGMOD Record* **18**, No. 2, 348–357.

Chen, P.P.S. [1976] The Entity Relationship Model: Towards a Unified View of Data, *ACM Trans. on Database Systems* **1**, No. 1.

Chou, H.–T and Kim, W. [1986] A Unifying Framework for Version Control in a CAD Environment, *Proc. Int'l Conf. on Very Large*

Databases, Kyoto, Japan.

Chou, H.–T. and DeWitt, D.J. [1985] An Evaluation of Buffer Management Strategies for Relational Database Management Systems, *Proc. Int'l Conf. on Very Large Data Bases*, Stockholm, Sweden.

Codd, E.F. [1970] A Relational Model of Data for Large Shared Data Banks, *Communications of the ACM* **13**, 377–87.

Codd, E.F. [1972a] Further Normalisation of the Data Base Relational Model, in *Data Base Systems* (ed. R. Rustin), Courant Computer Science Symposia Series **6**, Prentice Hall International, Englewood Cliffs, NJ.

Codd, E.F. [1972b] Relational Completeness of Database Sub-Languages, in *Data Base Systems* (ed. R. Rustin), Courant Computer Science Symposia Series **6**, Prentice Hall International, Englewood Cliffs, NJ.

Codd, E.F. [1974] Recent Investigations into Relational Database Systems, *Proc. IFIP Congress*.

Codd, E.F. [1979] Extending the Data Base Relational Model to Capture More Meaning, *ACM Trans. on Database Systems* **4**, 397–434.

Copeland, G.P. and Khoshafian, S.N. [1985] A Decomposition Storage Model, *Proc. ACM SIGMOD Conf. on the Management of Data*, Austin, TX.

Copeland, G.P. and Maier, D. [1984] Making Smalltalk a Database System, *Proc. ACM SIGMOD Conf. on the Management of Data*, Boston, MA.

Cox, B.J. [1986] *Object-Oriented Programming: An Evolutionary Approach*, Addison–Wesley Publishing Co., Reading, MA.

Crozier, M., Glass, D., Hughes, J.G., Johnston, W. and McChesney, I. [1989] Critical Analysis of Tools for Computer Aided Software Engineering, *Information and Software Technology* **31**, No. 9, 486–496.

Dadem, P. *et al.* [1986] A DBMS Prototype to Support Extended NF2 Relations: An Integrated View on Flat Tables and Hierarchies, *Proc. ACM SIGMOD Conf. on the Management of Data*, Washington, D.C., 356–366.

Dahl, O. and Nygaard, K. [1966] Simula, an Algol-based Simulation Language, *Communications of the ACM* **9**, 671–678.

Date, C.J. [1981] Referential Integrity, *Proc. VIIth Int'l Conf. Very Large Data Bases*, Cannes, France.

Date, C.J. [1983] *An Introduction to Database Systems*, Vol. II, Addison–

Wesley Publishing Co., Reading, MA.

Date, C.J. [1990] *An Introduction to Database Systems*, Vol. I, 5th Edition, Addison–Wesley Publishing Co., Reading, MA.

Deshpande, A. and Van Gucht, D. [1988] An Implementation for Nested Relational Databases, *Proc. Int'l Conf. on Very Large Data Bases*, Los Angeles, CA.

Deux, O. [1990] The Story of O_2, *IEEE Trans. on Knowledge and Data Engineering* **2**, No. 1, 91–108.

Downs, E., Clare, P. and Coe, I. [1988] *Structure Systems Analysis and Design Method*, Prentice Hall International, Hemel Hempstead, England.

Dyke, R.P. and Kunz, J.C. [1989] Object-Oriented Programming, *IBM Systems Journal* **28**, No. 3, 465–478.

Eswaran, K.P., Gray, J.N., Lorie, R.A. and Traiger, I.L. [1976] The Notions of Consistency and Predicate Locks in a Data Base System, *Communications of the ACM* **19**, No. 11.

Fagin, R. [1977] Multivalued Dependencies and a New Normal Form for Relational Databases, *ACM Trans. on Database Systems* **2**, No. 3.

Fagin, R. [1979] Normal Forms and Relational Database Operators, *ACM SIGMOD Int'l Symposium on Management of Data*, 153–160.

Fikes, R. and Kaehler, T. [1985] The Role of Frame-Based Representation in Reasoning, *Communications of the ACM* **28**, No. 9, 904–920.

Fishman, D.H., Annevelink, J., Beech, D., Chow, E., Connors, T., Davis, J.W., Hasan, W., Hoch, C.G., Kent, W., Leichner, S., Lyngbæk, P., Mahbod, B., Neimat, M.A., Risch, T., Shan, M.C. and Wilkinson, K. [1989] Overview of the IRIS Database Management System, in *Object-Oriented Concepts, Databases and Applications* (eds W. Kim and F.H. Lochovsky), Addison–Wesley Publishing Co., Reading, MA.

Fishman, D.H., Beech, D., Cate, H.P., Chow, E.C., Connors, T., Davis, J.W., Derratt, N., Hoch, C.G., Kent,W., Lyngbæk, P., Mahbod, B., Neimat, M.A., Ryan, T.A. and Shan, M.C. [1987] IRIS: An Object-Oriented Database Management System, *ACM Trans. Office Inform. Syst.* **5**, No. 1, 48–69.

Fox, S., Landers, T., Ries, D.R. and Rosenberg, R.L. [1984] *DAPLEX Users Manual*, Report CCA–84–01, Computer Corporation of America, Cambridge, Mass.

Garcia–Molina, H. and Salem, K. [1987] SAGAS, *Proc. ACM SIGMOD Conf.*, 249–259.

Garza, J.F. and Kim, W. [1988] Transaction Management in an Object-Oriented Database System, *Proc. ACM SIGMOD Conf. on the Management of Data*, Chicago, IL, 37–45.

Goldberg, A. and Robson, D. [1980] *Smalltalk-80: The Language and its Implementation*, Addison–Wesley, Reading, MA

Gray, J.N. [1978] Notes on Database Operating Systems, in *Operating Systems: An Advanced Course* (eds R. Bayer, R.M. Graham and G. Seegmuller), Springer–Verlag, New York.

Gray, P.M.D. [1984] *Logic, Algebra and Databases*, Ellis Horwood, Chichester, England.

Guttag, J.V. and Horning, J.J. [1977] The Algebraic Specification of Abstract Data Types, *Acta Informatica* **12**, No. 3.

Hall, P.A.V., Owlett, J. and Todd, S.J.P. [1976] Relations and Entities, in *Data Base Management Systems* (ed. G.M. Nijssen), North–Holland Publishing Co., New York.

Hammer, M.M. and McLeod, D.J. [1975] Semantic Integrity in a Relational Database System, *Proc. 1st Int'l Conf. Very Large Data Bases*, Framingham, MA.

Hammer, M.M. and McLeod, D.J. [1981] Database Description with SDM: A Semantic Data Model, *ACM Trans. Database Syst.* **6**, No. 3.

Harland, D.M. [1988] *Rekursiv: Object-Oriented Computer Architecture*, Ellis Horwood, Chichester, England.

Harmon, P., Maus, R. and Morrissey, W. [1988] *Expert Systems: Tools and Applications*, Wiley, New York.

Hasemer, T. and Domingue, J. [1989] *Common Lisp Programming for Artificial Intelligence*, Addison–Wesley Publishing Co., Reading, MA.

Haskin, R. and Lorie, R. [1982] On Extending the Functions of a Relational Database System, *Proc. ACM SIGMOD Conf. Management Data*, 207–212.

Heath, I.J. [1971] Unacceptable File Operations in a Relational Database, *Proc. ACM SIGFIDET Workshop on Data Description, Access and Control*.

Herlihy, M.P. [1986] Optimistic Concurrency Control for Abstract Data Types, Proc. *5th ACM Conf. on Principles of Distributed Computing*, in *Readings in Object-Oriented Database Systems* (eds S.B. Zdonik and D. Maier), Morgan Kaufmann, San Mateo, CA.

Herlihy, M.P. and Wing, J.M. [1987] Axioms for Concurrent Objects, *Proc. 14th Symposium on POPL*, 13–26.

Herlihy, M.P. and Wing, J.M. [1988] Linearizable Concurrent Objects, *ACM SIGPLAN Notices* **24**, No. 4, 133–135.

Hewitt, C.E. [1985] Viewing Control Structures as Patterns of Passing Messages, *J. of Artificial Intelligence* **8**, No. 3, 323–364.

Hoare, C.A.R. [1972a] Proof of Correctness of Data Representations, *Acta Informatica* **1**, 271–281.

Hoare, C.A.R. [1972b] Notes on Data Structuring, in *Structured Programming* (eds O.–J. Dahl, E.W. Dijkstra and C.A.R. Hoare), Academic Press, New York, 83–174.

Hoare, C.A.R. [1978] Communicating Sequential Processes, *Comm. of the ACM* **21**, No. 8, 666–677.

Hoare, C.A.R. [1985] *Communicating Sequential Processes*, Prentice Hall International, Hemel Hempstead, England.

Hornick, M and Zdonik, S. [1987] A Shared Segmented Memory System for an Object-Oriented Database, *ACM Trans. Office Inform. Syst.* **5**, No. 1, 70–95.

Hudson, S.E. and King, R. [1986] CACTIS: A Database System for Specifying Functionally Defined Data, *Proc. Int'l Workshop Object-Oriented Database Systems* (eds K. Dittrich and U. Dayal), Pacific Grove, CA.

Hughes, J.G. [1988] *Database Technology: A Software Engineering Approach*, Prentice Hall International, Hemel Hempstead, England.

Hughes, J.G. and Connolly, M.M. [1987] A Portable Implementation of a Modular Multiprocessing Database Programming Language, *Software–Practice and Experience* **17**, 533–546.

Hull, R. and King, R. [1987] Semantic Database Modelling: Survey, Applications and Research Issues, *ACM Computing Surveys* **19**, No. 3, 201–260.

Ichbiah, J. *et al.* [1979] Rationale for the Design of the Programming Language Ada, *ACM SIGPLAN Notices* **14**, No. 6.

Ishikawa, Y. and Tokoro, M. [1986] Orient84/K: An Object-Oriented Concurrent Programming Language for Knowledge Representation, in *Object-Oriented Concurrent Programming* (eds Y. Yonezawa and M. Tokoro), MIT Press, Cambridge, MA.

Kaehler, T. and Krasner, G. [1983] LOOM: Large Object-Oriented Memory for Smalltalk-80 Systems, in *Smalltalk-80: Bits of History, Words of Advice* (ed. G. Krasner), Addison–Wesley Publishing Co., Reading, MA.

Kaiser, G.E. [1988] Transactions for Concurrent Object-Oriented Programming Systems, *ACM SIGPLAN Notices* **24**, No.4, 136–138.

Katz, R., Chang, E. and Bhateja, R [1986] Version Modelling Concepts for Computer-Aided Design Databases, *Proc. ACM Conf. on the Management of Data*, Washington, D.C.

Kent, W. [1978] *Data and Reality*, North–Holland Publishing Co., New York.

Kent, W. [1983] A Simple Guide to Five Normal Forms in Relational Database Theory, *Comm. ACM* **26**, No. 2.

Khoshafian, S.N. and Copeland, G.P. [1986] Object Identity, *Proc. ACM Conf. Object-Oriented Programming Systems, Languages and Applications (OOPSLA)*, Portland, OR.

Khoshafian, S.N. and Valduriez, P. [1987] Persistence, Sharing and Object-Orientation: A Database Perspective, *Proc. Workshop on Database Programming Languages*, Roscoff, France.

Kim, W. [1989] A Model of Queries for Object-Oriented Databases, *Proc. Int'l Conf. on Very Large Data Bases*, Amsterdam, The Netherlands.

Kim, W. [1990] Object-Oriented Databases: Definition and Research Directions, *IEEE Trans. on Knowledge and Data Engineering* **2**, No. 3, 327–341.

Kim, W. and Lochovsky, F. (eds) [1989] *Object-Oriented Concepts, Applications and Databases*, Addison–Wesley Publishing Co., Reading, MA.

Kim, W., Ballou, N., Chou, H.-T., Garza, J.F. and Banerjee, J. [1988] Integrating an Object-Oriented Programming System with a Database System, *Proc. ACM Conf. Object-Oriented Programming Systems, Languages and Applications (OOPSLA)*, San Diego, CA, 142–152.

Kim, W., Ballou, N., Chou, H.-T., Garza, J.F. and Woelk, D. [1989] Features of the ORION Object-Oriented Database System, in *Object-Oriented Concepts, Databases and Applications* (eds W. Kim and F.H. Lochovsky), Addison–Wesley, Reading, MA.

Kim, W., Garza, J.F., Ballou, N. and Woelk, D. [1990] Architecture of the ORION Next Generation Database System, *IEEE Trans. on Knowledge and Data Engineering* **2**, No. 1, 109–124.

Kim, W., Kim, K.C. and Dale, A., Indexing Techniques for Object-Oriented Databases, in *Object-oriented Concepts, Databases and Applications* (eds W. Kim and F.H. Lochovsky), Addison–Wesley, Reading, MA.

Korth, H.F., Kim, W. and Bancilhon, F. [1988] On Long-Duration CAD Transactions, *Information Sciences* **46**, 73–107.

Kung, H.T. and Robinson, J.T. [1981] On Optimistic Methods for Concurrency Control, *ACM Trans. on Database Systems* **6**, No. 2.

Lang, K. and Pearlmutter, B. [1986] OakLisp: An Object-Oriented Scheme with First Class Types, *Proc. ACM Conf. Object-Oriented Programming Systems, Languages and Applications (OOPSLA)*, Portland, OR.

Langworthy, D.E. [1988] Evaluating Correctness Criteria for Transactions, *ACM SIGPLAN Notices* **24**, No. 4, 139–141.

Lecluse, C. and Richard, P. [1989] The O_2 Database Programming Langauge, *Proc. XVth Int'l Conf. on Very Large Data Bases*, Amsterdam, The Netherlands, 411–422.

Liskov, B. *et al.* [1981] CLU Reference Manual, in *Lecture Notes in Computer Science* **114** (eds G. Goos and J. Hartmanis), Springer–Verlag, Berlin.

Liskov, B. [1972] A Design Methodology for Reliable Software Systems, in *Tutorial on Software Design Techniques* (eds P. Freeman and A. Wasserman), IEEE Computer Science Press, New York.

Liskov, B. and Guttag, J. [1986] *Abstraction and Specification in Program Development*, MIT Press and McGraw–Hill, Cambridge, MA.

Liskov, B. and Zilles, S.N. [1974] Programming with Abstract Data Types, *ACM SIGPLAN Notices* **9**, 50–9.

Liskov, B. and Zilles, S.N. [1975] Specification Techniques for Data Abstractions, *IEEE Transactions on Software Eng.* **SE-1**, 7–19.

Luger, G.F. and Stubblefield, W.A. [1989] *Artificial Intelligence and the Design of Expert Systems*, Benjamin/Cummings Publishing Co., Redwood City, CA.

Maier, D. and Stein J. [1987] Development and Implementation of an Object-Oriented DBMS, in *Research Directions in Object-Oriented Programming* (eds B. Shriver and P. Wegner), MIT Press, Cambridge, MA.

Maier, D., Stein, J., Otis, A. and Purdy, A. [1986] Development of an Object-Oriented DBMS, *Proc. 1st Int'l Conf. on Object-Oriented Programming Systems, Languages and Applications*, Portland, OR.

Martin, B. [1988] Concurrent Programming versus Concurrency Control: Shared Events or Shared Data, *ACM SIGPLAN Notices* **24**, No. 4, 142–144.

Matthews, D.C.J. [1985] An Overview of the Poly Programming Language, *Proc. Workshop on Persistence and Data Types*, Appin Scotland, 255–264.

McCarthy, J. [1960] Recursive Functions of Symbolic Expressions and their Computation by Machine, *Comm. ACM* **3**, No. 4.

McGettrick, A.D. [1982] *Program Verification Using Ada*, Cambridge Univ. Press, Cambridge.

McLeod, D. and Heimbigner, D. [1985] A Federated Architecture for Information Systems, *ACM Trans. on Office Information Systems* **3**, No. 3.

Meyer, B. [1986] Genericity Versus Inheritance, *Proc. ACM Conf. Object-Oriented Programming Systems, Languages and Applications (OOPSLA)*, Portland, OR.

Meyer, B. [1987] Reusability: The Case for Object-Oriented Design, *IEEE Software*, March Issue, 50–64.

Meyer, B. [1988] *Object-Oriented Software Construction*, Prentice Hall International, Hemel Hempstead, England.

Milner, R. [1984] A Proposal for Standard ML, *Proc. 1984 ACM Symposium on Lisp and Functional Programming*, ACM, New York, 184–197.

Minsky, M. [1975] A Framework for Representing Knowledge, in *The Psychology of Computer Vision* (ed. P. Winston) McGraw–Hill, New York.

Moon, D.A. [1986] Object-Oriented Programming with Flavors, *Proc. ACM Conf. Object-Oriented Programming Systems, Languages and Applications (OOPSLA)*, Portland, OR.

Morrison, R. [1982] S-Algol: a Simple Algol, *Computer Bulletin* **II**, No. 31.

Morrison, R., Brown, A.L., Carrick, R., Connor, R.C.H., Dearle, A. and Atkinson, M.P. [1987] Polymorphism, Persistence and Software Reuse in a Strongly Typed Object-Oriented Environment, *Software Engineering Journal*, November Issue, 199–204.

Moss, J.E.B. [1981] Nested Transactions: An Approach to Reliable Distributed Computing, Ph.D. Thesis, Laboratory for Computer Science,

MIT, April 1981 (available as *Technical Report No. MIT/LCS/TR-260*).

Moss, J.E.B. [1985] *Nested Transactions: An Approach to Reliable Distributed Computing*, MIT Press, Cambridge, MA.

Mylopoulos, J. and Levesque, H.J. [1984] An Overview of Knowledge Representation, in *On Conceptual Modelling* (eds M.L. Brodie, J. Mylopoulos and J. Schmidt), Springer–Verlag, New York.

Mylopoulos, J., Bernstein, P. and Wong, H.K.T. [1980] A Language Facility for Designing Interactive Database-Intensive Applications, *ACM Trans. on Database Systems* **5**, No. 2, 185–207.

Navathe, S. and Cheng, A. [1983] A Methodology for Database Schema Mapping from Extended Entity-Relationship Models into the Hierarchical Model, in *Entity-Relationship Approach to Software Engineering* (eds G.C. Davis *et al.*), Elsevier North–Holland, New York.

Neuhold, E. and Stonebraker, M. [1988] Future Directions in DBMS Research, *Tech. Report 88–001*, Int'l Computer Science Inst., Berkeley, CA.

Ng, P. [1981] Further Analysis of the Entity-Relationship Approach to Database Design, *IEEE Trans. on Software Engineering* **7**, No. 1.

O'Brien, P., Bullis, B. and Schaffert, C. [1986] Persistent and Shared Objects in Trellis/Owl, *Proc. Int'l Workshop Object-Oriented Database Systems* (eds K. Dittrich and U. Dayal), Pacific Grove, CA.

Ontologic Inc. [1989] *Object Database for C++*, Ontologic Inc., Boston, MA.

Ozsoyoglu, G., Ozsoyoglu, Z and Matos, V. [1988] Extending Relational Algebra and Relational Calculus with Set Valued Attributes and Aggregate Functions, *ACM Trans. on Database Systems* **12**, No. 4.

Papadimitriou, C. [1986] *The Theory of Database Concurrency Control*, Computer Science Press, New York.

Parnas, D. [1972] On the Criteria to be used in Decomposing Systems into Modules, *Comm. ACM* **15**, No. 12.

Pomberger, G. [1984] *Software Engineering and Modula-2*, Prentice Hall International, Hemel Hempstead, England.

Pu, C., Kaiser, G. and Hutchinson, N. [1988] Split Transactions for Open-Ended Activities, *Proc. 14th Int'l Conf. Very Large Data Bases*, Los Angeles, CA, 26–37.

Reimer, M. [1984] Implementation of the Database Programming Language Modula/R on the Personal Computer Lilith, *Software–Practice and Experience* **14**, 945–956.

Rowe, L.A. [1981] Issues in the Design of Database Programming Languages, *Proc. of Workshop on Data Abstraction, Databases and Conceptual Modelling*, Pingree Park, CO, Part 74, 180–182.

Rowe, L.A. and Shoens, K.A. [1979] Data Abstraction, Views and Updates in RIGEL, *Proc. ACM SIGMOD Conf.*, Boston, Mass., 71–81.

Rowe, L.A. and Stonebraker, M. [1987] The POSTGRES Data Model *Proc. 13th Int'l Conf. Very Large Data Bases,*, Brighton, England, 83–96.

Sakai, H. [1983] Entity-Relationship Approach to Logical Database Design, in *Entity-Relationship Approach to Software Engineering* (eds C.G. Davis, S. Jajodia, P.A. Ng and R.T. Yeh), Elsevier North–Holland, New York, 155–187.

Samples, A., Ungar, D. and Hilfinger, P. [1986] SOAR: Smalltalk without Bytecodes, *Proc. ACM Conf. Object-Oriented Programming Systems, Languages and Applications (OOPSLA)*, Portland, OR.

Schaffert, C., Cooper, T., Bullis, B., Kilian, M. and Wilpolt, C. [1986] An Introduction to Trellis/Owl, *Proc. ACM Conf. Object-Oriented Programming Systems, Languages and Applications (OOPSLA)*, Portland, OR.

Scheuermann, P., Scheffner, G. and Weber, H. [1980] Abstraction Capabilities and Invariant Properties Modelling within the Entity-Relationship Approach, in *Entity-Relationship Approach to Systems Analysis and Design* (ed. P. Chen), North–Holland, 121–140.

Schlageter, G., Unland, R., Wilkes, W., Zieschang, R., Maul, G., Nagl, M. and Meyer, R. [1988] OOPS: An Object-Oriented Programming System with Integrated Data Management Facility, *Proc. IEEE 4th Int'l Conf. Data Engineering*, Los Angeles, CA, 118–125.

Schmidt, J.W. [1977] Some High Level Language Constructs for Data of Type Relation, *ACM Trans. on Database Systems* **2**, 247–261.

Schmidt, J.W. and Mall, M. [1980] *Pascal/R Report Bericht Nr. 66*, Inst. fur Informatik, Univ. Hamburg, Hamburg, West Germany.

Schoman, K. and Ross, D.T. [1977] Structured Analysis for Requirements Definition, *IEEE Trans. on Software Eng.* **SE-3**.

Schwartz, P.M. and Spector, A.Z. [1984] Synchronizing Abstract Data Types, *ACM Trans. on Computer Systems* **2**, No. 3.

Seidewitz, E. and Stark, M. [1986] General Object-Oriented Software

Development, *Report No. SEL–86–002*, Software Engineering Laboratory, NASA Goddard Space Flight Centre.

Shipman, D.W. [1981] The Functional Data Model and the Language DAPLEX, *ACM Trans. on Database Systems* **6**, No. 1.

Shopiro, J.E. [1979] Theseus - A Programming Language for Relational Databases, *ACM Trans. on Database Systems* **4**, 493–517.

Sibley, E.H. and Kerschberg, L. [1977] Data Architecture and Data Model Considerations, *Proc. AFIPS National Computer Conf.*, Dallas, Texas.

Smith, J. *et al.* [1981] MULTIBASE: Integrating Distributed Heterogeneous Database Systems, *Proc. National Computer Conf.*, AFIPS **50**.

Smith, J.M. and Smith, D.C.P. [1977] Database Abstractions: Aggregation and Generalisation, *ACM Trans. on Database Systems* **2**, No. 2.

Smith, J.M., Fox, S. and Landers, T.A. [1981] *Reference Manual for ADAPLEX*, Computer Corporation of America, Cambridge, MA.

Smith, K.E. and Zdonik, S.B. [1986] Intermedia: A Case Study of the Differences Between Relational and Object-Oriented Database Systems, *Proc. ACM Conf. Object-Oriented Programming Systems, Languages and Applications (OOPSLA)*, Portland, OR.

Snyder, A. [1986] Encapsulation and Inheritance in Object-Oriented Programming Languages, *Proc. ACM Conf. Object-Oriented Programming Systems, Languages and Applications (OOPSLA)*, Portland, OR.

Stefik, M. and Bobrow, D.G. [1986] Object-Oriented Programming: Themes and Variations, *AI Magazine*, January Issue, 40–62.

Stepp, R.E. and Michalski, R.S. [1986] Conceptual Clustering of Structured Objects: A Goal Oriented Approach, *Artificial Intelligence* **28**, 43–69.

Stonebraker, M. [1987] The Design of the POSTGRES Storage System, *Proc. 13th Int'l Conf. Very Large Data Bases*, Brighton, England, 289–300.

Stonebraker, M., Anton, J. and Hanson, E. [1987] Extending a Database System with Procedures, *ACM Trans. on Database Syst.* **12**, No. 3, 350–376.

Stonebraker, M., Wong, E., Kreps, P. and Held, G. [1976] The Design and Implementation of INGRES, *ACM Trans. on Database Syst.* **1**, 189–222.

Straw, A., Mellender, F. and Riegel, S. [1989] Object Management in a

Persistent Smalltalk System, *Software–Practice and Experience* **19**, No.8, 719–737.

Stroustrup, B. [1986] *The C++ Programming Language*, Addison–Wesley, Reading, MA.

Taylor *et al.* [1988] Foundations for the Arcadia Environment Architecture, *Proc. SIGSOFT 88: 3rd Symposium on Software Development Environments.*

Teorey, T.J. and Fry, J.P. [1982] *Design of Database Structures*, Prentice Hall International, Englewood Cliffs, NJ.

Teorey, T.J., Yang, D. and Fry, J.P. [1986] Logical Design Methodology for Relational Databases, *Computing Surveys* **18**, No. 2.

Traiger, I.L., Gray, J.N., Galtieri, C.A. and Lindsay, B.G. [1979] Transactions and Consistency in Distributed Database Systems, *IBM Research Report RJ2555.*

Tripathi, A., Berge, E. and Aksit, M. [1988] An Implementation of the Object-Oriented Concurrent Programming Language SINA, *Software–Practice and Experience* **19**, No. 3, 235–256.

Tsichritzis, D.C. and Lochovsky, F.H. [1982] *Data Models*, Prentice Hall International, London.

Ullman, J.D. [1982] *Principles of Database Systems*, 2nd Ed, Pitman, London.

Van de Reit, R.P., Wasserman, A.I., Kersten, M.L. and De Jonge, W. [1981] High Level Programming Features for Improving the Efficiency of a Relational Database System, *ACM Trans. on Database Systems* **6**, 464–485.

Ward, P.T. [1989] How to Integrate Object Orientation with Structured Systems Analysis and Design, *IEEE Software*, March Issue, 74–82.

Wasserman, A.I. [1979] Design Goals for PLAIN, *Proc. ACM SIGMOD Conf. Boston*, 60–70.

Wasserman, A.I. [1980] The Design of PLAIN - Support for Systematic Programming, *Proc. AFIPS*, NCC **49**, 731–740.

Wasserman, A.I. *et al.* [1981] Revised Report on the Programming Language PLAIN, *ACM SIGPLAN Notices* **16**, 59–80.

Wegner, P. [1989] Object-Oriented Programming: Learning the Language, *Byte*, March Issue, 245–253.

Weihl, W.E. [1985] Linguistic Support for Atomic Data Types, *Proc.*

Appin Workshop on Data Types and Persistence, Persistent Programming Research Group, Report No. 16, Univ. of Glasgow, Scotland.

Welsh, J. and Bustard, D.W. [1979] Pascal-Plus: Another Language for Modular Multiprogramming, *Software–Practice and Experience* 9, 947–957.

Wileden, J.C., Wolf, A.L., Fisher, C.D. and Tarr, P.L. [1988] PGRAPHITE: An Experiment in Persistent Typed Object Management, *Proc. ACM SIGMOD Conf. on the Management of Data*, Chicago, IL.

Wilkinson, K., Lyngbæk, P. and Hasan, W. [1990] The IRIS Architecture and Implementation, *IEEE Trans. on Knowledge and Data Engineering* 2, No. 1, 63–75.

Wirth, N. [1982] *Programming in Modula-2*, 2nd Ed, Springer-Verlag, Berlin.

Woelk, D. and Kim, W. [1987] Multimedia Information Management in an Object-Oriented Database System, *Proc. 13th Int'l Conf. Very Large Data Bases*, Brighton, England, 319–329.

Woelk, D., Kim, W. and Luther, W. [1990] An Object-Oriented Approach to Multimedia Databases, in *Readings in Object-Oriented Database Systems* (eds S.B. Zdonik and D. Maier), Morgan Kaufmann, San Mateo, CA.

Yang, C.–C. [1986] *Relational Databases*, Prentice Hall International, Englewood Cliffs, NJ.

Yokote, Y. and Tokoro, M. [1986] The Design and Implementation of Concurrent Smalltalk, *Proc. ACM Conf. Object-Oriented Programming Systems, Languages and Applications (OOPSLA)*, Portland, OR.

Yokote, Y. and Tokoro, M. [1987] Experience and Evolution of Concurrent Smalltalk, *Proc. ACM Conf. Object-Oriented Programming Systems, Languages and Applications (OOPSLA)*, Orlando, FL.

Yonezawa, Y. and Tokoro, M. (eds) [1987] *Object-Oriented Concurrent Programming*, MIT Press, Cambridge, MA.

Yonezawa, A., Briot, J. and Shibayama, E. [1986] Object-Oriented Concurrent Programming in ABCL/1, *Proc. ACM Conf. Object-Oriented Programming Systems, Languages and Applications (OOPSLA)*, Portland, OR.

Yonezawa, A. Shibayama, E., Takada, T. and Honda, Y. [1987] Modelling and Programming in an Object-Oriented Concurrent Language ABCL/1, in *Object-Oriented Concurrent Programming* (eds Y. Yonezawa and M. Tokoro), MIT Press, Cambridge, MA.

Index

serial schedule 187, 194
serializability 181, 186, 187, 192,
    200, 206
serializable 59, 181
set 63, 174
shadow 193
    copy 196
    object table 196
    page table 204
    paging 204
Shan, M.C. 256
shared intention exclusive 191
Shekita, E.J. 254
Shibayama, E. 266
Shipman, D.W. 41, 47, 148, 264
SHM 39
Shoens, K.A. 162, 263
Shopiro, J.E. 162, 264
Sibley, E.H. 41, 264
side effects 244
signature 155
Simula 57, 121
SINA 179
single-class indexing 220
single-valued 139
single-valued function 41
slot 237, 241, 248
slot value 242
Smalltalk 57, 122–127, 179, 222,
    245
    environment 128
Smalltalk-80 170, 176
Smith, J. 11, 39, 89, 94, 120,
    208, 264
Smith, D.C.P. 11, 39, 89, 94,
    120, 208, 264
Smith, K.E. 120, 264
snap-shot 173, 201
Snyder, A. 140, 264
soft crash 201
software
    engineering 3, 48, 51, 197
    failure 201

management 49
    reuse 74
spatial modularity 193
specialization 13, 14, 57, 71, 86,
    121
specification 48, 128
    of data types 1
Spector, A.Z. 211, 263
SQL 100, 142, 160, 248
SQL ASSERT 100
SSADM 51
Stark, M. 82, 120, 263
static binding 132
static type checking 66, 123
statically typed language 123
Stefik, M. 251, 264
Stein, J. 122, 141, 228, 254, 260
Stepp, R.E. 224, 233, 264
stepwise refinement 48, 80
Stewart, P. 253
Stonebraker, M. 167, 177, 262,
    263, 264
Straw, A. 176, 264
strong type checking 36, 60, 67
strongly typed language 66, 75
strongly typed object-oriented lan-
    guage 121
Stroustrup, B. 121, 128, 264
structural information 238
structural semantics 228
structure independence 170
structured knowledge
    representation 238
structured knowledge
    representation schemes 237
Structured Systems Analysis and
    Design Methodology
    (SSADM) 51
structured systems design
    methodologies 56
structured systems development
    methodologies 51
Stubblefield, W.A. 251, 260